To Shirley Lang

fortunate mother
of a most intelligent
son

Thomas Boylston Adams

A NEW NATION

A New Nation

THOMAS BOYLSTON ADAMS

Globe Pequot Press

Chester, Connecticut

Illustrations on pages 6, 11, 32, 37, 81, 94, 100, 105, 172-173, 177 and 192 are published with the kind cooperation and permission of the Massachusetts Historical Society. The copy photographer is Stephen J. Kovacik.

Illustrations on pages 69 and 133 are published with permission of the U.S. Department of the Interior, National Park Service, Adams Historical Site, Quincy, Massachusetts.

The illustration on page 52 is published with the permission of the artist, George Dergalis.

The illustration on page 57 is published with permission of The American Antiquarian Society, Worcester, Massachusetts.

The illustration on page 128 is published with permission of the U.S.S. Constitution Museum Foundation.

The illustration on page 260, is published with the permission of The Associated Press.

The illustration on page 272 appeared in *American Architect and Building News.*

The illustration on page 283 is published with permission of the Boston Athenaeum.

Library of Congress Catalog Card Number 81-82607

ISBN 0-87106-959-8

Designed by David Ford

Gettysburg / November 1863

Fourscore and seven years ago
our fathers brought forth on this continent,
a new nation, conceived in Liberty,
and dedicated to the proposition
that all men are created equal.

Abraham Lincoln

CONTENTS

PREFACE

*H*istory is the imperfect record of an unaccountable number of uncontrolled experiments. Under the name of experience it is the daily guide of every individual. The law calls it precedent and bases its opinions on it. Nations shape their courses by it. Its defect is the impossibility of applying to social problems the techniques of definition and limitation essential to the scientific method.

Between mankind and perfect understanding lies the uneasy fact that the subjects of each experiment are the performers of it. Its planners and directors are its chief beneficiaries—or its victims. They stand to win or lose their jobs by its result. And since winning or losing a job may mean, in the simple Arab phrase, "your head or mine," emotions direct as much or more than reason. What is true of its leaders is true of all society. In every experiment, as it progresses, life, liberty, property and control of the experiment itself are at stake.

This interferes with the essential element of rationality; self-criticism and the impartial testing of theory by the objective observation of its effects. A scientist in his laboratory, having with care arranged an experiment, when he tries it and it fails, feels no sense of guilt. He may abandon it altogether or he may try again, after careful check of his apparatus. If he then succeeds and offers his hypothesis and his proofs to the world, he knows it will be subjected to further questioning and testing. Proof of the behavior of controlled elements is possible even on the gigantic scale of atomic fision. Equally it is possible in the observation of microcosms in a test tube.

The correct observation of human events as they unfold is more difficult. But it is not impossible. It is the occupation of a considerable segment of mankind which is engaged in gathering what is called the news. It is the preoccupation of much of the rest of mankind, which follows the news avidly, to consider its effect on itself in every aspect, from the most immediate weather report to the most distant report of conditions on the opposite side of the globe or even outer space. And along with the news comes its interpretation, as each human mind considers it and as the considerations of many minds affect the conclusions of others.

It is in this interpretation that history finds its function. Familiarity with past experiments can suggest useful hypotheses as to the progress and wisdom of present experiments. Were total familiarity possible and all the facts of past experience available, the application of historical knowledge of developing events could approach a science. They are not. Therefore the scientific interpretation of history continues to elude mankind.

But a method that offers promise of useful results is to narrow the field. It is possible, within limits almost scientific, to isolate certain instances in recorded history and determine the origin and results of action. All the facts cannot be available because the actors have vanished and there is only a partial transcript of what they said and thought. But the scene can be recreated fairly accurately from available evidence and the parts of the principal actors written again—often with the revealing addition of their secret thoughts now discovered from diaries and private letters.

Now the audience is no longer part of the play. It can, if it tries hard enough, learn to be objective observers. It can learn to use the mind for hypothesis and testing. It can learn how to fail without a sense of guilt. It can observe the tendency to repeat errors because of emotional involvement in them. It just possibly can learn how better to conduct its own affairs. For the great hope that lies in every experiment is that it will lead to another; wiser, more copious, more useful to mankind.

The goal is worth striving for. The progress of scientific discovery and control of material things has placed in human hands cosmic power. The abuse of that power can end the human experiment for a very long time—possibly for all time as measured by human standards. The ambitions and quarrels of mankind must be placed under better control to permit survival. If we fall into any of the old bogs we are done for.

Attempts to control human destiny by arbitrary application of theory, based on imperfect knowledge and mere guesswork, tend to become oppressive and tyrannical. Failure to attempt solutions tends towards anarchy. Neither a universal church nor a monolithic state has ever quite satisfied any but those in control of the experiment. Socialist experiments such as the first year or two of Plymouth Plantation or Brook Farm have satisfied nobody. The American experiment in democracy may offer a middle road. But such human factors as greed, ambition and stupidity remain. The defense of theory can precede its formulation and dogma is often made a substitute for thought. Perhaps Americans, relieved by the First Amendment to their Constitution from restraints placed on the thinkers of former ages, can learn better. If they fail, the failure is their own. The opportunity is clear in the study of their own history.

A NEW NATION

NOVEMBER 1963

*W*inter is coming. On this November afternoon the sky is perfectly clear over Walden, the water is perfectly transparent near shore, green-blue farther out, and blue beyond. The northwest breeze turns up the surface in a myriad wavelets. The sun's rays, steeply slanting through the red oak woods, red oak woods but half stripped of leaves—half the shriveled recollection of summer still hangs on their branches—catch them in sudden flashes. The pond is unusually low this year. The wavelets patter against the stony shore, six feet of stones and pebbles below the usual bank. In the cove there is the faint tinkle of thin, wind-broken ice. Under this shadowed south shore the sunlight has not found its way today.

One thinks of Thoreau and Gandhi, of the power of thought, of the durability of an idea. Here Thoreau pondered the Indian Vedas, considered the strength of every little man, discovered the power of non-violence. A generation, two generations pass and in jail in South Africa, Gandhi reads *Civil Disobedience*. He returns to India, labors. Then, suddenly the harvest. India free, mankind awaking to the possibilities of earth, he falls by the assassin's bullet.

One thinks of the flag-covered coffin in Washington; of the great crowd as it passes; of the sea of faces as it passes to Arlington. Over the whole nation the faces are sad. The churches are crowded, the streets are empty. Especially one sees the young and sad faces in the Harvard Church, this church built to remember the companions of this man whom we mourn, these companions who died so little time ago in that most recent war against the powers of darkness.

Youth we have buried today, and hope. But youth and hope

1

will spring again. The red oak buds are eternal. But have we buried greatness today? And the thought comes—only the living can answer that question. If the test ban treaty is made the turning point of history, if the world struggles out of fear into understanding, if the atom is made the servant of all mankind, then we have buried greatness. If the dark, unfathomable depths of hate are dried up, if the terrible darkness of prejudice is made light, then we have buried greatness.

The memory of him we mourn is in the hands of the living. A nation that turns to selfishness, cynicism and death will not long remember him, or be remembered. If the soul of Lincoln lives, and the nation ceases not to strive to make all men equal under just laws, and law and justice rule, then this new martyr will live.

The pond is all in darkness now. The wind has ceased. There will be ice on the cove in the morning. The day still lives only in the white mist of bare maple branches high up on the opposite shore, where the daylight still lingers. We shall walk home in the dark, through woods deep in leaves, moist-smelling, soft with the recent rains. And tomorrow there will be a new day. What sort of day?

THE BEGINNING

*T*he origins of democracy in America are many and their sources dim. Somewhat they go back to the wild peoples that inhabited the dark forests of Europe after the last ice age; somewhat to the Mediterranean Sea and the Aegean, to ancient Greece and classical Rome. Mostly they stem from the Protestant Reformation; specifically and definitely for Massachusetts and New England, from that group of reformers and religious enthusiasts known as Puritans. A small group of these, to escape the conformist pressures of established church and arbitrary state, fled England and settled in Holland early in the seventeenth century.

Their spiritual guide and intellectual leader was a man named John Robinson. His influence and the influence of the few that he taught, like that of the Apostles, far exceeded their numbers. Indeed it is immeasurable. For the teacher affects eternity. He never can tell where his influence stops.

Nobody knows what Robinson looked like. Something of what he said is matter of record, and it made a great impression on his hearers. Twenty and thirty years later some of them could repeat it word for word. The whole number of his congregation was about three hundred. They met at Robinson's house in Choir Alley in Leyden, and there, after some dozen years of exile in a foreign land, they made the decision to emigrate to America. There was not money enough to take the whole group. So it was decided that the strongest should go, leaving the weaker and larger part in Holland under Robinson's care.

Those who went have been known ever since as the Pilgrims. It was thus they knew and considered themselves. The fact is clearly stated in that extraordinary record titled *Of Plimoth*

Plantation. It was written by William Bradford, their leader in the New World. He describes their departure from Leyden. "So they left that goodly and pleasant city which had been their resting place near twelve years; but they knew they were pilgrims, and looked not much on those things but lift up their eyes to the heavens, their dearest country, and quieted their spirits."

They had need to quiet their spirits. Edward Winslow, then a young man, taking with him a young wife who would not survive the first winter, remembered in detail. He wrote it long after, nearly thirty years after, when he, too, had made his mark in the New Canaan. He was Bradford's assistant and wisest ambassador, being then returned to England where the Puritan Revolution was triumphant under Cromwell. He gives us Robinson's words, his farewell spoken in the large room in the Dutch house, where the exile group was gathered for the last time.

"We are now ere long to part asunder, and the Lord knoweth whether we shall see each other's faces again. But whether the Lord hath appointed it or not, I charge you before God and His blessed angels, to follow me no further than I follow Christ, and if God shall reveal anything to you by any other instrument of His, be as ready to receive it as ever you were to receive any truth by my ministry. For I am very confident the Lord hath more truth and light yet to break out of His holy word."

He went on to explain that there was no absolute certainty of revelation. The trouble with the Lutherans was they could not be drawn to go beyond what Luther saw. "They will die rather than embrace whatever part of God's will was revealed to Calvin. As for the Calvinists, they stick where Calvin left them. Yet were these two now living they would be as ready and willing to embrace further light, as that they had received." Then he went on to urge them to be very careful what they received for truth, to examine and weigh it and to check with each other and to compare. He stressed the responsibility of each individual to discuss and to question. He stressed toleration of other points of view, "rather to study union than division."

The Beginning

These ideas took hold and have continued. It is the best of the Puritan ideal. It is the spirit that is never sure it is right, that never closes its ears to rational argument, that never ceases to search for more truth and light and out of its passionate doubt finds the driving force to cross immense oceans and inhabit new worlds. It has appealed to emigrants ever since. Plenty who came after, like some who crossed on that first voyage, carried with them baggage of prejudice and dogma. But more than a majority came to accept Robinson's ideas, and still do. His ideas crossed the ocean. He never did. Prophets more often see the promised land than set foot on it.

After the Pilgrims left Holland but had not yet sailed from England, Robinson wrote them a letter and in it is a significant phrase, "Whereas you are become a body politic, using amongst yourselves civil government, and are not furnished with any persons of special eminence above the rest to be chosen by you into office of government, let your wisdom and godliness appear, not only in choosing such persons as do entirely love and promote the common good, but also in yielding unto them all due honor and obedience in their lawful administration." This phrase is echoed in the document now world famous, known as the Mayflower Compact, wherein the first settlers of New England "combined themselves into a civil body politic for their better ordering and preservation" and agreed to submit themselves to just and equal laws; which laws would be of their own making.

Here is the foundation of democracy; the obligation to discuss problems and to question truth; which is more than a right; it is a duty, for neither God nor all his regiments of angels can stand between mankind and its own acts; to form a body politic whose authority is derived from the governed; to obey the elected representatives as long as they perform their appointed task—"do love and promote the common good." It derives directly from the covenant between fellow believers traditional in the reformed churches. That it should be extended to political action is clearly set forth by Robinson before the departure of the Pilgrims from England. In this seed is expressed, as in the genes which control inheritance, the doc-

Edward Winslow — The only true likeness of a Plymouth Pilgrim.

trine of inherent, unalienable right which was to be developed into its ultimate expression in the Declaration of Independence.

What became of these ideas when they got to America is a long story. They did not live happily ever after. But they did live. The Pilgrim company was by no means a perfect model of equality or democracy. Along with some men of a little property there were indentured servants with no property at all but a pair of hands and no prospects but the expectation of future opportunity and liberty. There were women, who had no legal vote and no prospect of getting it. But it was unique in one respect. There was no representative of the King or of any recognized civil authority.

The only license for the voyage of the *Mayflower* was a charter from the King to settle in the northernmost parts of Virginia. That charter was made void because their landfall was Cape Cod and the very imminent prospect of death by drowning on Nantucket shoals forced them to sail north instead of south. They were obliged to think for themselves and act independently. That had always been their intention and circumstances favored their intention. The tools of their future were discussion, doubt, self-discipline and democracy. These became the pattern for the English colonies in America. Authority was the pattern for the French and the Spanish colonies, as it had also been and long continued to be for the Jamestown colony in Virginia.

This was the beginning. The Pilgrims' universe has changed and grown ever since. It would not be intelligible, not comprehensible, to this, its first part. It will not cease from change. As it changes, the perception of each of its parts changes, and as the perception changes the shape of the whole is changed. Nothing is static, least of all the past. Some fragments of it recede into oblivion. Other fragments rush out of lost time and move the present world. The science of history is the discovery, the examination and the calculation of the mass, the velocity and the direction of these fragments.

THE LIGHT HERE KINDLED

*T*he first Thanksgiving was the best. It was celebrated on a date uncertain, probably early October 1621 at New Plymouth in New England. It was the age of innocence; the new beginning. Paradise lost might yet be regained. In a new Eden mankind was to have a second chance.

It was indeed a new Eden. "They began now to gather in the small harvest they had, being all well recovered in health and strength and had all things in good plenty. Some were exercised in fishing, about cod and bass and other fish, of which they had good store. And now began to come in store of fowl of which this place did abound. And besides waterfowl there was great store of wild turkeys, of which they took many, besides venison etc. They had about a peck of meal a week to a person, Indian corn to that proportion."

The writer is William Bradford, who for most of the rest of his life was to be the annually re-elected Governor of the Plymouth colony. He was a widower of thirty-two years, his wife Dorothy having drowned in Provincetown harbor the previous December. Of those who had left England in the *Mayflower* just half survived. But no one had died since spring. The children were thriving. There were twenty-five of them and twenty-five others, mostly young bachelors. Marriageable girls were in short supply. Of married couples there were just four, and one of these was the union of a recent widow and widower.

Providence now smiled on their enterprise. There had been no sickness all summer, and no hunger since the English-speaking native Squanto had come into their midst, taught them how to tread eels out of the mud, net herring in the brook and to set corn. The Indians were friendly; at least those were with whom they had any immediate contact. Some Cape Indians had shot

8

arrows at them on their first landing at Eastham, they heard rumors of a great and warlike people to the south, the Narragansetts, and they knew that a fearful sickness had almost completely eliminated the Indian population of the region where they were settled and to the northward.

They knew almost nothing about Indian politics. Of the extent of the continent which lay to the west they had absolutely no idea. Who or what might inhabit that incredible wilderness they were better off not trying to guess. So with the good sense and the boldness which marked most of their actions after Bradford took over the management of affairs, they settled on a policy of cultivating the friendship of Massasoit, Chief of the Wampanoags. They knew he had about a hundred naked warriors under his direct command. He seemed to enjoy a sort of vague sovereignty over other tribal chiefs. With him they made a treaty. So Edward Winslow, Bradford's ablest lieutenant, was able to write to a friend, "We walk as peaceably and safely in the wood as in the highways of England, we entertain the Indians familiarly in our houses, and they as friendly bestow their venison on us."

Their sole means of communicating with the Indians, except for a few grunts and signs, was through Squanto. He had been kidnapped some six years before from that very place, sold in Spain for a slave, redeemed by a charitable priest and somehow made his way to England where he became a member of the household of an English merchant, "the worshipful John Slany." Sent on an exploring expedition to North America in 1619, he jumped ship at Martha's Vineyard, made his way back to Plymouth and found all his people dead of a plague. He lived disconsolate among Massasoit's people; when the Pilgrims arrived, he threw in his lot with them. He lived among them for less than two years, then died of that mysterious sickness that destroyed Indians, not whites.

He was certainly at Plymouth on Thanksgiving Day of 1621. It would be more correct to speak of Thanksgiving Days. Following the old medieval custom Bradford proclaimed a period of feasting. He sent four men on a fowling expedition "so we might after a more special manner rejoice together after we had gathered the fruit of our labor." Those four men in one day shot enough wild geese, ducks and turkeys to feed the whole company for a week. Not only did they feed the fifty whites but also Massasoit and ninety of his men, with their wives and children. Massasoit's contribution was five deer and a barrel or two of oysters. On the table, too, were cod and bass and fat eels, clams and lobsters, dandelion greens and other wild herbs known to the Indians and now forgotten or destroyed by an industrial age. Certainly there was thick and heady wine made from "grapes white and red, very sweet and strong."

They entertained and feasted the Indians for three days. According to the old English custom they had games, marching, and target practice. The Indians danced. The Pilgrim army amounted to about a dozen men. They were armed with matchlock guns and in Myles Standish had a formidable commander. But their real shield and defense, indeed their survival, was arranged by a most extraordinary sequence of luck. Squanto, by being kidnapped, was saved from the plague that wiped out his entire tribe, the Pokanokets. And his many adventures thereafter caused him to reappear at Plymouth just in the nick of time. Bradford called him "a special instrument sent by God for their good beyond their expectation." Squanto's diplomatic skill and his facility with languages made it possible for ninety Indian warriors to move freely among a mere handful of whites "for we have found the Indians very faithful in their covenant of peace with us; we often go to them and they come to us; some of us have been fifty miles by land to the country with them." These good relations lasted just exactly as long as Squanto. When he died the following year misunderstandings developed, soon reaching the stage of violence, fanned by Captain Standish's hot and jealous nature. The serpent was loosed in Eden.

But paradise was not entirely lost. The sane and decent character of Bradford pervaded the acts of Plymouth Plantation, tempered the cruelty of the Puritan theocracy that dominated Boston and Salem. Plymouth hanged neither witches nor Quak-

A SERMON PREACHED AT PLIMMOTH IN NEVV-ENGLAND

December 9. 1 6 2 1.

In an affemblie of his *Maiefties faithfull Subiects, there inhabiting.*

VVHEREIN IS SHEVVED

the danger of felfe-loue, and the fweetneffe of true Friendfhip.

TOGETHER VVITH A PREFACE,

Shewing the ftate of the Country, *and Condition of the* SAVAGES.

Rom. 12. 10.

Be affectioned to loue one another with brotherly loue.

Written in the yeare 1621.

LONDON

Printed by *I. D.* for IOHN BELLAMIE, and are to be fold at his fhop at the two Grey-hounds in Corne-hill, neere the *Royall Exchange.* 1 6 2 2.

Deacon Robert Cushman's sermon, Plymouth 1621. Published London 1622.

ers. It passed no laws against gay apparel. Roger Williams, before he went to Providence and founded his tolerant plantation, found refuge there. Democracy got a good start at Plymouth, beginning with the famous Compact. The world may yet rediscover that enlightenment in race relations that was first revealed at Plymouth.

For one brief moment of Indian summer, that gives each fall promise of another spring, on that first Thanksgiving red man and white sat down together in peace and cheerfulness. The golden afternoon arrested the spirits of all men. Savage competition was for a moment stilled like the sea currents resting at full flood before they are seized with the madness of the ebb. Freeborn American and freedom-seeking European, under the magical sky, shared equal plenty, rejoiced in hope, forgot the miserable past and perched on the narrow edge of an unmeasured land, cut off from custom by ocean and the shock of new ideas, dared to believe in the brotherhood of man and a loving God. It was but a moment. And Bradford put it in words of immortal measure, "as one small candle may light a thousand, so the light here kindled hath shone unto many, yea in some sort to our whole nation."

THANKSGIVING HAS TWO FACES

*N*ovember is the pious month. In November politicians, editorialists and sometimes historians spout platitudes as if Plymouth Rock itself were Old Faithful geyser. It would be better, each November, to remember also certain realities of the American experience that began with the Pilgrims.

My Lai is now a household word. It means massacre. It is not remembered that My Lai is in one of the worst and oldest American traditions. On a winter day in 1623 Myles Standish and a half dozen men from the Plymouth Colony arrived in Quincy Bay, a part of Boston Harbor. Under pretense of trade they lured some of the local Indians into their stockade. Suddenly shutting the gates, they stabbed and murdered two chief warriors, hung another with rope and then shot or hacked to death three others.

This is called "The Wessagusset Affair." No white man had been attacked by any Indian. The alleged reason for the massacre was a plot suspected against the settlement at Plymouth. It is a plot whose existence is substantiated only by the testimony of those who committed the murders. It was said to be a preventive action. As such it has been condoned by historians. It bears a ghastly resemblance to the Tonkin Bay lie that was used as justification for the Vietnam escalation and the bombing of Indochina.

One notable protest was made at the time. John Robinson, the Pilgrims' spiritual leader, wrote from Holland "concerning the killing of those poor Indians"—"where blood is once begun to be shed, it is seldom stanched off a long time after." And of their military man, "there is cause to fear there may be wanting

13

that tenderness of the life of man (made after God's image) which is meet."

Robinson's warning has turned out to be unfortunately true. The record of Americans in dealing with weak groups of people of different race has been often savage. The Pilgrims got us off to a bad start.

This is much the worst, really the only serious crime that can be charged up against the Pilgrims. They were, compared to later settlers of Boston bay under Endicott and Winthrop, decidedly tolerant, almost gentle. And there is another part of their story pertinent to later times. We are accustomed to celebrate their fortunate landing. Material success has always pleased Americans inordinately and a turkey dinner is one of its symbols. But it is also appropriate to remember the flight of the Pilgrims from their homeland.

In many respects the Pilgrims resembled those called draft resisters. They found intolerable a society whose aims they totally deplored. In protest they risked life and property and took the chance of exile.

Tudor and Stuart England required complete compliance with the King's will. Dissent was a crime and the crime of advocating dissent in others was worse still. For "devising and circulating seditious books" men were hanged and disemboweled. As with the famous Pentagon Papers case, revelation of anything but officially authorized truth was fraught with risks. Assembly to discuss unauthorized truth was a crime punishable by fine and imprisonment.

The whole system seemed rotten to a gradually enlarging group of serious people. Those who felt deeply the guilt of association with the corruption of government fled to Holland. But their flight was little noticed by their contemporaries. To the authorities the chief interest of the refugees was the opportunity to confiscate their property. The populace called them "Brownists," a term of contempt like the Vietnam-period word "hippy," and occasionally enjoyed watching the humiliation or execution of one of them.

Looking back into history we can see portents where contemporaries saw only subjects for ridicule or active dislike. For when conditions become sufficiently intolerable so that an appreciable number of people flee their country things may be getting serious. It is like the flight of geese southward. So it proved with the Pilgrims. Within their generation there was a complete overthrow of the regime that forced them out. The notion of divine right on which it was based was discredited and the King was beheaded.

For intolerable governments have a tendency to destroy themselves while building up and enriching other nations. America has commonly been the beneficiary of such social profligacy. Those we call Pilgrims were but the firstcomers. The Reformation continued to send refugees for well over a hundred years, both Protestant and Catholic. And the repressions of liberty in 19th-century Europe kept up the flood, aided by economics and military conscription. The flight from fascism has been a major fact in the enrichment of American society, science and culture throughout the 20th century.

Only black slaves found America intolerable in the 19th century. But the increasing flight of slaves from the South foreshadowed the Civil War. The flight of young men to escape the American draft during the Vietnam period was a similar portent. It revealed a society ill at ease, a society that depended more than formerly on repression to hold itself together. There could be no Thanksgiving till the strange unnatural tide of young Americans away from their country stopped. Till again America was a land that pilgrims came to. Not a land they fled.

CHRISTMAS COMES TO BOSTON

*T*he peculiar quality of the American character was set at the beginning and still builds along the old lines. We are a mixing people, a federalizing type. We have accepted inter-racial toleration not necessarily because we liked it but because it worked. After it worked we discovered we liked it. We liked it in the most practical and agreeable way. The girls and boys got married and along with their genes their customs got mixed.

On board the *Mayflower* was a girl called Priscilla Molines. At least that is the way her father spelled the family name. But her father died in the great sickness of the first winter and Miss Molines became Miss Mullins and later became Mrs. John Alden in a romance almost as famous as Juliet's with Romeo, but more successful. On the next boat to sail into Plymouth were some others with French "outlandish" names. There was Phillipe de la Noye. And Moisse Symonson. And Edouard Bompass. They were French-speaking Walloons from the Low Countries. Their names soon became Delano and Simmons and Bumpas. The French Delanos from Massachusetts later got mixed up with the Dutch Roosevelts in New York and by adding a Franklin made a President of the United States.

Dutch and French words were familiar in the Old Colony. Simply to survive in Holland, the Pilgrims had been obliged to learn something of the language. Brewster knew Latin and Dutch and could converse with the learned men of the University of Leyden. Bradford and Winslow were fluent in Dutch and could read Latin. But the hardships of the New World were no encouragement to learning. Reading and writing were taught at the primary level. Beyond that communication was oral. A new language began to develop, American.

Captain Hewitt, R.M.S. Britannia, starts for home after delivering the
first copy of Dickens' *Christmas Carol* to America.

The dominant group was Puritan and English and the language and prejudices of the dominant group took over—with modifications. The modifications are important for they set the pattern we still follow. They were encouraged by the necessities of frontier living. The language became phonetic and staccato. There were no dictionaries to anchor sounds. The prejudices were tempered by amazement at unlimited space and by the human sympathy engendered by the endurance of much suffering. As Dido remarked to Aeneas when, to her own great disadvantage, she fished him out of the sea, "Non ignara mali miseris succurere disco," which means, in American, "Brother, I've been wet myself and I'm sure glad to give a helping hand."

Unity was necessary for survival and the most effective means of achieving unity was by some measure of toleration. Brutality had been tried at Jamestown in Virginia and it did not work. Military discipline was the accepted means of managing affairs in the French and Spanish empires to north and south. But by the nature of their religious beliefs and the Congregational organization of their church the Pilgrims were predisposed to democracy and toleration.

Yet tolerance is not the easiest virtue to come by. Probably it is the latest and the last in any society. Nothing makes people so sure as uncertainty and the way to salvation is confused by signs pointing in different directions. So Christmas at Plymouth in early days was not exactly gay.

The first Christmas celebrated in New England was marked by a singular act of charity. On that day the Pilgrims, who did not believe in Christmas celebrations of any kind, ran out of beer. But Captain Jones of the *Mayflower*, no Puritan himself, insisted on sharing his stock with them. During the next three months, in the great sickness which killed half the company, he continued the same charity, declaring that those sick who had need of beer should have it "though he drank water homeward bound."

The fear of drinking water was well founded. The germ theory of disease was not yet imagined. But it was an observed fact that those who drank water were prone to mysterious, innumerable ills, dysentery and the like, very often fatal. Water kept in casks aboard ship developed a rotten taste; became after awhile so foul that rats would not drink it. Already by that first Christmas day, six of the Pilgrim company were dead.

It was a grim Christmas day, that first one in New England, so meagerly celebrated. It was a work day, of course. Strict Puritans observed none of the old holidays, which were closely associated in their minds with religious persecution and corruption in church and state. In the afternoon it blew up a great storm of wind and rain. The task force ashore, trying to set up the very first house, must needs rough it as best they could for two days, before a boat could be sent from the ship to fetch them.

The next Christmas was less grim; but not gay. By now the Pilgrims had invented their own great feast of Thanksgiving—and that was enough of holidays! It lasted a week! So, as Governor Bradford wrote, "on the day called Christmas," when some newcomers by the latest ship staged a sit-down strike, he took positive action. At first he admonished them. Then, with the faithful who had survived the great sickness, he quietly set the example of going to work in the fields. But on returning for dinner he found the recalcitrants playing ball; whereupon he took away the ball, saying, "If they made the keeping of Christmas matter of devotion, let them keep their own houses, but there should be no gaming or reveling in the streets." And later he added a footnote, "since which time nothing hath been attempted that way, at least openly."

In England the great Puritan poet John Milton might write his exalted "Ode on the Morning of Christ's Nativity." In New England, untempered by art or poetry, firm prejudice had its way. Remembrance of Christmas and the generous deed of Captain Jones receded into the mists of time. The message of good will must wait a century or two. For soon the mild restraint of Bradford in the Old Colony became rigid law in the Bay Colony as the great Puritan migration took over all the land from

Cape Ann to Cohasset. Fierce Endicott and stern Winthrop condemned even "gay apparel" and to take notice of Christmas was made a crime.

That law was repealed after the Restoration of Charles II. But the custom of work on Christmas day was unbroken. In the taverns along the waterfront the sailors might get a little drunker than usual on Christmas night; but respectable people paid no attention. Then came the French. Louis XIV revoked the tolerant Edict of Nantes when Boston was barely fifty years old. Many of his most enterprising and industrious subjects fled France, driven into exile by their bigoted Sun King. Some came to Boston, bringing their language, their customs and along with their Bibles their volumes of the urbane essays of Montaigne.

There was no controlling these French. Their credentials as Protestants were as good or better than the English Puritans. Their faith had been tested in a persecution even more savage, more thorough. Yet they celebrated Christmas! Samuel Sewell wrote in his famous diary, "This day I spoke with Mr. Newman about his partaking with the French Church on the 25th of December on account of its being Christmas as they abusively call it." The French Church was decorated with pine and hemlock, with holly and with laurel in December. On the 25th, when the rest of Boston went about its business as usual, the French congregation came together and sang joyously. Then they went home and drank wine—another heresy. The sign of strong faith in old Boston was strong drink, rum if you could get it, if not, hard cider. But heresy is catching. Bostonians discovered that they liked wine and the importation of Madeira became a big business. Much more gradually they discovered that they liked to celebrate Christmas.

The French were the first distinct group to follow the English settlers into Boston. They spoke a strange language, met for religious services in a small building on School Street. As soon as they could afford to they built, in accordance with the new fire laws, a brick church. And they afforded it surprisingly soon. Trade made the wealth of Boston and the French were adept at trade. The persecution in the homeland had scattered members of one family, the Faneuils, to Holland, to Ireland, to England, to New Rochelle in New York and to Boston, where one of them, Andrew, became the city's richest merchant. His great house, standing among seven acres of gardens and fruit trees, where the One Beacon Street tower rises today, was the showplace of the town.

The French Church survived a generation. How long French survived as a spoken language in Boston is uncertain. Probably less long, although Peter Faneuil, nephew and heir of Andrew, ordered, as late as 1738, "1 handsome, large, octavo Common Prayer Book of a good letter and well bound, with one of the same in French for my own use." But the assimilation into the American scene was nearly complete. The order was placed on Faneuil's London agents and like most of his business correspondence was in English. Trinity Church had just been founded. The Faneuil family maintained pews in both the old French Church and the new Trinity.

Faneuil Hall remains to this day abiding evidence of the generous invasion of Puritan Boston by the French race. Less obvious are certain inheritances of brown eyes and dark complexions and innumerable corruptions of French names, such as Appolus Rivoire, which was soon turned into Paul Revere. For some reason, probably because of Peter's munificent gift, the Faneuil name retained its ancient French spelling. On the corner of Peter's gravestone it is chiseled as it was pronounced in his lifetime, Funel.

But Boston had to wait yet a century to shake off its old Puritan prejudice. The glorious celebration of Christmas as the brightest and most cheerful of the year's holidays, the feast of forgiveness of trespasses and hope for the kingdom of a merciful God, came to Boston on a day in January 1844 in a small packet wrapped in brown paper in the special care of Captain Hewitt of the Royal Mail Steamer (paddle wheel) *Britannia*. It was addressed to C.C. Felton, Professor of Greek at the University in Cambridge, and could be delivered only by hand. The sender was Charles Dickens. Within the package was a little volume set between red covers, brightly illustrated by George Cruikshank. The title was *A Christmas Carol* and this was the first copy to reach America.

It was a gift in return for hospitality, an acknowledgment of the genesis of an idea. Boston had a hand in the making of *A Christmas Carol*. It snows but seldom in London. The number of white Christmases in a century are few indeed. Dickens was only thirty years old when he wrote his famous story. And in that story there are descriptions of many a Christmas and almost always either it is snowing or there is snow on the ground. The air is seldom clear and bright in southern England in winter, and the sun almost never shines. The warm moist air of the Gulf Stream condensing over cold land sees to that. And in Dickens's day the burning of coal assured a constant fog.

Yet Dickens had vividly in mind a snow scene which, like a theme and variations, pervades his story. Boston provided it. In January of the previous year, after a fearful Atlantic crossing on one of the very first Cunard liners, which nearly lost its smoke stack and so the ship in a conflagration, Dickens, with his young wife, had arrived at the old Long Wharf.

A crowd of newspaper reporters and a gentleman from the *Transcript* jumped aboard and surrounded him. He was the greatest celebrity to come to the city since Lafayette. The rage for his works was like a forest fire. Oliver Twist, Mr. Pickwick, Fagin, Bill Sikes, Little Nell and Barnaby Rudge were as familiar in Boston as the State House. He was besieged with questions. The gentleman from the *Transcript*, Dr. Palmer, asked just one, "Did Mr. Dickens have hotel accommodations?" Then Dr. Palmer hailed a cab and galloped to the Tremont House where he engaged the best suite. For the next two weeks the *Transcript* was the horse's mouth.

That night there was a full moon and it was very cold. After a gin sling and a sangaree and a beefsteak, Dickens set out to explore. He was wrapped to the ears in a shaggy fur coat and ran down School Street, into Washington and back via Temple Place over the shining, frozen snow. All the time he kept up a continual shout of uproarious laughter, never stopping, reading the street signs as he ran, delighting in the strange architecture of this new world. And the next day he was still more delighted, "The air was so clear, the houses so bright and gay, the signboards were painted in such gaudy colors, the bricks were so very red, the stone was so very white, the blinds and area railings were so very green, the knobs and plates upon the street doors so marvelously bright and twinkling ... " This reality that Dickens saw became part of the dream *A Christmas Carol.*

Of course the young genius was feted within an inch of his life. The doors along Beacon Street opened and sucked him in. Black waistcoats were the uniform of the gentlemen in Boston. Dickens wore waistcoats red and green with fathoms of gold chains. This became the fashion. At one formal table he pulled out a pocket comb and staring into a big dining room mirror arranged his long black hair. Long hair became the fashion, though hair doing in public had to wait another century. But the shock of the combing was nothing to the shock at the historian Prescott's great dinner when the talk turned on two famous beauties. "Well, I don't know," said Dickens, "Mrs. Norton perhaps is the more beautiful, but the Duchess of Sutherland, to my mind, is the more kissable."

Dickens left Boston in a flurry of snow, sleighbells and good wishes. He left behind him the best friends he made in America, Felton, later President of Harvard, the poet Longfellow and all the great of New England's flowering. "Boston is what I would like the whole United States to be," he wrote. The rest of the country he found crude, commercial, sharp dealing, dreary. He was disgusted by the universal chewing and spitting of tobacco, even on the floor of the Senate in Washington. The sight and smell of slavery horrified him.

He returned to England in June in the safety of a sailing ship. Already on that long and delightful Atlantic crossing the idea of a Christmas story was stirring in his mind. Over its composition he excited himself in a most extraordinary manner. As summer moved into fall he walked about the black streets of London thinking about it. Many a night he walked fifteen and twenty miles, weeping, laughing and weeping again. The story was in the hands of the printer in time for Christmas publication.

Twenty-five years later he returned to Boston and stayed at the magnificent new Parker House. But he stayed as royalty does, protected from the public eye by faithful attendants, venturing out incognito to visit favorite friends. He was alone now, separated from his wife, seeking by public readings to gain the dollars denied him by the lack of copyright. He suffered from an unremitting cold, which he tried to cure by dozen mile walks to Cambridge and back with his adoring friend and American publisher, James T. Fields. He slept little and worked all the time, preparing his readings, writing new stories. Coming onto the stage at Tremont Temple he sometimes was so worn he had to be lifted up by his manager. But as he entered the glare of the gaslights he suddenly revived, threw off all appearance of illness and became the most extraordinary personality ever to appear on a Boston stage.

Dickens was a wonderful actor. He lived the parts, created them anew, embellished the people his extraordinary imagination had given the world. The Temple was packed at every reading. It was the greatest show on earth. Mr. Pickwick, Dick Swiviler—Dickens really was Dick Swiviler—came alive as their creator put aside his book, acted each person, improvised lines when his own text was insufficient for the thrill of the moment.

The greatest triumph was on Christmas Eve 1868. The reverberations of Dickens's performance that night to the standing room only crowd in Tremont Temple have come down to this day. "Out upon Merry Christmas," said Scrooge."What's Christmas time to you ... "? No one ever again in Boston would be so dull, so stupid, so mean as to decry Christmas. When at last Dickens, as the Ghost of Christmas Yet to Come, brought his audience to the so quiet Cratchit house and showed the empty chair of Tiny Tim, there was unrestrained weeping. One young woman, in deep mourning, fainted and was carried out. But then the awful ghost vanished.

Christmas Comes to Boston

Abruptly it was Christmas Day. Scrooge—and Boston—was a new man. Feasting and jollity, kindness and sharing, filled the air. Tiny Tim did not die after all. No! He waved his little crutch and cried the toast "God bless us everyone!"

THE TAX THAT FAILED

*W*hen the Peace of Paris in 1763 ended French dominion in North America, Britain became the greatest empire since Rome. And George III, a cheerful young man in his early twenties, who had just succeeded to the throne, seemed to be about to show the world a new golden age of Marcus Aurelius.

But the tax burden left by the wars was very great. George and his Ministers decided the American colonies should share it. London conveniently forgot that the Americans already had been taxing themselves and sending levy after levy of men for half a century to fight the French and Indians. So George Grenville, the Empire's Treasurer, cast about for a means of raising money. He hit on revenue stamps. He thought he was being considerate as well as clever. Since the tax would hit everybody about equally, nobody in particular could complain.

The rage, the shouts and the violence that greeted the act surprised Grenville and the licentious, loose-living legislature he represented. The government of England then was anything but an efficient tyranny. It was tyranny of a sort, a rather ratty sort, careless in its administration and indiscriminate in its results. Taxes were levied without consulting most of the people. But property, for those who had any, was carefully safeguarded. And life and liberty, even of the destitute, enjoyed the limited protection of habeas corpus and trial by jury. Spain, France and even the miserable German Principalities, where most of the burden of taxation fell on those who could not complain, were much better organized. They approached, but could hardly equal Russia, where everybody was taxed by the tyrant who in his person was the state, and nobody dared complain.

The Tax That Failed

The one feature that all these systems had in common was that their subjects were used to them. They had developed gradually through the ages, modified from time to time by revolts or repressions as this or that group or individual gained the upper hand. They contained no surprises. The serf or peasant was born to his yoke. The tenant farmer to his rent. The lord to his manor. The king to his uneasy throne. And the colonies were used to their system, too. They taxed themselves for their own protection and improvement. The King, who protected and regulated trade, was entitled to customs duties. That was all.

Grenville made the worst single mistake that any taxing authority can make. He surprised and hurt everyone at once. It was as if, just at dinner time, he had managed to slip a tack onto the seat of every chair in the American colonies. His tax required that nobody could read a newspaper, graduate from school or even give money to a school, take any action in law, get married, die, play cards or take a drink of anything but cold water or home brew without making a special contribution to the King. And to make matters much worse, and to insure that the wound would continue to sting even after the tack was pulled out, all payment of the tax had to be made to England in hard money. Gold and silver were scarce already. Payment of the tax would, in a few years, drain the colonies of specie and bring on a disastrous inflation.

The perfect situation was thus created for the tax resister. Town and country were equally alarmed. The interest of the tavern brawler was made equal with that of the rich merchant. The farm hand had reason to be as bitter in his protest as the owner of the farm, the shipwright and the rigger as the builder of the ship. And Boston, renowned for ships, for trade, for argument and learning, for dissident puritanism and just plain cussedness, was the ordained eye of the building hurricane.

The first uneasy breaths of hot air, and action hotter yet, began to stir just at the corner of Washington and Essex Streets. The distillery of Chase and Speakman was located there. On the second floor was a private room where met "the

27

loyal nine," a very select and very secretive group known as the Caucus Club. Among them were the printer of the *Boston Gazette*, a sea captain, half a dozen tradesmen and two distillers. From here originated the actions and, so the Tories said, "the courage from the steams of their poisonous rum" of the Boston mobs that soon controlled the town.

Sam Adams was not a member. But he was a frequent guest and it is pretty well understood now that it was he who was the brains and gave the orders to the caucus. Sam's second cousin John was not a member either but he was agreeably entertained there with "punch, wine, pipes and tobacco etc and patriotic toasts." In the open square opposite grew a great oak tree. The acorn had been planted more than a century before in the first year of the Puritan Revolution that had liquidated Charles I. Patriots enjoyed reminding English kings of that.

On a steamy August morning in 1765 a crowd began to assemble under this tree. Hanging by the neck from a high branch was a dummy, elegantly dressed in blue swallowtail coat and knee breeches. Staring up at it was Sam Adams. An officer of the crown approached him and asked whose was the effigy. "I do not know—I cannot tell—I want to inquire" was the bland reply.

Sam needed to feign more than nearsightedness. The effigy was clearly labeled "Andrew Oliver." It represented the man who had been designated Stamp Master for Boston. And Sam knew a great deal more than he was prepared to admit about the plans for the rest of the day.

Things turned out almost, but not quite, as planned. The sheriff arrived to take down the dummy. The crowd prevented him. All day it hung there. Towards evening certain respectable tradesmen, decently dressed, took it down, laid it on a bier, and at the head of an orderly mob, paraded to the Old State House where the Governor was sitting in Council. They marched three times around the State House and gave three cheers for "Liberty and Property."

Then the more respectable element went home. The rest proceeded to Oliver Street where they pulled down a building on Oliver's Wharf, said to contain stamps. With the wreckage they proceeded to Fort Hill and built a bonfire. Then they beheaded and burned Oliver's dummy and on the way home smashed the windows of Oliver's house.

A similar and much worse outrage was perpetrated a week later with the looting of Lt. Governor Hutchinson's house. Hutchinson barely escaped with his life. The history of the Commonwealth that night suffered irreparable loss. For in the house, and destroyed by the senseless mob, was a great number of original documents, the best record of the beginnings of the Bay Colony.

Violence had now gone much too far, farther than its originators had intended. Miraculously, order was restored. Mobs and marches continued for the rest of the summer. But they were controlled, as by a regiment of soldiers. Respectable citizens, not too subtly disguised as roughs, appeared in the ranks. The mobs moved, turned or stopped in response to quietly spoken orders, appeared or disappeared from the streets at the sound of a whistle. And the Royal Governor, with his stamps and his tax collectors, fled down the harbor and took refuge on Castle Island.

The rest of the country caught the fever. The Stamp Act was completely nullified. The British Parliament, admitting defeat, repealed it. To save face, at the same time it passed an act declaring that it could, at its pleasure, "bind the colonies in all cases whatsoever." This, being merely a declaration, the colonies ignored. They went right ahead in uproarious celebration of the glorious fact of the death of the tax.

Had the British Parliament there let matters rest, there would have been no American Revolution. Total calm descended on the Empire. The health of George III was drunk in bumper after bumper from one end of the continent to the other. Crowds assembled around the Liberty Tree to cheer his name. A vicious tax had been nullified by universal and simultaneous action. It had been repealed by the common consent of those who imposed it and those who would not endure it. It was a result unique in the life of this nation. It was a condition and a happy result that would not be repeated, in all probability, to the end of time.

CHAMPAGNE TOWNSHEND AND TAXES

*G*eorge III was, perhaps, sufficiently stupid to dismember the British Empire all by himself. But he had the assistance of a very clever man. Charles Townshend is a statesman who has left nothing but mistakes to account for his fame. His wit, his eloquence and his indiscretion were famous. When he staggered to his feet in the House of Commons, word was passed to the lobby and the members rushed in to hear him, as to a play.

Townshend took over the job of Treasurer of the British Empire in 1766. The Stamp Tax on the American colonies had just been repealed by common consent of the taxers and the taxed. Not a single penny of revenue had it produced. It had been made perfectly clear, and all parties were agreed, that unless the British sent an army along with the stamps the act could not be enforced. And as yet neither Britain nor the colonies were ready for war.

Then Townshend made a famous speech and proposed the Acts that bear his name. When he finished, the House clapped and roared in rapture. "A half bottle of champagne, poured on genuine genius, kindled a wonderful blaze. It was at once proof that his abilities were superior to those of all men, and his judgment below that of any man," was Horace Walpole's comment.

The debate that followed gives the flavor of the curious club that was then the House of Commons. It was made up of country squires, who owned immense tracts of land farmed by tenants, and the younger sons of the nobility. A change of ministry occurred not because the people got fed up with the notorious bribery and corruption but because one or another power group was dissatisfied with its share of the loot.

Champagne Townshend and Taxes

Ex-Treasurer Grenville, whose Stamp Tax had failed, was furious at Townshend's clever jibes at the way he had managed affairs. He shouted, "You are cowards. You are afraid of the Americans. You dare not tax America." Townshend shouted back, "Fear? Cowards? Dare not tax America? I dare tax America!!"

The taxes he thought up were a lot cleverer than Grenville's clumsy effort. They were wrapped in the comfortable cloak of tradition. According to old theory the Crown, which supplied navy and protection on the seas, was entitled to regulate trade and levy customs duties. This theory, unfortunately for the colonials, had been supported by some of their best thinkers. The trouble with the Stamp Tax, it was claimed, was that it was a *direct* tax and unconstitutional. So when the theory was turned around and *indirect* customs taxes were imposed, some new arguments had to be invented.

Actually the colonies were not too stirred up by the new and added customs levies on certain specified items like glass, tea, paper and paint. The people in the back country hardly noticed the difference in price. They were used to being fairly regularly gouged by the seaport traders anyway. But the traders, especially the big merchants like John Hancock, who owned fleets of ships, discovered they were in deep trouble. The taxes they would have to pay were bad enough, would eat up their profits and drain the colonies of specie. But how the money was used was the stickler.

A good chunk of it, nearly half, was used to increase the number of revenue cutters and customs inspectors in an effort to stop smuggling. Some more was used to pay judges and royal governors. This was a very real peril. Formerly these officials had been paid by the colonials and had tenure "during good behavior." Now they had tenure "at the King's pleasure" and since he was paying their keep they would become mere creatures of his will. A foreign hand was reaching out to control the daily life of the people. For well over a century, especially in New England, the people had directed their own affairs, become used to independence. They were not about to let it go without a fight.

The BOSTONIAN'S Paying the EXCISE-MAN, or TARRING & FEATHERING

Boston tars and feathers the British tax collector.

Champagne Townshend and Taxes

The devil in Townshend's acts was their enforcement. Townshend was too smart to tax everybody at once and directly. He chose instead to use the invisible tax, the tax on trade. And the only shock was to the professional importers, suddenly faced with a shipload of customs inspectors fresh out of Scotland, tough, well paid and unbribable men. Always before the customs had been sinecures of English lords and gentlemen. They sold licenses to collectors who were native Americans. And the native Americans accepted presents of rum and money from other native Americans so that His Majesty's customs ended up in a deficit.

Smuggling had always been a part of colonial life, a profitable and rather exciting game to be played with His Majesty's enforcers. It was commonly regarded as a special kind of unalienable right. Now Townshend proposed to change the rules. Sam Adams was beside himself. He considered arranging a particular reception for the royal tax commissioners, possibly with tar and feathers. But Sam was a thoughtful revolutionary. His appearance was plain and middle class. He was a superior scholar in Latin and Greek and the tactics of the Roman general Fabius, who gave the adjective fabian to our language, appealed to his subtle mind. He was "cool, abstemious, polished and refined," but like the Protestant reformer Calvin, "inflexible, uniform and consistent." He did not believe in getting too far ahead of public opinion. He preferred to mold it first.

The methods he used for molding agreeably filled the lack of theater and religious pageantry in Puritan Boston. It happened that the commissioners arrived on Guy Fawkes and Gunpowder Plot Day. They were allowed to land peacefully at the foot of State Street and escorted through town by a trained mob carrying signs "Liberty, Property and No Commissioners." They were lighted on their way by bonfires where "Devils, Popes and Pretenders" in effigy were being burned with joyous shouts and occasional bloodcurdling Indian war whoops.

During their stay the commissioners got little sleep. Marchers would parade around their houses blowing conch shells. Their honest efforts to collect port duties raised more and more resentment. Public opinion was excited by a boycott of British goods. And the mob's taste for excitement—and loot—was whetted by the occasional enforcement of the boycott by raiding the store of some Tory merchant. To add gaiety to the scene John Hancock provided liberty caps, banners and rum, and on very special occasions, fireworks.

This pageantry and propaganda successfully united the great middle class, hardworking tradesmen and artisans, against the common enemy, the distant British legislature and its self-serving burdensome taxes. A crisis came when the commissioners framed John Hancock and impounded his sloop *Liberty* on a charge of smuggling Madeira wine. At a nod from Sam Adams there was a riot. The *Liberty* was liberated. And the commissioners fled to Castle Island and the protection of a British man-of-war. Thence they wrote scare letters to England. The ministry responded with an order for troops. And presently a fleet of naval ships sailed into Boston, anchored off the foot of State Street and trained its guns on Faneuil Hall and the Old State House. Then the tax commissioners, escorted by four regiments of infantry in red coats, with bayonets fixed, returned to their office at the Custom House.

The fat was in the fire. It was now to be a trial of force. Pay taxes or fight.

FROM TEA TAX TO ARMS

*T*he decision of the British government to send troops to Boston in 1768 to enforce the collection of customs duties was a direct challenge to the American people. It was an unheard-of interference with traditional liberties; a real shocker. It was proposed to make use of "writs of assistance" to ferret out smuggled goods. These writs permitted royal officers to search any warehouse or private house for contraband. They were general writs, a crass, brutal violation of ancient English law as built up since Magna Carta. James Otis had clearly shown this seven years before in a very eloquent and famous plea before the Superior Court of the colony. He had electrified his hearers. In the words of John Adams, "He hurried away everything before him. American independence was then and there born; the seeds of patriots and heroes were then and there sown."

The Acts of Trade which now were being resuscitated by the British Parliament, and to which the Townshend Acts were an addition, were part of an ancient theory of empire management too long disregarded to be viable. Their purpose was to keep colonies forever in subjection, mere feeders of raw materials to the mother country. If enforced, they would wreck the profitable coastal and West Indies shipping business to the Spanish and French islands. And they would raise the prices of molasses and rum, without which New England could not live. The cost of living was threatened with a dangerous increase. Far more serious, the safety of every man in his own house was threatened. And almost every man chose, in some degree, to fight. The ablest and the most energetic men chose to fight to the bitter end, no matter what that end might be.

There was a general boycott of English goods. There was

enthusiastic support of the long popular and generally approved activities of smugglers. The Harvard Corporation voted to let the graduating class take degrees dressed in homespun instead of imported black broadcloth. The students made the interesting decision to give up drinking tea in favor of native rum. The various colonies formed Committees of Correspondence. These in effect were standby governments that could take over in case of revolution. And in Boston soon was felt the "dangerous, ruinous and fatal effects of standing armies in populous cities in time of peace."

By 1770 the launching stage was set for American Independence. The rocket was on its pad. For two years busy Patriots had been loading in the fuel, so generously supplied by the British Ministry. Incident followed incident. When there were no incidents, the ingenious contributors to *The Journal of Events*, written in Boston and printed in New York, invented them. The brawls of the soldiers, the high living and scandalous behavior of the officers got steady publicity.

Even the Tories were shocked. Of the 29th Regiment Governor Hutchinson wrote, "They are in general such bad fellows that it seems impossible to restrain them from firing upon an insult or provocation given them." The morals of the young, as befitted a Puritan city, became a chief preoccupation. The *Boston Evening Post* reported the grief of one sober Patriot who discovered "in the morning a soldier in bed with a favorite granddaughter." Hardly a day passed without a story being circulated of a soldier assaulting a woman. And the soldiers retorted that assault was quite unnecessary since the town's virtue was so easy that not an officer or private "down to a drummer, that cannot have his bedfellow for the winter; so that the Yankee war, contrary to all others, will produce more births than burials."

More serious incidents occurred. There was a row between the town paupers and the soldiers about a barracks. At night a drunken soldier might be beaten up. And one day there was a riot with the ropewalk workers and a civilian was killed. The count was coming down, steadily, relentlessly, and each time

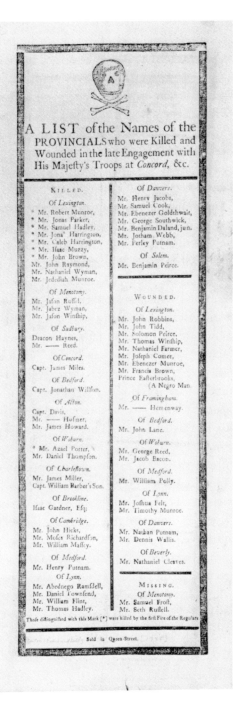

A LIST of the Names of the PROVINCIALS who were Killed and Wounded in the late Engagement with His Majefty's Troops at *Concord*, &c.

KILLED.

Of Lexington.
* Mr. Robert Munroe,
* Mr. Jonas Parker,
* Mr. Samuel Hadley,
* Mr. Jona' Harrington,
* Mr. Caleb Harrington,
* Mr. Ifaac Muzzy,
* Mr. John Brown,
Mr. John Raymond,
Mr. Nathaniel Wyman,
Mr. Jedediah Munroe.

Of Menotomy.
Mr. Jafon Ruffel,
Mr. Jabez Wyman,
Mr. Jafon Winfhip,

Of Sudbury.
Deacon Haynes,
Mr. —— Reed.

Of Concord.
Capt. James Miles.

Of Bedford.
Capt. Jonathan Willfon.

Of Afton.
Capt. Davis,
Mr. —— Hofmer,
Mr. James Howard.

Of Woburn.
* Mr. Azael Potter,
Mr. Daniel Thompfon.

Of Charleftown.
Mr. James Miller,
Capt. William Barber's Son.

Of Brookline.
Ifaac Gardner, Efq;

Of Cambridge.
Mr. John Hicks,
Mr. Mofes Richardfon,
Mr. William Maffey.

Of Medford.
Mr. Henry Putnam.

Of Lynn.
Mr. Abednego Ramfdell,
Mr. Daniel Townfend,
Mr. William Flint,
Mr. Thomas Hadley.

Of Danvers.
Mr. Henry Jacobs,
Mr. Samuel Cook,
Mr. Ebenezer Goldthwait,
Mr. George Southwick,
Mr. Benjamin Daland, jun.
Mr. Jotham Webb,
Mr. Perley Putnam.

Of Salem.
Mr. Benjamin Peirce.

WOUNDED.

Of Lexington.
Mr. John Robbins,
Mr. John Tidd,
Mr. Solomon Peirce,
Mr. Thomas Winfhip,
Mr. Nathaniel Farmer,
Mr. Joseph Comee,
Mr. Ebenezer Munroe,
Mr. Francis Brown,
Prince Eafterbrooks,
    (A Negro Man.

Of Framingham.
Mr. —— Hemenway.

Of Bedford.
Mr. John Lane.

Of Woburn.
Mr. George Reed,
Mr. Jacob Bacon.

Of Medford.
Mr. William Polly.

Of Lynn.
Mr. Joshua Felt,
Mr. Timothy Munroe.

Of Danvers.
Mr. Nathan Putnam,
Mr. Dennis Wallis.

Of Beverly.
Mr. Nathaniel Cleaves.

MISSING.

Of Menotomy.
Mr. Samuel Froft,
Mr. Seth Ruffell.

Thofe diftinguifhed with this Mark [*] were killed by the firft Fire of the Regulars

Sold in Queen-Street.

A list of the men killed in Concord fight. A powerful argument for revolution.

the church bells rang out a loud alarm. Zero hour came on a miserable night in March 1770. Wet snow mixed with the muck on the streets. A ragtag crowd was amusing itself firing snowballs at the sentry in front of the Custom House. Their aim was good. The sentry whistled for help. More soldiers came running. The crowd pressed closer. Ammunition harder than snow was passed up. It began to come—a paving stone—a brick—then a well-aimed log with a nail in it. A soldier was knocked flat. He picked up his gun and let fire into the mob. Suddenly there were many shots and then there were five crumpled bodies lying in the trampled, dirty snow.

Such was the Boston Massacre. The Revolutionary rocket was off the ground. Mobs formed. A packed town meeting sent demands to the Governor. Sam Adams was spokesman for the delegation. After much whispering between Governor Hutchinson and the commander of the King's troops, it was agreed to send one regiment out of the city. Sam Adams paused a long moment, then spoke in cool and even voice, "If you can send one you can send two." Sam later reported, "He turned pale. I saw his legs shake under the table. I rejoiced at the sight."

The royal authority folded completely. Both regiments went down the harbor to Castle island. There were just nine British soldiers left in the town of Boston, and they were in jail under indictment for murder. But there was no rioting; no suggestion of summary vengeance. Since then, from the French Revolution to the last murderous overthrow of government in the unhappy 20th century, there is no similar example of restraint. Some things do not improve.

The Revolutionary rocket was on its way to the stratosphere. But it did not go into orbit. The second stage did not fire. The best counsel in the colony was procured for the accused soldiers. Tried eight months later they were acquitted. The only useful propaganda that was got out of the Massacre was Paul Revere's famous engraving and an annual oration to commemorate the event.

Suddenly the whole climate of opinion changed. The British Parliament, responding to the agonized appeals of the London merchants, repealed the Townshend Acts, all but the tax on tea. The non-importation agreements among the American colonies began to lapse. A short harvest in Europe required heavy shipment of grain from America and for the first time since Jamestown was founded in 1607 the balance of trade was reversed and gold moved westward across the Atlantic. Prosperity began to dilute the spirit of liberty. Not much remained but a principle and the tax on tea. Principle alone makes a thin drink and John Adams, returning to his quiet farm in Quincy after his successful defense of the Massacre soldiers, could only hope, rather wanly, that the tea he had drunk at John Hancock's house had paid no tax—been honestly smuggled.

The Revolution might not again have got off the ground. But the British government was equal to the emergency. In the summer of 1773 it sent over enough solid fuel for a dozen rockets. Expediency got the better of common sense. Almost everybody who was anybody in England owned shares in the East India Company. And that included members of Parliament, both Lords and Commons. The Company was on the edge of bankruptcy. Its warehouses were bulging with tea because of the closing off of the American market. To bail it out the government agreed to let its tea leave England without paying the usual export tax. But it insisted that the American port tax be collected. It thus created a monopoly. East India Company teas would undersell all others—even smuggled tea. The merchants to whom the tea was consigned—who happened to be Tories—would undersell the Patriots and run them out of business. And once the tea got into the hands of retailers there would be no telling where it came from and the staunchest Patriot might drink the stuff and not choke.

Suddenly, as in stamp tax days, the whole country was united. The economy of the colonies was threatened by the use of a monopoly power that might destroy at will. The tea reached Charleston, South Carolina, and was stored in bond in a damp warehouse where it rotted. The tea ships entered New York harbor and prudently turned round and sailed home. The ships destined for the City of Brotherly Love never got into the Delaware River because of a casual remark dropped to a pilot, "What think you, Captain, of a halter round your neck, ten gallons of tar decanted on your pate—with the feathers of a dozen wild geese laid over to enliven your appearance."

Stubborn Governor Hutchinson of Massachusetts took a different tack. The tea was consigned to his sons. He let the tea ships enter the harbor and the Patriots let them tie up at Griffin's Wharf, but they posted guard night and day to prevent any tea being landed. At the end of three weeks—by law—the tea must be landed and pay tax—or the ships must sail home or be confiscated. But they could not sail without a permit from the Governor. He refused the permit.

When this news reached a mass meeting in the Old South Meeting House, Sam Adams rose and said simply, "This meeting can do nothing more to save the country." There was a war whoop from the gallery. War whoops answered from the street. And in the December dusk a troop of bogus Indians rushed to the tea ships and dumped their cargoes—worth about a million dollars—into the sea.

This time the Revolutionary rocket took off in real earnest. It is still in orbit.

LEXINGTON WAKES THE WORLD

*T*he defect of empire is that its government is separate from the governed. Democracies may be just as stupid, or even more so, but they feel pain sooner. The body of the British Empire was suffering severe cramps on the morning of the 19th of April 1775 but its nervous system was fast asleep in London. It was sleeping so soundly that it could not hear the voice of its greatest statesman, old William Pitt, shouting in its ear, "I trust that it will be impossible for free men in England to see three millions of Englishmen slaves in America."

It was anything but impossible. The voting for members of Parliament was so rigged that the people of England had almost no say in the government. One young member of the House of Commons remarked, and was much commended for his speech, that it was no shame that America had no representative in Parliament for after all, neither did Manchester nor Sheffield. William Pitt himself had been a member from Old Sarum, a rotten borough with almost no inhabitants, where sheep grazed over the ruins of an ancient city. Seats in Parliament were traded like real estate at an auction. The ministers of George III ruled by open bribery.

General Gage, their proconsul sent to Boston to close the port, force payment for the destroyed tea and starve the inhabitants into submission and enforce new coercive measures known as the Intolerable Acts, was a fit representative of such a crew. He had diligently spread the opinion that the inhabitants of New England were sanctimonious cowards. He greatly offended them when they set aside a day of fasting and prayer to deplore the King's acts, by issuing a manifesto against hypocrisy. And a dispatch sent to London read "as to what you hear of their taking arms it is merely bullying and will go no further than words. Whenever it comes to blows, he that can run fastest will think himself well off." The conclusion was that any two royal regiments could beat the whole force of the Massachusetts province.

It was in such a mood that the royal troops, magnificently dressed in their conspicuous red-topped uniforms, marching into the Common in Lexington at four in the morning of the 19th of April 1775, encountered a group of local militia drawn up in ragged ranks, and dispersed it with gunfire. Who fired first has been a subject of discussion ever since. The best opinion seems to be that it was some Yankee sniper with a bad aim firing from a too distant cover to do any damage. But whoever fired the first shot, there was almost instantly thereafter a volley from the royal troops that killed eight Americans. The troops then went on to Concord and what happened after to them at the hands of the Minutemen has been the subject of poetry, pageants and rhetoric ever since.

The success of the Patriot resistance that day was considerable. The success of the Patriot assault on public opinion in America and throughout the world in the weeks and the months that followed was stupendous. Sam Adams, when he heard the guns of Lexington, exclaimed, "Oh what a glorious morning!" He was bubbling over with excitement and glee. The thing had happened at last. The King's troops had committed the overt act that would rouse the people to implacable fury, that would unite the nation to drive the foreigner from the land.

Sam had inside knowledge of what would happen next. He knew that the propaganda machine that had made much of a minor riot and turned it into the Boston Massacre was tuned up and ready. He knew that Warren's able pen was filled with ink; that half a dozen others on the Committee of Safety knew how to seize and exploit an incident; that Isaiah Thomas and his printing press were on their way to Worcester. Massachusetts could put up a good fight but it could hardly hope to win alone. It must be joined by the sober Quakers of Pennsylvania, by the Tory-inclined great families along the Hudson River, by the aristocracy of Virginia. If opinion in Great Britain could be swayed in favor of the colonies, it would help. The Tory stranglehold on Parliament might be loosened.

The amount of powder and shot, and the number of local militia, might be enough to drive a task force out of Concord. It would take armies of disciplined men, arsenals of weapons and the French navy, too, to drive the British from their American colonies. The new democracy was ready to seize its advantage. It had one great weapon, the press, and a strong arm in men who knew how to use it. Expert leader of these was Dr. Joseph Warren. He had been conspicuous in the attack on the British Regulars as they fled into Charlestown. Before dawn of the next day, and ever increasing day after day thereafter, his fame was carried by word of mouth all over eastern Massachusetts. It was told how he had rushed into the thick of the fight to rescue a wounded man; how he had knocked down a British soldier; how a musket ball had grazed his head.

The account of the battle was to be more important than the battle itself. Warren set to work to write it, omitting his own heroic deeds. "The barbarous murders committed on our innocent brethren on Wednesday the 19th instant have made it absolutely necessary that we immediately raise an army to defend our wives and children from the butchering hands of an inhuman soldiery . . . " he began. And the last shots after the retreating British were hardly fired before this circular, in the name of the Committee of Safety, was being carried to every town in the colony. It was a remarkable document. Its purpose was to raise an army. It concentrated as much on brutalities to be expected as those already committed. It omitted facts, leaving them to be supplied by rumor; a wise choice. Three or four thousand people had actively participated in the running fight, thousands more had witnessed it, and for every witness's account there were sure to be repetitions and exaggerations raised to the tenth power.

The next step was for the Provincial Congress to assemble an official record of the affair. A committee was appointed to take depositions from participants. For three days it worked, interviewing about a hundred persons. One great point was made clear. At Lexington, and at Concord too, the British had fired first. The deposition of Paul Revere was not used—until Longfellow made it famous nearly a century later—probably because Revere, at the moment carrying one end of John Hancock's trunk and being behind a house, merely heard a volley of shots and could not swear as to who fired them.

Even as these depositions were being collected a committee of the Congress, presided over by Dr. Benjamin Church who, it later turned out, was in the pay of the British, wrote the official account of the battle. Reading it two centuries later, it is clear that, like the player queen in *Hamlet*, Church protests too much. He also knew too much about just what the British did and why. Thus concealing his identity as a spy, he admirably served the purposes of the Revolution by piling atrocity on atrocity, demonstrating the innocence of the inhabitants and the brutality of the soldiers.

The whole bundle was rushed by courier from Maine to Georgia. Isaiah Thomas, who at the last moment had smuggled his press out of Boston in pieces and reassembled it in Worcester, produced the very famous broadside "Americans, forever bear in mind the battle of Lexington . . . "

Meanwhile, General Gage had written a restrained and minimized dispatch to the Ministry in London. "I have now nothing to trouble your lordship with but an affair that happened here on the 19th . . . " This he sent off by a British heavy loaded full-rigged ship. Four days later a fast American schooner in ballast left Salem, under cover of dark slipped through the British fleet and cracking on all sail reached England two weeks before the lumbering British official carrier.

The American account was printed all over Britain. The Ministry was flooded with inquiries it could not answer. And when Gage's tame version was finally received, it simply was not believed.

Public opinion was violently affected. The Paris press seized on the story, made the most of it. Here was a chance to get in some licks at England, perhaps even recover the lost empire in Canada! In Venice, as the gondoliers passed one another along the Grand Canal, they shouted the news, and in the Piazza San Marco the printed version passed from hand to hand of "la grande scaramucia a Concordia." The sound of the shot was indeed started on its way round the world! It would reach Indonesia and Africa in the 20th century. Stocks fell in London. Merchants petitioned Parliament. The tide of feeling rose and rose against the war. At last William Pitt, recently raised to the peerage as Earl of Chatham, made a great speech that expressed for millions silent and unrepresented of his countrymen, for other millions of the oppressed throughout the world, the emotion of the time and for the ages. "If I were an American, as I am an Englishman, while a foreign troop was landed in my country I never would lay down my arms—never! never! never!"

WAR MADE UNAVOIDABLE

*O*n the 19th of April 1775 there were perhaps just two people in the world, in positions of responsibility, who were completely ready, willing and eager to cry "Havoc!" and let slip the dogs of war. They were Samuel Adams and George III. Adams had lived and worked for almost twenty years with only one end in mind, the complete independence of the American colonies. He welcomed the crisis. So did George III. He had ordered the expedition that was making all the noise. The half dozen or so men dying on the fresh spring grass were of no account. To his mind, formed in the stubborn mold of teutonic feudalism, they were peasants. To complete the work he was prepared to send his English peasants as long as the supply held out and then, if necessary, hire whatever more might be needed from his German connections in Hesse.

George III's mind was not quite out of the 17th century. It hankered after the absolutism of the Stuarts; but he was willing to settle for the rule of a Parliament of land barons. These he could control, for he had skill at bribery. The rest of the population, and very decidedly the population overseas, were just subjects to be ruled.

In February the news had come to him of John Sullivan's exploit of capturing the store of British powder at Portsmouth, N.H. After his first apoplectic reaction to this effrontery from trouble-making colonials, he discovered a grim satisfaction in the turn events had taken. "I am not sorry," he wrote Lord North, "that the line of conduct seems now chalked out. The New England Governments are in a state of rebellion. Blows must decide whether they are to be subject to this country or independent."

Just as eager for blows was Sam Adams. He was sure the sun

46

was setting over the old world and rising over the new. Populism would take the place of monarchy. He was well into the 19th century, and even had a foot in the 20th. He enjoyed revolution. The manipulation of mobs was his sport. He was adept at persuading the youthful rich, like John Hancock, to join in the fun. His interest in property was as absent as Lenin's. Except it provided a handle on power he had no use for it. Whatever disasters lay ahead, nothing could be as bad as the usurpations of a colonial government ordered from London.

The rest of the world looked on, some with dismay, all with apprehension. George Washington, taking command of the forces besieging Boston, where the "Ministerial" army was pent up, continued at his officer's mess to drink the King's health. The flag which he raised showed thirteen stripes, but in the canton still the Union Jack, symbol of unbroken union with Britain. The trouble was all to be blamed on the King's advisers. Throw the rascals out and all would be well. The good King would, like a good parent, hear and heed his children's complaint. This was the earnest theme of John Dickinson's famous "Letters of a Pennsylvania Farmer." "Everything may be attributed to the misrepresentations and mistakes of Ministers and peace can be established only by acknowledging that half a dozen are fools and knaves."

The great Lord Chatham had been shouting the same message all the new year. It was he who had ordered the forces that had wrested North America from France. With good reason had Pittsfield and Pittsburgh been given his name. Now all his great work was being swept down the drain in a cloudburst of Ministerial stupidity. The cause of America, he said, was the cause of all Irishmen, Catholic and Protestant alike. If Americans were foes, then all good men at home soon would be. Foreign war was at the door. France and Spain were watching their chance.

The Lords woke up for a minute, just long enough to shake their heads. In the Commons Edmund Burke loosed his great oratory, warned that a fierce people of their own stock could never be beaten. It was wasted effort. Half the members were already bought by the King's friends. Most of the rest were moved, as were the Lords, by a sense that their prerogatives were at stake, their sinecures endangered, that a monstrous thing—one member dared mouth the word—democracy, was raising its head. The motion to withdraw the troops was lost; motions to impose new penalties on New England were passed—further restrictions on trade and fishing. That last backfired. The unemployed fishermen, joining Washington's army, not long after made possible the night crossing of the Delaware and victory at Trenton.

There is a curious footnote to the tragedy. Benjamin Franklin, Agent for the Colonies during the previous ten years in London, was giving up and going home. All his efforts at conciliation had failed. Except he had the protection of certain powerful men in England, notably Lord Chatham, he might have been in real trouble. It was whispered that some in the Ministry would be glad to see him locked up in Newgate Prison. For he was in bad odor with the government. Some old letters of Thomas Hutchinson, last Royal Governor of Massachusetts, had fallen into his hands. These showed plainly that Hutchinson had been one of the chief instruments to persuade the King to close the port of Boston and garrison his troops there. Their publication in Massachusetts caused a furor. The repercussion was a vicious attack on Franklin in the Privy Council and talk of his arrest. So he was lying low that spring of '75 waiting for his ship to sail.

Then he received an unusual invitation. Miss Howe, sister to the General who would soon take command of the British troops in Boston and of Lord Howe, Admiral of the fleet going to America, asked him to play chess. She wrote that she had heard of his reputation as a chess player and would like to test his skill. Franklin accepted and they played a game or two. Then the cat was slipped out of the bag. Franklin's reputation as a fixer was even greater than his reputation as a chess player. Would he see her brother? Lord Howe was sent for and presently put Franklin in touch with two British merchants, themselves professional fixers. They offered Franklin a large sum of

money and any office he cared to name in the colonial government to smooth out affairs in America. He replied that God
Almighty could not do that unless the troops were withdrawn
from Boston.

What was in the mind of the Howes nobody knows. The
episode may shed some light on the lack of enthusiasm they
showed later on in prosecuting the war in America. It is also an
indication of the customary way government business was
done. Whether the King ever heard of the attempt to conciliate
is doubtful. It was probably one last effort, by some of his loyal
and discreet servants, to save him from himself.

Unavoidable war is a state of mind. It had complete hold on
the mind of George III. It also is a cancer that spreads fast in
the body politic. Soon it was no longer possible to throw all the
blame for the war on the King's Ministers. Behind the motion
was a motor. George Washington gave up drinking the King's
health. Stars took the place of the Union Jack in the canton of
his flag.

4/19/72—NIXON, PRESIDENT — KISSINGER, SECRETARY OF STATE

*T*he uses of cruelty and terror in the management of human beings should be well understood. They have been tried often enough. Francis Bacon admired the cold-blooded gamesmanship of Henry VII in suppressing revolution, because he spared most noblemen, but "for rascal people they were to be cut off every man, especially in the beginning of an enterprise, he therefore hanged them all for the greater terror."

Americans are proud to believe that on the 19th of April 1775 a notorious incident of such a management attempt backfired on its clumsy perpetrators. This time the people did not come off second best. The terror was brief and the indignation excited by the cruelty of shooting down farmers—peasants to George III—on Lexington Common has lasted more than two centuries.

Yet for ten years and during the administrations of two Presidents, each one of whom enjoyed one landslide electoral triumph, America engaged in such another attempt to use cruelty and terror to gain its ends. The immensity of the cruelty and the long duration of the terror anesthetized the soul of America. The shooting of eight decent men on a spring morning is a comprehensible atrocity. The atrocity of killing a million or more people by bombs falling from planes out of sight in the sky—children, women, men and some soldiers, is harder to take in.

It is harder to take in but it had the same result. "Oh what a glorious morning!" Patriot Sam Adams happily remarked as John Hancock's chaise bobbled out of a little wood back of Lexington on its way to Philadelphia and the momentous Second Continental Congress. There had been a slight delay in starting. Paul Revere had been obliged to go back for John Hancock's trunk, which in the scramble of departure from Buckman's Tavern had been forgotten. John Hancock, who was not a very bright man, thought Sam was talking about the weather. Sam had to explain that he was seeing visions. The morning was glorious because the unforgivable act was being committed by the King's troops—the heavy firing was witness—and nothing now could hold back the independence of America.

George III and Lord North, establishment men existing in a comfortable cultural environment out of sight and hearing of the action, did not see visions. Like the sound practical men who recommended bombing to American Presidents, they toted up the odds and settled on a reasonable policy. The measure of force at their disposal was so overwhelming that resistance would be absurd. Boston would quickly "come to its senses" taken over by British troops and blockaded by a British fleet, just as the Vietnamese would, according to the game plan, "be bombed to the peace table."

The management men left humanity out of their calculations; either the humanity that can feel for the pain of others or that can understand the reaction of others to pain. We can see their mistake now. It is all perfectly clear to us two centuries later. We can see the folly of a remote governing clique, simply because it is in monopolistic possession of an arsenal of offensive weapons, thinking it can control the destinies of a far distant people without their consent. We can see, as Sam Adams saw even as the powder smoke was rising in a slow white cloud over Lexington, that the act of cruelty would have its certain result, arousing in the people an intense rage of resistance that could only end in the independence of America.

Did Ho Chi Minh exclaim "Oh what a glorious morning" on February 7, 1965, the day President Johnson ordered air strikes on North Vietnam? It could be. Premier Kosygin of Russia was in Hanoi when the strikes began and he promised more aid to Ho Chi Minh. Two days later China announced that she would

President Nixon as King Richard by Boston artist George Dergalis.

"definitely not stand idly by" if North Vietnam were invaded. The act of terror was having the result that should have been expected; it was creating the resistance that would eventually force American withdrawal.

It took seven years to persuade the British government that its policy of oppression could not win. It had lost two armies in America, London had been devastated by the Gordon riots, its economy was in collapse, unemployment, rampant inflation and starvation were destroying the work force, Ireland was in revolt, and France, Spain and the Netherlands had joined the war. No wonder that Lord North, hearing the news of Washington's victory at Yorktown, threw up his arms like a man shot and cried, "Oh God! It is all over!"

It was indeed over. Yet the British would soon again recover mastery of the seas when Admiral Rodney destroyed the French fleet in the West Indies; the main British army was still intact in New York and the colony continued to profess allegiance to the Crown. But the nation at home was on the edge of chaos. It was saved by peace with America.

For more than seven years America bombed Indochina. It dropped twice as many tons of bombs as were dropped in Europe in the Second World War. It destroyed farm lands, towns, cities. It obliterated monuments of ancient civilizations. Forests were ripped up, whole landscapes defoliated. People were killed in numbers uncounted and unknowable with indiscriminate savagery. The dead and the maimed are guessed at in millions.

America's great expeditionary force came, lost the lives of more than fifty thousand young Americans and left. But the bombing continued in stubborn pursuit of a management objective as discredited and ruinous as ever were the policies of George III.

The 19th of April 1972 was not a glorious morning in the Unites States of America.

FREEDOM AND THE PRESS

*T*he most dangerous weapon in the arsenal of civilized man is the printing press. It is the highest priority job in every modern totalitarian system to control what the people read. A free press is more feared by modern masters of tyranny than guided missiles with atomic warheads. Such old bunglers of despotism as the Russian Tsars spent a good chunk of the national income trying to stamp out unauthorized printing. And that pigheaded amateur of tyranny, George III, lost his American empire to its explosive force. The curious can still see the instrument of his discomfiture, set up and ready to go, on the floor of the American Antiquarian Society in Worcester.

Isaiah Thomas was just one, but one of the ablest and most persistent, of the printer-publishers who carried the idea of the Revolution to the American people. In his ultimate success he was typical of that new breed of men the new nation has so persistently produced, the diligent applier of new techniques to the problems of mass use. His career is a case study for business schools. So, for that matter, is Paul Revere's. But Paul Revere's usefulness for such study has been hopelessly damaged by a poet who made him so famous as a post rider that his skill as a copper master must forever rest in the shade. Isaiah Thomas was a post rider, too, and spread the alarm on the night of the 18th of April '75, but his name fits no convenient meter and is difficult to rhyme.

Yet his activities on that tremendous night of revolution, and for two days before, were a lot more complicated and of more importance than those of Revere that Longfellow has made so posthumously famous. For Thomas not only helped spread the alarm and was present at Lexington but he wrote his own potent account of it and printed it in Worcester within a fortnight.

That was no mean feat. The press and type which he used were smuggled out of Boston, with the help of the heroic Dr. Joseph Warren, over the Charlestown ferry under the nose of the occupying British army, dumped into a cart and dragged over fifty miles of dirt road to Worcester. There they were carried into the cellar of a friend's house and stored till the printer himself, arriving on foot from Lexington, could set up the press, write the copy, set the type and produce the first number of the Worcester edition of the *Massachusetts Spy* which during the previous five years had become the most widely circulated newspaper in the colonies.

The radical point of view had paid well while the *Spy* was established in Boston. "Banned in Boston" has always been a useful advertising slogan. The British authorities made enough threats to close down the press to keep the paper circulating rapidly. They even, according to Thomas, threatened his life and destruction of his press by mob violence. Considering the temper of the local mob at that time, ably manipulated by Sam Adams, that threat may perhaps be dismissed as from the mouth of the wolf threatened by lambs.

But the prosperity made by approaching danger became disaster when it arrived. There can be no doubt that once hostilities had broken out and martial law been declared the press would have been seized by the soldiers. It was better to have it in Worcester than not have it at all, but in Worcester there was only bad ink, little paper and few subscribers. John Hancock, passing through on his way to the Continental Congress, took time out to write to the Committee of Safety that an immediate supply of paper be sent to Thomas. Enough did arrive so that he could carry out a famous commission for the the Provincial Congress titled "Narrative of the Excursion and Ravages of the King's Troops under the command of General Gage on the nineteenth of April 1775." This account, complete with depositions of many eyewitnesses to the fact that the British had fired first and without provocation on unresisting citizens, was quickly sent off to the places where it would do the most good, including King George and all the provincial governors. If King George read his copy it seems to have made little impression. But the impression it made on the colonies was to unite them in opposition and bring about the Declaration of Independence.

This same Declaration of Independence caused a good deal of excitement in Worcester and some unexpected and unforseeable problems to the enterprising printer. Isaiah Thomas, always on the alert for news, intercepted the courier from Philadelphia with a first copy in his pouch. On the offer of a free drink the courier stopped while Thomas read the Declaration from the porch over the door of the meeting house to an impromptu crowd. Two days later there was an official celebration "when the arms of the Tyrant in Britain, George III of execrable memory were committed to the flames." The fourteenth toast that afternoon was "perpetual itching without the benefit of scratching to the enemies of America." Twenty-four toasts in all were drunk in good sound New England rum and the next day Ben Russell, the indispensable assistant at the press, woke up to find that he had enlisted in the army.

Since he was only sixteen, too young for service, after some effort by Thomas, he was released from his contract. Presumably it was young Russell who set in type the *Spy's* account of the affair which concludes, "The greatest decency and good order was observed and at a suitable time each man returned to his respective home."

But the war nearly ruined Thomas. The scattering of his customers out of Boston made the collection of subscriptions almost impossible. He was forced to lease his press to pay debts. His wife ran away with a British officer. It was a bad time. But within four years he had got a new and faithful wife, recovered control of the *Spy* and begun to establish himself as the foremost printer-publisher in America. He was then thirty-one years old.

His was a peculiarly American genius. He was never content. He kept forming partnerships, really branch offices of his busi-

Strong arm of freedom — the printing press of Isaiah Thomas.

ness in other towns, re-established himself in Boston with the firm of Thomas & Andrews. Almanacs, children's books, school books as well as newspapers and magazines came from his presses; then histories, Bibles and at last music. To sell his product he set up bookstores. Needing paper he built a paper mill. Then he began to write a book, now a classic, the *History of Printing*. No learned society at that time in this country was equipped to aid him in his special enterprise so he founded his own, The American Antiquarian Society. It still flourishes, one of the major centers of historical research, possessor of one of the greatest collections of American printing. Two centuries later the President of that Society, appropriately in succession to Thomas, was Russell Wiggins, for many years editor of *The Washington Post*, the newspaper that revealed the Watergate horrors and destroyed that cheap would-be tyrant Nixon. Time changes the costumes and the players. The great themes continue to be acted out on the world's stage. The press of Isaiah Thomas, standing in the hall of the Society, is still a symbol and a sign "No tyrants wanted."

AN AMERICAN INVENTION

*T*he *news* paper is an American invention. The English finally accepted the idea and put the news on the front page instead of advertisements. The French still offer opinon instead of news. No *news* paper has ever entered Russia except as contraband. The Russians simply do not know the meaning of news. In that country, and half the world beside, there are only propaganda and rumor.

George Jones, a Vermont boy, deserves most of the credit for the invention. It was he who perceived the possibilities in the news—just the news. There was a destiny at work in the Vermont hills when he was born. Two other boys were growing up near by, Horace Greeley and Henry Raymond. All three would slip, as water drops on the hills must eventually slip into the sea, into the hurrying tides that swirled about New York City. And their shifting relationships would change history.

Comets and earthquakes are supposed to introduce great men to the world. George Jones arrived on a flood. It was in the year that *Constitution* was fitting out in Boston for its epic fight with *Guerriere*. Madison was President. On a summer's day the sky turned to darkness at noon over Poultney, Vermont. The rains descended and a flood came. Whole buildings rose from their foundations and floated away like ships. The thriving industries along the Poultney River were laid waste.

One only survived. It was a woolen mill. The foreman of the mill and his young wife were recent immigrants from Wales, land of magicians. To them was born a son as the floods receded. There was, perhaps, something of magic in the survival of that one mill, the prosperity of the foreman, who became the proprietor, and the good start young George had. But the luck of the Joneses ran out. By the time George was twelve the business was bankrupt, both his parents were dead and he was keeping alive by working in the general store of Amos Bliss.

At the back of the store was a hand press where Bliss put out the *Northern Spectator*. It was an example of the beneficient press which Jefferson celebrated, "Here we are not afraid to tolerate any error so long as reason remains free to combat it." Whether what it peddled was reason or error depended entirely on the politics of the reader. Political feeling ran high in those days between Democrats and Federalists. The two parties even held separate celebrations of the Fourth of July. In Poultney the celebrations began separately but ended together in a glorious fight. Poultney had 1900 inhabitants. To take care of these it had ten distilleries. Whiskey was cheap and applejack was cheaper and people made the most of the home product.

Into this rural scene walked one day Horace Greeley, just half a year older than George Jones. Out behind the shop, planting potatoes, was the editor. "Be you lookin' for a 'prentice printer?" "We-ell, I reckon I be." And that was the beginning of the career of the great editor, publisher and politician, a mighty force in his time, now most remembered for a single sentence, "Go West, young man, go West."

It was the beginning of a lifelong friendship. The sensible Jones was attracted to the imaginative, passionate Greeley. Unknown to them a third boy was leaving his father's farm to enter the university at Burlington. His name was Henry Raymond. A few years later all three, separately, had drifted to New York City. Horace Greeley had founded the *Tribune* and it was prospering mightily. He needed a business manager and hired Jones. He needed an assistant editor and hired Raymond.

But Greeley was wildly eccentric. Causes flourished in his paper, though the news perished. It suited the taste of the age and he made money. He offered Jones a partnership. Jones thought a bit about Greeley's business methods, decided to go instead into banking in Albany. Raymond, too, went to Albany, throwing up his job as Greeley's assistant, getting elected to the Assembly and there becoming Speaker.

Banking was then a business almost as freewheeling as the

An American Invention

Fourth of July in Poultney. A man put up a sign that said "Banker" and began to speculate with his customers' money. If he was sharp enough and honest, he—and his customers—did rather well. Jones was both honest and able.

But a new law was in the works to regulate the banking business. Jones asked his friend Speaker Raymond to oppose it. "What will you do if the banking law passes?" asked Raymond. "I don't know," said Jones. "Would you go to New York and start a paper with me?" "I might." "Then," said Speaker Raymond, laughing, "I'll see that the law passes."

It did. Jones closed up his banking business and raised the capital to open *The New York Daily Times*, with Raymond as editor. Raymond, as far as the world could see, ran the paper. It took a party line, was deep in politics, helped make Lincoln President, supported him through the Civil War. But it kept building up its news gathering service. It became the paper people read to get the news. Then Raymond suddenly died. All the world assumed the *Times* was for sale. The great editor, Horace Greeley of the *Tribune*, made an offer. "Not while I am on top of the sod," Jones answered.

Jones quietly continued his work of making the *Times* a great *news* paper. The rapport he had worked out with Raymond he continued with a new generation of editors. He was the ideal boss. He let the editors decide on the policy of the paper. But he insisted on the news. It had to be true; well and truly reported.

The great test came in a famous battle with Tammany Hall. Political malefactors had got control of city and state. They were milking the public for millions. Yet respectable people were annoyed at the *Times'* attacks on Boss Tweed and his ring. It was bad publicity for the financial heart of the country. Better sweep the whole matter under the rug. Threats were made; of punitive ordinances, taxation, sabotage, against Jones' life. He calmly continued to support his editors.

Then a break came. The secret books of the Tweed ring came into the possession of the paper. An emissary of Boss Tweed approached Jones, offered in modern equivalent something like fifty million dollars to buy the *Times*. Jones refused with the remark, "I don't think that the devil will ever bid higher for me than that."

In the end the devil lost out to the *news* paper. The facts on the front page beat him, and his agent, Boss Tweed, went to jail. More important, a great American invention was established, a creation of new techniques applied to problems of mass use. It has served the country well. When the devil made his most recent try, in the Nixon era, to take over the national government, it defeated him. The independent newspaper is a weapon of more value than atomic bombs in maintaining the independence of the people of the United States.

POSTERITY WILL SCARCELY CREDIT . . .

*G*unpowder, on the day of Lexington and Concord, was in the same relation to the embattled farmers as oil to the contending nations of the world in the latter part of the 20th century. It was the necessity without which resistance could not be sustained. It was the object of the enemy attack. The lack of it on the American side limited the force of counterattack. The possession of it made possible the retreat of the British and ensured the long continuance of the war.

Powder was the scarcest commodity in Massachusetts, and the most precious, on the 19th of April '75. Of the first year of the Revolution John Adams wrote, "We were distressed to a degree that posterity will scarcely credit for powder." And indeed posterity has not yet grasped the fact. So much has been said and still is being said—and rightly enough—about the courage of the combatants, the epochal importance of the small battle, the great cause at stake—that the nation has forgotten why the battle occurred.

The British expedition to Concord was no fool's errand, though it was planned and carried out by fools. There was an important store of powder in Concord, as the British spy service well knew. To capture it would be a severe blow to the rebel cause. The British Ministry had a clear objective in view. It was to intimidate and starve the Americans into submission at the least possible cost. The easiest way to do this was to cut off the supply of gunpowder. That on hand would soon be used up. A British blockade could stop more coming in. Its manufacture was almost unknown in the colonies. The country was dependent on imports for the one commodity without which its independence could not be maintained.

So along with the orders to close the port of Boston as reprisal for the famous tea party came a general order absolutely prohibiting the export of gunpowder to any colony. General Gage immediately raided the powder house in Charlestown and confiscated the supply there. He planned to do the same thing in Portsmouth, but an American, General John Sullivan, got there first. King George, when he heard of that exploit, came closer to apoplexy than at any time before or after. But for the most part the royal orders were effective. Whatever powder was lying about unguarded was grabbed for the King. Just two days after Concord fight fifteen marines from a British armed schooner picked up and carried away the store of powder in the magazine at Williamsburg, Virginia.

It was the field artillery of Lord Percy's relieving force, drawn up above Lexington Green and loaded with a fresh and abundant store of powder in the afternoon of the 19th of April 1775 that proved the fact of British power. Under the protection of those brightly polished, light-wheeled brass guns Colonel Smith and his men, exhausted by their run from Concord, fell "panting like dogs." The cannonball the Regulars then let fly did no damage except to the church, crashing through the front and out the back above the pulpit. But the loud report, the sudden belch of royal superfluity, warned the Patriots to keep their distance.

They had no field guns. Already those who had followed the retreat were low on the great essential, powder. James Hayward had left Acton early in the morning. In his horn was a pound of powder; in his pocket forty musket balls. He was at the bridge in Concord and was one of those ducking behind stone walls and firing at the redcoats as they hurried past Merriam's Corner in Lincoln. He was actively engaged for about three hours. Coming into Lexington, just on the east slope of Fiske Hill, he went to a well beside a house for a drink of water. A grenadier came out of the house, leveled his gun and said, "You are a dead man." Hayward said, "So are you." Both fired point blank. Both were killed. In Hayward's pocket were left two musket balls. In his horn just enough powder for one more shot.

Hayward's short supply of ammunition was typical for most of those who saw action that day. The Minuteman carried with him a pound of powder, loose or in cartridges. When that was gone his reasonable choice was to go home. There was no general reserve from which to replenish. Even the dead or wounded were probably in like case. Both sides were firing as fast as they could. And it took a lot of shot and a lot of powder to do damage with a smooth bore flintlock without a rear sight. The powder to fire the shot heard round the world was brought by each individual from small store hoarded at home. When that was gone, there was no more to be had.

So the first thing George Washington asked when he took command of the Continental Army in July 1775 was "How much powder do you have?" He was told three hundred eight barrels. But a month later it was discovered there had been a mistake. The inventory had included all the powder that had been used up at Lexington, Concord and Bunker Hill! There were only ninety barrels left! Just about enough to issue each man in the army besieging Boston twelve cartridges over and above what he had in his pocket and leave something to put in the few available cannon. If the British should find out and attack, the war could be over in a dozen or maybe two dozen volleys.

Washington heard in silence. According to John Sullivan he remained speechless for half an hour. Then what could be done was done fast and secretly. Urgent expresses were sent out to all the colonies to send every ounce of powder to Boston they could buy or beg. Privateers were armed to capture British supply ships. Frantic efforts were begun to find saltpeter and begin manufacture of powder. Paul Revere made crude engravings to illustrate the process. A man was found in Canton, Massachusetts, who had once operated a small powder mill. He was put to work, made a quantity of explosive, but not very well. It was of inferior grade, but of a grade sufficient to blow up the mill.

Philadelphia was more successful. Twelve months later enough powder was being made in this country, or had been smuggled in from the West Indies, to relieve the crisis and carry on the war. But from the first to the last of the siege of Boston the cause of independence was in jeopardy and all Washington's efforts hamstrung by the lack of powder. It is a point to ponder. The lifeline of 20th century civilization now extends to the Middle East. The dangers of finding alternatives to oil as the prime source of energy have to be weighed against the dangers of a war breaking out to control the supply of oil. The risks and possibilities of developing and using alternative sources of energy can be calculated with some degree of certainty. The risks of dependence on the unstable governments of the Middle East are not subject to any reasonable calculation.

LET US NOW PRAISE FAMOUS MEN . . .

*W*e ought to call it Joseph War-
ren Day. Streets and counties, a dozen or so, bear his name.
Bunker Hill, where he fought, is marked by a granite monument. But the hurry of Boston business and the great city,
swarming over and around the site, changing out of recognition
the topography, allow little time to remember, even on the
17th of June, the eager, active man, the most conspicuously
American of the men who brought the American Revolution
into being.

He was killed in the prime of life. Dead, his heroic image,
overblown by oratory and graphics, carried the Revolution
which he had organized forward with a rush. And for the first
hundred years, while the republic struggled for a place in the
world among fiercely contending empires, his name was in the
mouth of every schoolboy. Then wealth, tending towards opu-
lence and vulgarity, taught the nation to forget the significance
of revolution. Sometimes, as in the aftermath of the Spanish
American War or in the Vietnam period, the great republic
assumed the manners of the imperial monster it set out to kill at
Bunker Hill. Educated by its mistakes the United States may
learn again to appreciate Warren.

We like him because he was like us, or what we would most
like to think we are. He was furiously energetic, utterly generous, worked at top speed all the time and yet was so good-
natured and so good-looking and so obviously an idealist that
he was popular even among the British and the friend of every
man and child in Boston and loved by every woman. He was
the best doctor in the city. And when every other conspicuous
Patriot leader had prudently left town and he was told the
British were about to arrest him, he stuffed a couple of loaded

pistols into his pockets and said, "I promised to visit old Mrs. Smith on Cornhill this evening."

Cornhill has vanished, to make room for City Hall Plaza. But some bits and parts of Warren's town remain, the Old State House, the Old South Meeting House, Paul Revere's house, Faneuil Hall, Copp's Hill and the narrow and interesting streets of the North End. Not only does Boston have more of a magnificent past to show its present citizens than any other city in America, it can show the forms and faces of the men who made it. Copley was the best portrait painter of his time or of most times and his picture of Joseph Warren, now hanging in the Museum of Fine Arts, is one of his best pictures. There is the speaking image of the man, portrayed with the psychological insight of which Copley was the master, who gave the order to hang the famous lanterns in the belfry of the North Church, who sent out Dawes, Revere and the rest to wake up Lexington and Concord.

On the morning of the day the Revolution began Joseph Warren was still in Boston. Orders had come out from England to take him into custody. But General Gage, the British military governor, had not dared act lest he precipitate war. That had nearly come in March, on the anniversary of the Boston Massacre. The streets were full of citizens ready for a riot. Word had been passed that an attempt might be made to take Warren, who was to deliver the oration. A band of redcoats came marching past the Old South just as Warren, unable to get through the crowd that thronged even the aisles of the church, was climbing through a window to the pulpit. About forty British officers were seated in the pews directly below him. They shuffled their feet, coughed, banged their canes on the floor and hissed "fie, fie." Someone in the back shouted "fire!" It looked as if revolution was going to start then and there. Luckily the panic was got under control and revolution was able to wait for a better moment, for the overt act of aggression, the British foray to Concord.

When Warren, on the 19th of April, mounted his horse for the last time in front of his house in Hanover Street, Patriot

farmers were already dead on the green in Lexington. Horse and rider boarded the ferry and as they left it on the Charlestown shore, Warren said to the ferryman, "Keep up a brave heart. They have begun it. That either party can do. And we'll end it! That only one can do."

He rode towards Lexington. Two British soldiers were trying to steal a horse from an old man. He rescued man and horse. He heard the news of the massacre on the town common and began to meet bands of militiamen. Hurrying on he organized the resistance to the British retreat, conferred with militia General Heath, did what he could to organize the mob of minutemen. When organization proved impossible he took part in the fighting, rallied the men again and again, rescued the wounded.

The Revolution had begun and Joseph Warren, President of the Massachusetts Congress, was in charge of it. The Continental Congress in Philadelphia was debating futile petitions to the King. For the next two months, until he was killed at Bunker Hill, Joseph Warren was the most important, as he was the most powerful, man in America. In fact he *was* the Revolution.

As head of the Committee of Safety, the generals of militia were responsible to him. As President of the Massachusetts Congress, civil authority was in his hands. As chief propagandist of the rebellion, the opinion of the nation and of the world, on which the whole future depended, was his responsibility.

Before the shooting stopped on the night of Concord fight he was writing the first of many manifestos. "By all that is dear, by all that is sacred give all assistance possible in forming an army to defend our wives and children from the butchering soldiers." His pen never stopped, yet he attended innumerable meetings, made countless arrangements. He got depositions to prove the British fired first, he chartered a vessel to hurry the news to England.

Then troops, supplies and advice began to pour into the area all around Boston. Sanitary conditions were frightful. Discipline was almost non-existent. Food was plenty here, short there. What with hot weather, lack of shelter, polluted water, dysentery was a constant threat. It was Warren's job to sort out the whole mess, devise a strategy in consultation with five militia generals, each nominally responsible to him but actually acknowledging no authority but their own, and always in danger of having that authority vetoed by their own men. In addition he operated an extremely efficient spy system.

Those spies brought alarming news. Gage was preparing an offensive. Crack troops had arrived from Britain The date set was June 18th. Something had to be done—and quickly. A council of war determined to fortify Bunker Hill. Warren dissented, arguing that the position was too exposed. He was right. From a military point of view it was a fantastically bad decision. British ships controlled the harbor and batteries could be moved to take the narrow causeway leading to the hill, cutting off retreat or reinforcements.

But on the night of the 16th of June a thousand men assembled on Cambridge Common, heard prayer from the President of Harvard, set off for the hill. Colonel Prescott, in command, decided to fortify not Bunker Hill, but the hill lower and in front of it known as Breed's Hill. This was a still worse and more dangerous position for the American troops; within range of the guns of the British ships, terribly exposed.

Strategically considered, the plan was sheer madness. Psychologically it was superb. On that day both sides were spoiling for a fight. They were like two teen-age gangs on the morning after snow. It was sufficient for one to build a fort. The other had to take it. General Gage pushed aside all prudent advice. And his arrogant officers were not forward in offering it. The British planned a frontal assault, perfectly confident the Provincials would run at their approach. General Putnam, now coming in with American reinforcements, knew better. "My men don't care much for their heads. But they're mortal afeared for their shins. Cover them breast high and they'll fight all day and all night too."

Joseph Warren could not be kept from such a necessary, however rash, endeavor. Putting aside all his duties of President of the Congress he hurried towards Charlestown, walked boldly across the causeway paying no attention to the ricocheting cannonballs, entered the farthest redoubt. He asked for a gun and with the Forlorn Hope withstood and repelled two British attacks, by his courage and example sustaining the battle. The third attack succeeded, the British losing men in a ratio of ten to one. Warren was killed. He was gone, as is a meteor, suddenly extinguished in a burst of light.

THE PRACTICAL EFFECTS
OF INDEPENDENCE

*T*he policy of the British Empire was to hold in check the development of industry in its American colonies. The products of agriculture and the forest were what the New World was wanted for. Cheap land was the bait to encourage settlement. The superiority of the Old World manufactures was so obvious, the number of trained artisans in England so many, and the wages they received so low, that competition from America seemed not only superfluous but futile. Even Benjamin Franklin, as a young genius making scientific experiments and setting up his post office in Philadelphia, was able to argue "the danger, therefore of these colonies interfering with their mother country in trades that depend on labor, manufactures etc. is too remote to require the attention of Great Britain."

This was the state of affairs up to the moment of the American Revolution. Farming, lumbering and the building of ships were encouraged. So were fishing and the coastal trade. But finished goods must come from England and world commerce must be carried in British ships.

The escape from this coil of manmade restrictions was by sea. The contrast fifty years later is vividly set forth by Edward Trelawney in his description of a visit to a Yankee ship with his friend, the poet Shelley. It is the only recorded case of Shelley taking a stiff drink. Trelawney was a great sailor and the two men were scrambling about the port of Leghorn in 1822 when an American schooner took their eye. Her lines were sweet and clean, her top sides bright painted; deck, spars and rigging taut and shining, a terrific contrast to the sloppy, dirty tubs of other nations.

Trelawney asked where he might get such another vessel. "I calculate you must go to Boston to get one," the Yankee mate answered. "There is no one this side of the water can do the job. Come aboard and look about." Once aboard he would not let them go till they had drunk, in good Medford rum, under the Star Spangled Banner, to the memory of Washington. "As a warrior and statesman," said Shelley, "he was righteous in all he did, unlike all who lived before or since; he never used his power but for the benefit of his fellow creatures."

"Stranger," said the Yankee, "truer words were never spoken; there is dry rot in all the main timbers of the Old World, and none of you will do any good till you are docked, refitted and annexed to the New."

But the New World in June 1775 was nothing but a promise. The vigorous enterprise that would suddenly transform it was just breaking out. The burst of energy that would outproduce all other nations was not yet released from tight bureaucratic control. Like a cloud of locusts the British Navy's ships lay in the water of the harbors and the bay of Massachusetts and its army swarmed over Boston and its islands and devoured its substance.

So when Joseph Warren, a typical well-to-do colonial subject of his Britannic majesty George III, dressed, before dawn on the hot June morning of the day of Bunker Hill battle, he put on a blue coat with brass buttons. The cloth of the coat, a fine broadcloth, was of British manufacture. So were the buttons. Even the pins with which he kept his wig in place were imported.

All well-dressed men in those days wore wigs. And it had been a nuisance when, on the 19th of April, one of his wig pins had been shot away. He had had to borrow a replacement. None were to be had in the shops. For at the first whisper of a shortage it is the items of commonest use, like imported wig pins or imported gasoline, that disappear from the market. Impeccably turned out in his London clothes, Warren arrived at the outermost trench. Having no weapon but a dress sword, also of British manufacture, he had to borrow a gun. It was a musket made in England a generation back and used in the old French war. When the precious, imported powder ran out he was shot dead as the redcoats swarmed over the barricade. Soldiers in war respect only the living enemy. That night the valuable blue coat with the expensive brass buttons was hawked on the streets of Boston by a British soldier.

The spirit of independence had been growing for a long time in America. But the habit of dependence on imports for all the finer things of life was fixed. With the sudden cut-off from the reservoir of English goods, there was not much to go on but spirit. Food, of course, there was plenty of, and things made of wood. But tools were breaking and getting scarce. Isaiah Thomas, when he fled from Boston to Worcester, could barely get out his *Spy*, the news and propaganda sheet that kept the Revolution boiling. Paper was hardly to be had; the ink was wretched; broken type could not be replaced. The small hoard of imported gunpowder was almost used up; the nearest cannon were at Ticonderoga, out of reach till frost should harden mud roads.

Yet within two years of the Battle of Bunker Hill, powder was being made; badly in Massachusetts, better in Pennsylvania. And cannon were being cast, well in Massachusetts, well, too, in Connecticut. As the Revolution came to an end, the Cabot family were setting up spinning machinery in Beverly, Massachusetts; Paul Revere was making plans for his foundry and copper mill in Canton. And the ships and the sailors were ready to carry these things and an infinity more of manufactured goods to Europe or around Cape Horn or the Cape of Good Hope to any port in the world. For the first time the world saw what free men operating within a free and democratic system of government could do.

THE BRITISH QUIT BOSTON

*I*t is the morning of the 17th of March 1776. We are on guard duty, as we have been interminably it seems, through a long winter. The place of our guard, appropriately enough, is called Plowed Hill. In front of us is a stiff redoubt, built of heavy timbers and plenty of mud. Mud is something we have plenty of. It is under our feet, and the best cowhide boots dripping with tallow won't keep it out. It is on the seat of our pants, on the back of our old leather coats. Our hands are grimy with it and it is in our hair, too. The only place it is not is in the old family flintlock. We keep that dry and bright and clean. And we keep our powder dry.

Across from us, half a mile or so, is Bunker Hill. It is fortified, too; more scientifically, we are told, than our hill. The British have crack engineers professionally trained in the art of war. All we have are some local surveyors, strong backs and Major General Lee who talks a good war. Now, as the fog begins to lift a bit, we can see a touch of scarlet over the edge of their fort. That will be one of their sentries. From time to time we lob a cannonball over their heads, just to keep them down. And they return the compliment. But not much damage is done. We have been at this now for ten months and hardly anybody has been killed. But enough have died to make you wonder. The food is good and plenty of it. Yet everyone has a cold and some die. Dysentery kills others. There's no way to keep clean. In some places the stink is pretty bad. And it is dull work. We have learned the hard way that war is mostly waiting in uncomfortable places.

There's a shout at the end of the line. That will be General Sullivan. More of a shout than usual. Of course. Saint Patrick's Day! We are mostly New Hampshire men. They call us Long

Faces. But there are Irishmen in the ranks. And we all are proud of our General. A real American. A self-made man. His father had to leave Ireland in a hurry. Nobody knows why. Probably some row with the British. He came from Dublin. And he met a beautiful girl on the boat. She was from Cork. They were married when they got ashore. Neither of them had a cent of money. To pay back their passage money they had to hire out to a farmer in the country back of Durham.

And now who owns the biggest house in Durham? Their son, of course. He is the greatest lawyer in the north country. They say he can charm the birds out of the trees. A jury would no more think of disagreeing with John Sullivan than an honest woman would give the time of day to a British soldier. He was his state's delegate to the Continental Congress, was a great man there for *Independence Now*. John Adams says he has left a draft with Mr. Jefferson saying just how the Congress should go about it. But they made him a general to get him out of politics. Out of politics! Hell will freeze over first.

Our General Sullivan is the handsomest man in the army. And he's done more for America than most men, except only perhaps General Warren that got killed over there in the fight for Bunker Hill. And Warren would have got killed a lot sooner if it hadn't been for Sullivan. It was Sullivan got the powder that made the fight last as long as it did. This is what happened.

He'd just got back from the first Continental Congress. It was a year ago last December; half a year before Concord fight. It was a bitter cold night, clear and cold, the stars so bright you could reach right up and touch them. There came a knock on the door. It was Paul Revere. He had a message from Joseph Warren in Boston. "There's a British man-o'-war getting under way and she's bound to Portsmouth to pick up the powder in the fort in the harbor."

Our John didn't stop but half a minute, just to pull on his boots. Within the hour he was aboard a gundalow, one of those heavy great barges rigged with a lateen sail, going down the river with the tide, and thirty picked men with him. It was near low water when they got to the fort and the nearest they could get to it was thigh deep. So overboard they slipped into that ice water. They crept ashore, knocked over the sentry, and in ten minutes they had the garrison tied up. Then they took the powder, ninety-eight kegs of it, and a heap of muskets and carried all aboard. They darsn't keep their boots on, lest a hobnail strike a spark and blow all up. So they came home in stocking feet. By the dawn of day that powder was hid under the pulpit of Durham Church.

When the King's Governor, Sir Thomas Wentworth, heard of it, he put out a writ of attainder for treason against all concerned. So what did John Sullivan do? He summoned his militia company, and he took his major's coat that he'd got from the King under his arm and his major's commission the King had given him, and he made a parade with fife and drum to Durham Common. And there he built a great bonfire and he threw the King's commission and the King's coat into the fire. And he sent word to Sir Thomas Wentworth to come and get him if he dared.

But here is himself now. "Morning, boys. You've had a rough night of it. But for sure the day will be better." There is just a sniff of smoke from the old sod in his talk. Now he's leveling his spy glass. The British burned a ton of powder last night. The cannonading never stopped. We expect an attack. There's more than ten thousand of them in Boston. They'll be coming up the river in their boats. Now that we've grabbed the Heights in Dorchester, they've got to do something. Well, let them come. We're ready.

But look! What's going on down there? The fog is lifting a bit down there at the water's edge. What's that great red patch on the water itself? It's a barge full of redcoats! It's not one, it's two, it's three barges! And they're not heading up river. They're heading for the ships in the harbor. And by the ships you can see more barges and redcoats going up their sides. Could it be? Can it be? Are they leaving? And suddenly the General laughs. He laughs and he lays down his glass. "Boys!

Those sentinels at the fort over there. They're dummies or I'll eat my hat and the gold braid on it."

And then he shakes hands with all of us, there in the trench. That's the difference! Over there on the other side of the river the officers are all Lords or Lords' sons. A British officer would rather shake hands with a rattlesnake than shake hands with a private soldier.

ONE OF THE MOST IMPORTANT
CHARACTERS IN THE WORLD

*G*eorge Washington came three times to Massachusetts. At first he came in 1756 as a soldier of the King, seeking the bubble reputation. Twenty-four years old, he had already sought it in the cannon's mouth. Now he came for the military recognition he deserved. It was the fatal weakness of Empire to withhold that recognition. He would not return again till he came as Commander-in-Chief of the Revolution.

He put up at the Cromwell's Head Tavern on School Street in Boston. Its sign hung so low that a tall man (George was six foot three) must bow as he passed the Lord Protector. He had entered town by a street two miles long lined by fine houses and opulent shops. There he bought a new suit, some yards of silver lace, a new hat and two pair of gloves. On his third and last visit in 1789, when he had been elected the first President of the United States of America, the street would be named in his honor.

The *Boston Gazette* announced, "arrived the Hon. Col. Washington, a gentleman who has deservedly a high reputation for military skill, though success has not always attended his undertakings." His mission was to establish his rank over a man who claimed a Royal Commission. There was the rub! A Regular Army officer of lower grade could give orders to a colonial officer, even if the colonial was fifty times more capable; even if, like Washington, he had saved the King's forces from total massacre in Braddock's defeat.

Governor Shirley, who was chief of the King's forces in America, gave his judgment in favor of Washington. But he said flatly that he could not get him a British Regular Army

George Washington by Joseph Wright. Painted for Thomas Jefferson.

commission. Washington went home, tried for another two
years to work out his impossible position as defender of Virginia and the Ohio territory, supported adequately neither by his
Province nor his King. Then he turned in his provincial commission, accepted election to the Virginia legislature and became an efficient and prosperous planter. For sixteen years he
did nothing to enhance his military reputation.

Yet that reputation grew and grew. In the Virginia legislature, where he almost never spoke and never failed to listen, his
opinion was sought on every military matter. When the split
came with the Mother Country, he was elected to the Continental Congress. There the Massachusetts delegation, with perspi-
cacity later ages have commended, propelled him into the dangerous honor of Commander-in-Chief of the rebel army.

The misgiving with which he took the job was real. He had
no experience in maneuvering armies in open country. The
British were unlikely obligingly to come into the woods to be
shot at. Controlling the sea they should be able to choose their
point of attack. And no untrained troops could stand against
the machine-gun-like fire of Regulars.

Posterity has a fancy vision of General Washington on a
white horse taking command of the Continental troops under a
great elm on Cambridge Common. There is no mention of the
scene in any contemporary account. The gaudy pictures were
all painted years after by imaginative artists for the sons and
grandsons of Patriots. We know only that Washington came
unannounced to Cambridge on a Sunday afternoon and rode off
at once to view the fortifications around Charlestown. He was
there till dark. Early the next day he was on the other side of
the Charles River reconnoitering the positions in Roxbury.
Naturally he was worried about the British. On a rising tide,
they could come up the river in their boats and by a hard strike
roll up the American forces on one side or the other. But when
he came back from his ride he was even more worried about the
American army he did not have.

Congress had supplied him with nine generals. One of these
felt he should have been chief. Two later betrayed him. Anoth-

er refused to accept his commission. A fifth stayed "sick" in quarters. The rest, as a contemporary wrote, "quarreled like cats and dogs." The troops were honest and serious but accustomed to tell their officers off in disputes and go home if they felt like it. There was very little gunpowder, not enough guns to go round, no supply, no organization, no sanitation, no discipline.

The next months were a long agony. There were alarms at the front, dysentery in the camp, failure to recruit. When enlistments expired at year end, nearly a third of the army laid down its arms and walked off. On the last day of December 1775 General Greene, in charge of the Roxbury sector, wrote "Nothing but confusion and disorder reign. We never have been so weak as we shall be tomorrow." At the new year he was left with seven hundred men to cover the whole front. At some points there were no defenders. Were the British asleep or just playing possum?

Washington thought they were not asleep. Desperately he planned an attack on Boston across the ice. He was deterred by a Council of War, and the ice melted. Then came the idea of seizing Dorchester Heights. The British had the same idea, but a fortunate storm swamped their boats and spoiled their plan. The Americans, approaching by land, got there first. Then it was all up with the British. With heavy guns trained on their fleet they had no choice but to board ship in March 1776 and sail away. George Washington was a hero. The whole country shouted his praise.

He had need of it. Military blunders on Long Island, the enormous advantage that sea power gave the attackers eroded his reputation. Only the desperate crossing of the Delaware on a Christmas night saved it from extinction. Not for six years and the victory at Yorktown, with the help of the French fleet and the French regiments, would he enjoy again entire success.

War over, he hoped for retirement. But that reputation of his, which had been so much his concern as a young man, and had grown, as it were, of its own accord, would not let him alone. His return to the life of a farmer, so much longed for, was brief. He could not avoid becoming President of the United States.

But the states were not united. Rhode Island even refused to join. There was jealousy between North and South. So six months after his inauguration he set out on a good will tour. There was a comic incident when he came to Boston. Governor John Hancock pleaded illness and did not make a courtesy call. So Washington declined to call on him.

Protocol was upset. Arrangements were in confusion. It took all the great men of Massachusetts to put Humpty Dumpty together again. Hancock was persuaded to make his call, recovering suddenly from his illness. And the next day Boston had the biggest parade and the greatest celebration of its young life.

John Adams had his wish, which in 1775 from Philadelphia and the Continental Congress, after his successful maneuver to make Washington Commander-in-Chief, he had written to Abigail his wife, "I hope the people will treat the General with all that Confidence and Affection, that Politeness and Respect, which is due one of the most important Characters in the World."

INDEPENDENCE AT LAST

*W*hy did it take so long? By six o'clock in the morning of the 19th of April 1775 eight Yankee farmers were dead on the green at Lexington. By four that afternoon the British were on the run out of Lexington, and the roadside all the way back to Concord was littered with their equipment, their wounded and their dead. And at dusk, as the last sweating redcoat staggered into Charlestown, Joseph Warren, chief of the resistance, sat down at a table in Cambridge to write an account of the battle that would wake up the world.

The news of the "butchering British soldiery," the need for men, for supplies, for an army to besiege Boston was rushed in every direction. Isaiah Thomas's smuggled press in Worcester printed scare headlines. In London the stock market crashed. In far-off Venice cafe society read about "the big fight in Concord."

But in Philadelphia, where the Continental Congress was assembling, two factions were cleaving the country. Independence was talked by some and the word was heard with horror by others. John Dickinson, an earnest, decent man, was sure the whole ruckus was a mistake. He came to call on the Massachusetts delegates in his coach drawn by four beautiful horses, invited them to dine with him at his country house. It was he who wrote the able essays signed "a Pennsylvania Farmer."

According to these, Farmer George, the beloved monarch, at his palace of Windsor, simply hadn't heard the news straight. If proper word could be got through to him from his devoted subjects in America, he would, of course, fire his corrupt ministers, and his excellent reign would return to its normal, peaceful course. These sentiments appealed to many of the delegates. New York and Carolina farmers were distrustful of mobs, especially Yankee mobs. The Virginia people were hot for action—but in Virginia. Massachusetts was a long way off and the winters up there were cold and hard cider was no substitute for mountain dew.

By a bare majority, measures were put through the Congress for the support of the resistance. The British Army holed up in Boston was referred to as the Ministerial Army. It was not the King's army. The King was a good sort but he had bad ministers. Townshend, the tax man, was dead. Providence had eliminated him. All really now that remained to do was to fire Lord North. All would then be well. Reconciliation would be easy. So Dickinson kept hammering away for one more petition to the King. "Let us behave like dutiful children who have received unmerited blows from a beloved parent. Let us complain, but let our complaints speak at the same time the language of affliction and veneration."

This wasted precious time. Reinforcements were coming from overseas to the British in Boston. Every post to the Congress brought news of some skirmish, urgent pleas for help. John Adams, that irascible Puritan, was beside himself. "From my soul I pitied Mr. Dickinson. His mother said to him, 'Johnny you will be hanged, your estate will be forfeited and confiscated, you will leave your excellent wife a widow and your charming children orphans, beggars and infamous.' " He decided something had to be done. Quick on the morning of the 14th of June, before the heat of the day, he interrupted the stale debate, nominated George Washington for Commander-in-Chief. That galvanized the Congress into action. Curiously the Virginia delegation demurred. But after a delay of twenty-four hours the motion was carried. Then all was hurry and confusion. A staff had to be recruited, subordinate generals appointed, some sort of military organization created. And with barely a week's preparation General Washington, escorted by the Philadelphia Light Horse, set out for Boston. A band played. The whole delegation from Massachusetts and delegates from the other colonies accompanied him to the edge of the city, to the beginning of the open road. There they bade him a formal farewell and turned back to their legislative delays. Washington got off his horse and into a light carriage, an open, four-wheeled phaeton. The driver clucked to the two white horses and they were off at a fast trot. The Revolution was at last rolling.

But not so fast that the Congress could not immediately return to its discussion of its olive branch petition to the King. Meanwhile, on the 17th of June, but unknown to the people in Philadelphia, the matter of forcible resistance had been clinched at Bunker Hill. No one around Boston after that had any doubt that peaceful reconciliation was impossible. Yet Washington, taking command "of the defenders of liberty" at Cambridge, in the name of the Continental Congress on the 2nd of July, still professed his and its loyalty to the King. Human nature could not quickly grasp the notion that the head of state could be false to his trust. It was like the trauma of impeachment of a President.

At last the petition to the king was got off at midsummer in the charge of a member of the Penn family. It prayed most humbly that the beloved monarch would listen to his good children and remember his duty to uphold the traditional rights of Englishmen anywhere on the globe. Some of those who signed it said it made them feel sick. It was almost a year before they could feel better by signing the Declaration of Independence.

It took that long for news to travel, for ideas to jell. The King, of course, refused even to receive the petition. He demanded, and got through Parliament, violent measures to put down the rebellion. Some of his ships bombed and burned Portland in Maine. That was persuasive. And Tom Paine made the cause simple and popular with his tract *Common Sense*.

Thomas Jefferson had spoken barely three sentences in the Continental Congress. But he had a reputation as a pen man. A committee delegated him to draft their statement of the necessity of division from the British Empire. His head was full of the political theory of John Locke. He had listened for a year to all the debates. Turning to neither book nor pamphlet, writing freely out of his genius and his memory, he created a concept of a new order as surely as Einstein's theorem split the atom. More powerful than the energy in the atom, more revolutionary than any words of Marx or Mao, it continues to challenge each individual to accept no destiny but the destiny he shapes for himself. For all men are born equal and their right to life, liberty and the pursuit of happiness is unalienable.

THE MAN WHO WOULD NOT BE KING

*W*hoever would be dictator of the United States must first overcome George Washington. The pattern of independence was cast before he was born. He stamped it on the new nation as firmly as the Allegheny and the Rocky Mountains are stamped on the face of the continent. The storms of ages may scour. The great impression remains.

Oliver Cromwell, fed up with delays and squabblings of a legislative body, called in his soldiers. He pointed to the Mace, symbol of the people's power, lying on the Speaker's table. "What shall we do with that bauble?" he cried. "Take it away!" Then he took over as England's dictator.

Napoleon Bonaparte did away with democracy even more thoroughly. He eagerly gave in to the demands of his army and became First Consul. Then he made himself Emperor. At the climax of the great coronation ceremony, to the considerable surprise of the Pope who had come to France for the occasion, he snatched the imperial crown out of his hands and with his own stuffed it onto his own head.

Washington set a different precedent. There comes a time after every war when the old order lies panting and there is a vacuum in the state. That is the moment of danger. The army demands pay and benefits. The people cry out for order and whoever can command the respect of the military is impelled, sometimes against his will, more often with it, to take over the government. The demand for military heroes is insatiable. No less than eleven of them have been Presidents of the United States.

But American Presidents have never become dictators. At times they have exceeded their just powers. So, for that matter, has Congress and the Judiciary, too. Power is poison in a choco-late cover. But always imposing between frail nature and temp-tation is the blazing remembrance of Washington's example, like the angel with the flaming sword that barred the way of Balaam's ass. After Cornwallis surrendered his army at York-town, the Revolutionary War was over. But there was not to be peace for yet two years. There was still a great force of British-ers bottled up in New York. The British navy once more con-trolled the seas, having defeated the French fleet that had made Yorktown possible. Americans still could not safely sail a fish-ing boat from Marblehead to Provincetown. Peace negotiations dragged on and on.

The Continental Army had nothing to do but build forts around New York and watch and watch and drill and drill and do guard duty. And grouse and grouse. The grousing was se-rious for the food was poor and not plentiful. Sanitation was terrible and there was a lot of sickness. Pay was in arrears. Much worse, pay was in the depreciating Continental currency. We still say "not worth a Continental damn."

General Washington went to Philadelphia in the winter of 1782 where the Continental Congress was sitting to see what he could do. It was not much. The colonies now called them-selves states, and the delegates were loaded with self-impor-tance. As the menace of an outside enemy receded, they grew bolder, vainer and less willing to cooperate. With no real pow-er to tax, the assembly was a bankrupt talkfest. So when Wash-ington went back to his headquarters at Newburgh, New York, he was probably not surprised, but he was certainly annoyed to be handed a communication from a trusted friend, one Colonel Nicola, suggesting that it was time for him to take over as King.

Washington blew up. He wrote a stiff letter. First he was insulted. He wanted to know just what defect in his own char-acter had ever suggested that he would fall for such a scheme. Then he was hurt. He felt acute pain that any such ideas should bubble to the surface in any army that he commanded. But of course he would do everything he could "in a Constitutional way" to see that the army got ample justice. And in closing he suggested in the polite, rather stilted phrases of an 18th century gentleman that his friend forever after shut up.

That quieted things down for a while. Warm weather came. There was more to eat, life was easier. The army was kept busy and felt useful building better quarters, fancier forts. But as another winter came on peace talk became persistent and peace itself became a concern, began to be felt almost as a menace to men too long in harness. Out of the shafts they might fall down. In February 1783 the rumor spread that the Congress, to get rid of a problem it could not solve, intended to disband the army by bits, leaving it at last impotent to do anything but straggle home and whistle for its pay.

This time no friendly officer handed the Commander-in-Chief a polite suggestion. This time mutiny was brewing. An anonymous letter was passed about the camp calling a meeting of officers. "Can you consent to be the only sufferers by this revolution? If you can, go, starve and be forgotten! But if you have sense enough to oppose tyranny, and spirit enough, awake and redress yourselves!"

Washington responded at once. He had to take notice of the proposed meeting, and did in his order of the day for the 11th of March 1783. He denounced "such disorderly proceedings." He then commanded a formal meeting to take place four days later to discuss the problem and to devise legitimate means to bring matters before Congress and get fair treatment. At once the anonymous writer put out another letter. It was even more strident. The tone is familiar to our own very recent past. Demands! Demands! And threats! Let Congress delay any longer and there will be a march!

On the 15th of March 1783 at precisely twelve o'clock the Commander-in-Chief entered the Newbuilding at Newburgh in full uniform, the old blue faded cloth and buff facings rubbed threadbare by much cleaning, the scabbard of his sword dented and dull, his epaulets irregularly glinting because of ineradicable tarnish. The assembly of officers fell instantly silent. The murmuring and the jostling ceased. The only sound was the heavy steps of the six foot three, two hundred pound soldier as his heels struck the boards on his way to the desk at the front of the room. He took from his pocket a paper and began to read.

"Gentlemen—By an anonymous summons an attempt has been made to convene you together—how inconsistent with the rules of propriety—how unmilitary—and how subversive of all order and discipline—let the good sense of the army decide."

Then he paused. He laid down the paper, took spectacles from his pocket and putting them on, as he was adjusting them said, very simply, "I beg your indulgence. I have grown gray in your service. I find now I am growing blind."

Some of the older officers looked at one another and looked down, then quickly at their feet. Even the youngest present felt a surge of emotion.

Washington went on. "The author of this piece is entitled to much credit for the goodness of his pen. . . . " and so continued with dignified sarcasm and good common sense demolishing the anonymous writer. He used strong language, which he rarely did. "My God! What can this writer have in view. . . . " He urged those present to express their horror and detestation of any man who would so attempt to overturn the liberties of our country. And he ended in the grand manner which was the natural manner of George Washington. "You will by the dignity of your conduct afford occasion for posterity to say, when speaking of the glorious example you have exhibited to mankind, 'had this day been wanting the world had never seen the last stage of perfection to which human nature is capable of attaining.' "

He folded his paper and walked slowly out of the room. Since that day there has been no more talk of a dictator for the United States.

DEBTS AND DANIEL SHAYS

*K*ing George and his taxes were washed overboard in the great storm of the American Revolution. But the Confederation of his former colonies was left a shattered hulk, dismasted, decks awash, wallowing in a sea of debt, ripped and torn by gales of inflation. The Continental Congress had no power to tax and its paper money depreciated as fast as it was issued. Every cent of hard money the Congress could scrape up by agreed-on requisitions from the several states was used to pay interest on the war debts owed abroad, mostly to Dutch bankers. There was not a penny to be spared for domestic relief. There was no federal government to bail out a bankrupt city like New York or a bankrupt corporation like Chrysler.

The army was disbanded. The treasury was empty. The new nation, with George Washington at its head, would not come into being till the making and the ratification of the Constitution in 1788. The last year before this happy solution, the bitter and dangerous year 1787, was grim.

Each state was sovereign and was free to solve its own problems in its own way — or to dissolve into chaos if it chose to. Several nearly did. Virginia, being of an agricultural mind, was accustomed to debt inherited from generation to generation, and settled in the familiar way, by paying off in depreciated paper, at about one dollar to a thousand borrowed. That left the real estate intact, ready to assume a new load of debt. Rhode Island went even further. Worthless scrip was declared sound money and creditors were ordered by the courts to take it. It did not jingle in the pocket but the government said it did. To refuse to take scrip was declared a crime. The too familiar situation was suddenly reversed. Creditors fled from the state

Elizabeth Freeman, "Mumbet" who saved the Sedgwick silver in Stockbridge.

with such property as they could carry pursued by eager debtors with bags full of nothing tendered in payment.

Massachusetts, being a trading state, opted for a sound currency. The profits of trade and customs duties eased the load for the seaport towns. But that was no help to up-country farmers. Taxes must be paid in hard money and there was none, except a man mortgage his farm to a big city banker. To make matters worse, the taxes levied by the state government were unfairly proportioned. Nearly half were a straight poll tax, so much per head, with the poorest man compelled to put up an equal share with the richest.

Redress lay in the hands of the State Legislature. The Representatives voted for a more reasonable apportionment. But the Senators killed the bill. The Senate was controlled by the mercantile interests. There was a property qualification to vote and a still higher one for the privilege of sitting in the Senate. The kindling was laid for a classic populist revolt. The match was struck in the Berkshire hills.

A plain and rather decent man gave his name to the rebellion. Daniel Shays was a destitute farmer. He had a lot of courage, abundant good nature and a cheerful disposition. His service in the Revolution began at Lexington and the furious fight at Bunker Hill. He was with the army that beat Burgoyne at Saratoga. He took part in the famous assault that took Stony Point on the Hudson with bayonets fixed to unloaded muskets. Cited for bravery he was made a Captain. And he returned from the wars to work a poor farm with nothing in his pocket but a little depreciating paper money and a promise of back pay at some future date. A few years later he could not raise $12.00 to pay a debt.

With a group of others in like case, he organized a ragged army and marched to Northampton in the autumn of 1786. Using the same tactics as Sam Adams with King George, this mob "persuaded" the judges to shut up the courts. This successfully prevented foreclosure of mortgages on farms. The idea spread like fire through dry brush. County courts were closed even as near to Boston State House as Concord by "embattled" farmers. Their intention was not especially belligerent. The object was to postpone court judgments till the spring when a new legislature would be elected that might pay more heed to just claims. No blood was shed.

The sorry episode that followed is now seen as through a glass darkly, like the removal of the Indians from the lands of their fathers by the encroaching whites. Facts are hard to come by because the losers wrote no history books. Such record as exists was written by their enemies and detractors. Theirs indeed are the plain and simple annals of the poor whose marker, if any exists, is a moss grown stone in a country graveyard. The Massachusetts government appears to have been impotent, unable to act promptly, almost powerless to act at all. This encouraged the insurgents. Shays' original band of oppressed freeholders was soon joined by every sort of ruffian and malcontent. The jails were opened to release debtors, and along with the debtors real criminals walked out. Shays led an attack on the Springfield arsenal to procure arms. This was barely frustrated by government forces.

Then affairs degenerated into looting and savagery. Houses were entered, hostages taken, and there were a few scattered skirmishes. Yet the sole cost in lives of the uprising — which lasted six months — was four men killed — two on each side. Shays' "army," without any discipline, had two main defects. It ran away when fired on and when not fired on got drunk. Neither was it very smart. On one occasion some "soldiers" demanded entrance into a fine house in Stockbridge. A black woman, Elizabeth Freeman, met them at the door, a fire shovel in her hand. Taking them down cellar she promised to brain anyone who broke a bottle, offered to serve them "like gentlemen" with glasses. Used to rum, they spat out the sour wine, went upstairs and began to ransack the house. "Real gentlemen like you," she said tauntingly, "would just naturally rob an old woman's trunk." To prove their gentility they left untouched Elizabeth's trunk in which she had hidden her employer's silver.

The rebellion was broken by General Lincoln, with the same

tactics that his wartime commander, George Washington, had used at Trenton. He surprised the rebels at dawn in the little village of Petersham after a forced march over mountains in a wild February blizzard. Half Shays' army was taken prisoner. Shays fled to Vermont. Some of the ringleaders were tried for treason and condemned to death. But in the spring elections John Hancock ran for Governor on a platform of total amnesty. He won by a heavy majority, showing clearly where the sympathy of the people lay. The insurgents were pardoned. The taxes that had caused the trouble were modified and so reduced by accommodations to accept notes from old soldiers instead of hard money as to lose their bite.

It was a bitter experience. It shocked the separate states into a sense of their predicament. It was a main factor in persuading them to throw up the idea of a loose confederation and form a federal union. Order and law had been preserved in Massachusetts by the merest whisker. It is a narrow road between chaos and despotism. It has to be paved with common sense. Nothing but taxes can control inflation. Yet unless the burden of taxes is fairly distributed there will be dangerous discontent. Suddenly in 1787 the people began to understand that taxtion with representation requires a sense of responsibility — sympathy and assistance to the unfortunate as well as protection for the profits of the shrewd and able.

THE CASE OF THE POOR BUTCHER

*W*hen a single interest takes over power in a state, that state is in trouble. The solution is to multiply the interests and divide the power. This was James Madison's theory of government which he wrote into the Constitution and it has worked. The contrary has left us some bad examples; the Sans Culottes who took over the French Revolution and the Bolsheviks who took over Russia. Governments work best when no single group gets the absolute upper hand.

Madison had good opportunity to observe the effects of single interest power at work in the Confederation that preceded the United States. New England was an excellent laboratory. There was the domination of the mercantile and hard money interest in Massachusetts that culminated in a minor civil war. And in Rhode Island a precisely opposite situation developed with the formation of the Country Party, a union of small landholders hell-bent to print paper money, extinguish debts and bury the merchants and bankers. In the process they nearly buried the laborers, the artisans, the clerks and themselves, too.

For a short time after the Peace of Paris in 1783 that ended the Revolution the former colonies seemed to be flooded with specie. The French soldiers and the British, paid in hard coin, had left most of it in America. The Dutch loans to the Confederation had provided the vital transfusion of gold to keep life in the new Republic. But mysteriously and suddenly, as money will when threatened, it disappeared. The poor blamed the rich for buying lavishly of silks and broadcloth, frippery and finery and sending America's gold and silver to pay for it abroad. The rich blamed the British navigation laws that discriminated against the new nation's trade. And the seaport merchants ran up bills in London and Liverpool and squeezed their country cousins hard to pay up on delinquent accounts.

The situation was peculiarly acute in Rhode Island. Its land was insufficient even to feed its population. It lived by trading with its neighbors, transshipping merchandise to and from the West Indies. It had no back country to provide large natural resources like timber and furs. It was a small state of small farms and small seaports. And the farmers controlled the vote. Its form of government was still as it had been since 1663 under the charter of Charles II, all power concentrated in a two-level legislature, and both levels elected twice a year. Government in Rhode Island was as nearly direct as government can be; a glorified town meeting, the only hitch being that the meeting members were elected by a single class, the freeholders, those who owned real estate. Everyone else was excluded from the vote.

The farmers formed a Country Party. In the legislature they outnumbered the representatives of the seaports two or three to one. They believed that the stagnation of trade was due to lack of money and the answer was to print as much as might be necessary. They hit on the figure of 100,000 British pounds—still the main medium of exchange. This convenient figure was printed and issued as a loan against real estate at four per cent.

The merchants screamed fraud and refused to take the paper except at a heavy discount. Infuriated, the Country Party passed a law that anyone who did not take paper at its face value should be fined 100 pounds. On a second conviction the culprit would be ineligible to hold public office. This was aimed directly at the freemen in the legislature who opposed the act, and would eliminate the minority. But the paper went right on depreciating and within three months of issue was worth barely one third of face value.

Now John Collins, the Country Party Governor, called the legislature into special session to check the opposition of "a combination of influential men against the good and wholesome laws of the state." Great events cast their shadows before! The state was good and wholesome a decade before the guillotine was invented to get rid of inconvenient minorities; a centu-

THE
CASE,

TREVETT against WEEDEN:

On INFORMATION and COMPLAINT, for refusing
Paper Bills in Payment for *Butcher's Meat,*
in Market, at Par with Specie.

Tried before the Honourable SUPERIOR COURT,
in the County of *Newport, September* Term, 1786.

ALSO,

The Cafe of the Judges of faid Court,

Before the Honourable GENERAL ASSEMBLY,
at *Providence, October* Seffion, 1786, on Citation, for difmif-
fing faid Complaint.

Wherein the Rights of the People to *Trial by Jury, &c.* are
ftated and maintained, and the Legiflative, Judiciary and
Executive Powers of Government examined and defined.

By *JAMES M. VARNUM*, Efq;

Major-General of the State of *Rhode-Ifland, &c.* Counfellor at
Law, and Member of Congrefs for faid State.

PROVIDENCE: Printed by JOHN CARTER. 1787.

Account of the case of butcher Weeden vs. cabinetmaker Trevett.

ry before the Gulag Archipelago. And the debate in the Rhode Island legislature has a familiar ring. Jonathan Hazard, addressing the opposition, said, "I wish you more prosperity elsewhere but if you insist on leaving the state I can't help it," an early version of the bumper sticker "America—Love it or leave it." The written remonstrance of thirteen protesters from Providence was refused even a hearing "because it was drawn in disrespectful terms." And the paper money went right on depreciating. Now it was worth one sixth of face value.

So another law was passed to put bite into the already enormous fine for refusing to take paper at face value. Offenses were to be tried by special courts of judges, no jury allowed, no appeal to any higher jurisdiction. And the judges were appointed by the legislature and had tenure only at the pleasure of the legislature! The first and last case tried under this statute is famous.

A butcher called John Weeden refused to take a pound note from a cabinetmaker named Trevett in payment for a piece of meat. He was defended by James Varnum, a noted lawyer, who took the case gratis, on principle. There was no defense against the fact, which was established, or the Act which was in accordance with Rhode Island law and the Charter of 1663. But in a noble defense, pressed with great eloquence, Varnum swayed five judges, against their will and their own interest, to the opinion that the law was unconstitutional because it denied the natural right of man to trial by jury, something secured by Magna Carta and the unremitting effort of brave men ever since. A testimony to the importance of Magna Carta, then invoked, is the gift by Britain to the United States of a corner of the famous ground of Runnymede where King John signed away his unlimited powers, a place now marked by a stone, against a background of laurel, that poignantly remembers John Kennedy.

The verdict for the defendant was greeted by "a universal clap" in the crowded Newport courtroom. The reward of the judges was to be summoned before the legislature to explain the reasons for their decision "if any they have in order that this Assembly on proper information may adopt such measure as may be agreeable to right and justice." Two of the judges suddenly became ill. The courageous remaining three bravely faced their censors. A judge is "accountable only to God and to his conscience," said Judge Howell. "When the General Assemblies attempt to overleap the bounds of the Constitution the Court has the power and *it is their duty* to refuse to carry such laws into effect." Judge Hazard, although an advocate of paper money, found himself obliged to strike down the law, being driven by "the energy of truth." The legislature then proceeded to censor the judges for giving "no satisfactory reason" for their decision. But they were not removed from office. Their decision held.

That killed the law. No twelve men would convict a fellow citizen for refusing to do what not one of them would do himself, swap a piece of good meat for a piece of unsecured paper. The great point was made, that an economic theory cannot be forced through at the expense of civil rights. It is to be feared it did not help the butcher. He went on relief, and what happened to him after we do not know. Probably, he, like the judges, who the next year lost their jobs, was a martyr for honesty and the first principle of the common law.

Thereafter the Country Party thrashed about like a landed shark eating its own tail. It made its depreciated paper legal tender, thus repudiating the state debt. Private debts could be liquidated by depositing a bundle of worthless notes with a judge, if the creditor refused to take it. Credit was extinguished. Merchants shut up shop or fled the state, carrying their goods with them. Trade stopped. Rhode Island was a separate nation, neither part of the British Empire nor of the new formed Union, and starving to death. Finally the legal tender laws were repealed. Two years late Rhode Island joined the United States.

Then President Washington made a good will visit and was received with cannon and bells and oratory. Neither the receipt of adulation nor the recollection of past foolishness much affected him. He simply said, "It affords me peculiar pleasure to observe that the completion of our Union, by the accession of your state, gives a strong assurance of permanent political happiness to the people of America."

So it was. The two violently opposed single interests in the state were quickly lost among the manifold political interests of all the states, and Rhode Island soon shared generously in the prosperity of the new nation.

HAMILTON CAGES THE BEAST INFLATION

*S*hays' Rebellion was the cataclysmic shove that created the United States. The American Revolution, pressing against ancient rule traditionally imposed from above, had been like the contact of earth plates that makes continents. Suddenly out of the depths of human experience rose a new world order, *novus ordo seclorum*, shuddering, heaving, groaning and cracking with fearful pains internally.

For a long moment in 1786, that dragged agonizingly into 1787, the loose Confederation of King George's former colonies skirted the edge of disaster. Moral persuasion was the only remedy immediately available to keep order. To back up 'suasion there was a poorly organized and reluctant militia. There was no national military force. "You talk my good sir, of employing influence to appease the present tumult in Massachusetts," wrote George Washington. "Influence is no government!" But influence was the most that one jealous state was prepared to offer another.

Massachusetts managed to resolve its troubles after a fashion by working out an uneasy compromise between debtors and creditors. And George Washington was pushed, the tallest peak in the new rising continent of human affairs, from his passionately desired retirement in Virginia towards a Constitutional Convention in Philadelphia. He had refused to go. He fumbled for excuses. He anticipated failure. He doubted that even a quorum of states would bother to come. But the earthquake and eruption under his feet and under the feet of the whole Continental Confederation could not be denied. It was organize or perish; create a working union or see hard fought independence crumble into anarchy among quarreling states.

Then in four months, in muggy, yellow fever prone Philadel-

Alexander Hamilton deplores democracy just before his duel with
Burr.

phia, two centuries of groping and striving for self-government culminated in the Constitution. It was a compromise that nobody liked entirely. Franklin summed it up, "I consent, Sir, to this Constitution because I expect no better, and because I am not sure that it is not the best."

Ratification was in doubt. Madison and Hamilton, with some help from John Jay, wrote and published in a New York newspaper, whence they were widely copied, the remarkable Federalist papers. They tipped the scale. Delaware was the first state to ratify, in December 1787, Pennsylvania the second and Massachusetts the third, in February 1788. By summer, New Hampshire came in, the ninth state, and the Constitution was declared in effect. Before winter, House, Senate and President of a new nation had all been elected.

It was indeed a wonderful year, *annus mirabilis*, one beyond the dreams of any ancient astrologer. It opened a new era in the world's history, even as the next year began the closing of another era with the collapse of the old order in France. Chaos, followed by terror, dictatorship, then general war, were the lot of Europe for the next generation. In America chaos stopped at the Berkshire hills. The new republic just rising beyond the western sea could not tolerate mob rule. It had to suppress it. But it could suppress it mercifully and extend pardon even to the leaders of the mobs.

A lesson was there well learned. Alexander Hamilton, no democrat, recognized the right of revolt. "If the representatives of the People betray their constituents, there is then no resource left but in the exertion of that original right of self defense which is paramount to all positive forms of government." The plight of the Shays rebels had been the direct result of the failure of the Continental Congress to make good its obligations. Its paper money had become almost worthless. Thus educated, by a shocking case history in the ultimate result of inflation, Hamilton undertook the new office of Secretary of the Treasury in the first administration under the new Constitution.

With half an eye anyone could see that inflation was the

absolute danger to the Republic. Indians on the frontier, hostile nations with fleets on the seas ready to attack were as nothing compared to the worm within. The loss of credit and the disappearance of any means of exchange but depreciating paper were destroying the farmer, the merchant and the artisan.

The next step would be hoarding and total paralysis, with neighbor set against neighbor. Already things had come to such a pass that President Washington, reputed to be one of the richest men in the country, had been obliged to mortgage his great estate just to get $3000 cash to transport himself and family to New York to take his new job.

What all the world could see Hamilton could see, who was brighter than most. Doubtless he could have solved his problem, or half solved it, in a dozen different ways. He chose a head-on approach, daring and efficacious. He proposed to substitute for the old Continental debts a new debt funded at six percent and backed by revenue-raising customs and reasonable taxes sufficient to make it good. He went a headlong step further and proposed to take over the debts of the states, too.

Of course the price of scrip rose; speculators made money. Then and thereafter critics have explained Hamilton's policies as stemming from everything from his social theories to his birth; as one biased observer put it, "the bastard brat of a Scotch peddler." But he stuck to his point; got his bills through; established the credit of the government and stopped the inflation.

Some fortunes were made. Hamilton's was not one of them. But in the return to stability all profited. It is easy to condemn Hamilton's moral character. It was dangerous; most of all to himself, for he died in an unnecessary duel. But it is hard to fault his performance. Washington backed his brilliant management of the country's economy and supplied whatever was lacking in character.

Then and now and hereafter the depreciation of the nation's credit can reach a point of danger. Beyond the point of danger lies nobody knows what — general chaos or arbitrary, perhaps savage measures — certainly something unpleasant. Shifts and expedients are of less and less effect. Guidelines are broken. Jawboning is of no avail. Nothing will work but a firm policy firmly maintained of fair taxes to pay just debts. It is sometimes unpopular, but in the end it works for everybody's benefit. Influence is no government.

THE PRESIDENTIAL OFFICE

*T*he door to the office of the President of the United States is very high. It has to be for it was shaped to admit the tall figure of George Washington. No greater figure has ever entered. It has been unnecessary to cut an entrance wider or higher.

The door opens into an enormous room. There, at a lonely desk, sits the President of the United States. At the end of, at the most, eight years he must leave. Not by the door at which he came in, but by another, specially cut to his size. Not many of the doors are as tall as the entrance way. One at least is wider. That is the door out of which was borne the body of the murdered Abraham Lincoln. His spirit will never leave the room—"with malice towards none; with charity for all; with firmness in the right as God gives us to see the right."

It used sentimentally to be said that the office of President of the United States was so great that it caused men to grow. "They grew with the office." Those who have lived well into the 20th century know better. It also causes men to shrink. Those elect who enter the great door, magnified many times by the mirage of the votes they have received, seem on inauguration day more than life size. So much of hope was cast along with the votes that the mirage is tinted very often the lovely pink of maple buds in spring. But then the door closes and the President is left alone with the weight of half the world on his shoulders.

The job of President of the United States is the biggest. Its bigness can be measured by the names of some of those who have held it and whose names accordingly appear on many lists, some of which may even be memorized by school children, but whose characters are no more remembered than last Tuesday's breakfast. Harrison and Harrison, Hayes, Fillmore, Arthur and Pierce, what did they ever do? Not really very much. The tide of events rolled over them. They are like smooth stones lying on the bottom of a stream. They make not even a ripple on the surface of time.

Some tremendous men make rather poor Presidents. If J.Q. Adams had left off public affairs after his single frustrated term of office, his previous diplomatic career might still have left him a reputation. But what makes him really live, and live ever more vigorously, as some modern states, whether super states or little disasters that support the super cruelty of petty tyrants, go on their mechanical way oppressing and destroying people, is his post-Presidential career. As a Congressman he fought the gag rule; he taught the white man that his right to free speech turned on the freedom of the black people. He may perhaps have taught Lincoln a turn of phrase, for a generation before the Second Inaugural he wrote, "In charity to all mankind, bearing no malice or ill-will to any human being, and even compassionating those who hold in bondage their fellow men, not knowing what they do."

To be a great President requires much more than administrative ability. Something the great President must have of the showman, the leader who can demonstrate as well as do. But if that were all, Aaron Burr would be a hero. More important than ability, either in engineering or in statecraft, is character. An American President has to know the difference between right and wrong; plain Harry Truman knew that, knew it much better than many better educated men. By the lights of later knowledge this or that action may be proved to have been wrong; but the motive that provoked the action was always right—the intended and expected advantage to the governed. Jefferson knew it, behind all his sophistries, philosophic or devious. It was the strength of Lincoln, underlying his humor, making his eloquence alive, not a thing dead as soon as spoken as is the noise of the professional orator. Theodore Roosevelt knew it, shaking his big stick, pushing his white fleet rambunctiously around the world. He knew the wrong of rampant imperialism. Democracy could not wait supine till kings, kaisers and tsars rolled it over. How different from the sanctimonious pietism of McKinley, which snatched the little brown brothers from the clutch of the tyrant Spain and made a fortune in sugar.

At the beginning of every Presidential term the American people believe for a silly moment that their votes have endowed a human being with something more than human wisdom. They have not, in fact, endowed him with anything except a big job. Whether he does it well or badly will depend for the most part on whom he persuades to work for him. No one man can do it alone. Woodrow Wilson, one of the best educated and most intelligent of Presidents, failed miserably when he had one of the greatest opportunities ever presented to any President, because he could neither take advice nor get on with the Senate. Crabbed little Coolidge, with a small opportunity, made the most of it. He sent Dwight Morrow as Ambassador to Mexico and added the good will visit of Charles Lindbergh. It went a long way to restoring democracy to inter-American relations too long poisoned by the crass imperialism that began with Presidents Tyler and Polk.

There are many doors that lead out of the office of the President. Very few of them are taller and broader than the door that leads in. Some are small and neat, some narrow and tall. Some are decorated with pillars and pediments. Some have no ornamentation but a plain Puritan frame. Some are strange indeed, crooked and twisted, with a doorsill under that is rotten. There is even a hole in the wainscot that appears to have been gnawed by a rat.

When Leverett Saltonstall wished Harry Truman well after his sudden elevation to the Presidency, Truman said just three words, "Pray for me." The American people can hardly do better on Inauguration Day than curb their expectations down to reasonable limits and ponder, with thoughtful consideration of recent history, a few words of John Adams. He was writing to his wife Abigail in the evening of the first night an American President would spend in the new nation's new official residence, the new White House in the new city of Washington, November 2, 1800. "Before I end my letter, I pray heaven to bestow the best of blessings on this house, and on all that shall inhabit it. May none but honest and wise men ever rule under this roof!"

THE UNITED STATES CRUSHES TERRORISM

*T*here are certain conditions which tend, by an inexorable progression, to violent solutions. Unless checked in their courses, their result among nations is war. Thus it came about that the infant United States, having achieved its independence by violence and war, found itself embarked on a new sea of troubles, the Mediterranean Sea. The release of ties with the British Empire brought it into rivalry with the ambitions of all trading nations. A foreign policy must be discovered and means developed to secure it.

Lining the north coast of Africa, like hawks perched along a cliff, were the Barbary States. The government of these States was organized along tribal lines and depended on the outcome of family rivalries and the complicated and murderous politics of the decaying Turkish Empire. The Sultans or Beys or Pashas, as they called themselves, of Morocco, Algiers, Tunis and Tripoli, lived in squalid splendor, exercising despotic power in Oriental courts complete with palace guards, lord high chamberlains and elaborate harems. Their revenues came from the organized robbery of the commerce that passed by their domains. Their protection was the mountains and deserts that guarded against attack by land, and a perilous coast, with harbors fortified by barriers of reefs and well-placed guns.

For centuries the rivalries of the European empires had allowed the continuance of this scourge. By payment of tribute a nation could secure safe passage of its ships. By payment of a little more, in time of war, it could secure the plundering of the ships of its enemy. Nations with strong navies paid less tribute. That put the United States in a tough position. Suddenly independent of Britain and without a navy of its own it was obliged to pay bribes and more bribes and must expect blackmail.

The first victim was an American brig named *Betsey.* The Peace of Paris was just made with Britain in 1783 when she was stopped by an Arab dhow because her papers were not "in order." Her crew were immediately chained up in jail and her cargo stolen. Slow and careful negotiations procured the release of the men unharmed after two years; and the ship. But the necessary bribe and the lost cargo cost many thousand dollars. And she was but the first of many. Hundreds more ships and their crews would suffer the same or a worse fate.

John Adams, one of the peace commissioners, was sent to Versailles to inquire of the French Foreign Minister, the Count of Vergennes, the best way of handling the Arab states. Why he went alone is not clear. Franklin was sick in bed but Jefferson, on this particular Sunday morning, went for a five mile walk. When Adams explained that his colleagues were "indisposed," Count Vergennes, smiling, inquired "very particularly" after their health. Evidently the old fox smelt a field mouse. To all Adams' questions he replied that he must make inquiry, "It was not in his department." Decidedly the French government was revealing no secrets about its dealings in the Mediterranean trade.

But on one point Vergennes was emphatic. The French King never sent the Barbary pirates any munitions of war—just money, or sometimes such harmless merchandise, convenient in a harem, as a cargo of looking glasses. And, he added, it was a lot cheaper to appoint consuls to the Barbary States than allow them to send ambassadors to your country. You would be expected to pay all the expenses of the ambassador and his suite, plus travel time! Adams returned from Versailles "well sprinkled with compliments, the holy water of courts," and not much wiser.

Even the Marquis de Lafayette was unable to ferret out accurate information. He could report only that the King of France paid less for "protection" than anyone else and not on any regular schedule of time or amount. His presents were apt to be, as from one friendly monarch to another, expensive watches or jewel-hilted daggers. The whole business, he reported, was purposely shrouded in mystery.

The Dutch were more explicit. Last year they had given the Emperor of Morocco supplies to equip two frigates including all necessary cannon, powder and shot and at least $100,000 in cash. Guided by these informations Jefferson and Adams settled on a policy of treating with the Barbary States that became, of necessity, the pattern of future negotiations. It was simple practicality—drive the best bargain possible till time and circumstances permit a better. Adams summed it up in a letter home, "I detest these barbarians as much as anybody, and my indignation against their piracies is as hot as that of anybody. But how can we help ourselves? As to fighting them what can we do? The contest is unequal. We have a rich trade for them to prey upon."

It was wise counsel. All the cards were in the hands of the Arab states. There was no suggestion of such a forum as the United Nations to appeal to. Quite the contrary. The suicidal rivalries of the competing European empires guaranteed immunity to the pirates. There was nothing to do but wait and work. It would be yet another four years before the United States could emerge as a real force in the world under its new constitution. And then a dozen more before it could gather strength to build a useful navy. "Some Americans say," Adams wrote, "we had better send frigates and fight them. I am afraid we shall make a great mistake in regard to these piratical states."

Fortunately the mistake was not made. The great personality of George Washington restrained those eager to act before action could produce any result but disaster. America bided its time. For a long time. Throughout the whole of George Washington's administration tribute was paid. It amounted to a very great sum; in some years as much as one fifth of the cost of running the government. And still the greed of the Sultans was not satiable. In the administration of John Adams a navy was begun. And it fell to the lot of Thomas Jefferson, reluctantly and cautiously, to use the power and resolve the problem.

But only after long and painful waiting. By 1801 more than

two million dollars had been spent to ransom the captives of Barbary, to pay tribute and to meet at each new emergency additional demands of blackmail. There was no relying on the word of the pirates. Any excuse or no excuse was reason enough to demand MORE. But a new weapon had come into the hands of the Americans. After a dozen years existence as a nation they had found strength to build an excellent small navy. Quite disregarding this fact Yussuf, ruler of Tripoli, in a fit of petulance when the American Consul refused to agree to a sudden new extortion, ordered the flagpole in front of the Consulate cut down. The Consul fled in a hired ship and war was on.

It was a tossup whether the other Barbary powers would join forces with Tripoli. Algiers was kept in good humor by a most extraordinary action. Frigate *George Washington*, sent to deliver a load of tribute, goods and money, unwisely tied up within the port. The Bey of Algiers summoned Captain Bainbridge and ordered him to convey an Embassy to Constantinople with presents for the Grand Sultan. He politely explained that if Bainbridge refused he would hijack the ship and put him and his crew in the prison always ready for such emergencies. Bainbridge, under this duress, agreed. So the American Flag was lowered, the Algerian flag was raised over it and in this piratical company were the Stars and Stripes first seen in the Bosphorus!

In response, the most powerful expeditionary force the United States would send overseas till 1917 was organized to protect the Mediterranean trade and deal with the temperamental Yussuf. Three frigates and a schooner were dispatched to blockade Tripoli. Within the next three years these were joined by a whole fleet of other craft, including the finest frigate of all, the *Constitution*. More than a thousand men were employed and the expense made President Jefferson groan. But the results were only so-so. The show of force persuaded the other Barbary States not to join Tripoli. Yet they quietly continued their customary depredations and ships out of convoy were not safe. As for Tripoli, the blockading of its port was an inconvenience, but its quick dhows, among its dangerous reefs, usually could avoid capture. Bombardment produced no more effect than bouncing tennis balls on a brick wall. The Bey would not abate one penny in his demands.

An order from Washington for more vigorous action produced an immediate and disastrous result. Frigate *Philadelphia*, now under command of Captain Bainbridge, chasing an Arab dhow off Tripoli, fetched up on a sunk reef. Four hours of frantic effort, even the jettisoning of most of her guns and cutting down the foremast, could not get her off. A council of war determined there was no course but to open the sea cocks, scuttle the ship and strike the flag. The crew were taken ashore, stripped of every possession, shackled and driven to work for their new masters with whips. The officers were likewise stripped, then locked up in the Bey's private jail.

The next day they looked out of their barred window and saw the *Philadelphia* riding safely at anchor off the harbor of Tripoli. It was a bad moment for Captain Bainbridge. The Tripolitans, taking advantage of the offshore night wind and the tides, small but certain, had succeeded in floating the ship. Now the entire effort of the U.S. navy would have to be to destroy one of its own finest frigates. And its crew of three hundred men were now hostage to the enemy. It was cold comfort to know that it was piratical custom to treat hostages as badly as possible without killing them. Thus maximum ransom could be extracted.

The American navy concentrated before Tripoli, even entered the Port and bombarded the town, but without causing much damage. A bomb ship, loaded to the gunwales with explosive, blew up too soon and cost the lives of a dozen brave men. The *Philadelphia* was finally destroyed by the famous exploit of Stephen Decatur, who sailed with a picked crew into the harbor under the guns of the fort, managed to board and burn her. School histories prefer to remember this gallant feat rather than the fact that its accomplishment succeeded only in preventing a ship, lost under questionable circumstances, from becoming an enemy ship. Its crew were still hostages in the hands of the enemy and the U.S. navy was diminished by one frigate—next to the *Constitution* its best frigate.

"It will take an army of 10,000 men and a squadron of ships to subdue Tripoli," wrote Bainbridge from his jail. But he reckoned without a Connecticut Yankee by the name of William Eaton. Eaton's career had been checkered. At sixteen he ran away from home to serve in the Revolutionary army. Then he spent seven years working his way through Dartmouth College, taught school, made political connections in Vermont, got a commission in the army, quarreled with his superiors, was court-martialed but the sentence not confirmed, and at last turned up in Tunis as American Consul. In this savage society he shone. When the Prince's high chamberlain attempted to bar his way to the Prince, over a little matter of protocol and bribes, he walked out, swearing at the top of his voice, "By God, I'm not come here to be insulted by a servant."

The consuls of the great nations were aghast. But the tactic worked. The chamberlain caved. Tunis and the United States were soon at terms.

From this base Eaton conceived the bold plan of winning the now formally declared war against Tripoli by a land attack. This would be organized to restore to the throne of Tripoli its "rightful" ruler, one Hamet, who had been deposed by younger brother Yussuf. Hamet had been living in exile in Tunis, where Eaton had met him, but the place having become too hot for him he had fled to Egypt.

Eventually Eaton got a vague sort of commission from President Jefferson as "a naval agent who might be useful" to the commander of the American squadron off Tripoli. The U.S. navy carried him to Egypt and landed him there with a dozen marines and a small bag of gold. He made contact with Hamet and organized an expeditionary force of Greeks, Arabs and disaffected Tripolitans. This wildly improbable army of some 500 bandits, expatriate revolutionaries and nine patriotic Americans, with camels and horses, set out to cross some 500 miles of desert and mountains to make contact with an American fleet that could approach land only during spells of good weather.

After the first couple of weeks' marching food grew scarce, water ran out. Mutiny was an almost everyday occurence. Progress dropped to barely ten miles a day. Somehow held together by the force of Eaton's personality this rabble reached the coast. Not a sail in sight! Eaton kept cool, kept off mutineers at pistol point and burned signal fires for a day and a night. Then the fleet came in, came close in shore, revictualed the army from small boats and the combined forces moved on by sea and land towards the powerfully garrisoned Tripolitan seaport town of Derna.

To Eaton's demand for surrender the commandant sent back the defiance, "My head or yours." After fierce fighting Eaton's army took the town. The naval guns helped prevent recapture by a strong relief force from Tripoli. Then in Tripoli the pirate king Yussuf had a sudden change of heart. He rushed to make peace with the United States. All captive Americans were set free. Promises were made to respect American ships. One small push more and an African empire would have fallen like a rotten apple into the lap of the United States.

But President Jefferson's political agent, Tobias Lear, from the comfortable cabin of Frigate *Constitution,* with pusillanimous caution, settled for much less. Fearing for the lives of hostages, he paid Yussuf sixty thousand dollars for their liberty. He forced Eaton to abandon Derna. He received in return a promise from Yussuf that he would grant amnesty to Eaton's Mahometan allies. This promise was not kept. Yussuf, after the Americans sailed home, had them murdered.

Eaton, with some reason, thought tougher terms should have been exacted. But the main point was gained. The terror attacks ceased. No more ransom money would be needed.

Hamet never did get back his throne. A congressional medal was talked of for Eaton. But partisan feeling was running high. Eaton was a Federalist and Federalists were poison to the administration. He was obliged to be content with the gratitude of the maritime state of Massachusetts, which granted him ten thousand wild acres of land in Maine. It also named the broad street that seems but a narrow way, lying as it does under the break of Beacon Hill, deep in the shadow of Boston State House, Derne, to remind the world forever of his exploit.

The world forgot. On modern maps, the old town in Africa which hides under the barren eastern ridges of the Jebel Akhdar mountains and was once a pirate's nest, is spelled Derna. Rock tombs above the town are the remaining vestige of Darnis, a settlement of ancient Greece. Overlooking the tombs and the town are the ruins of a fort.

The modern passer-by in Boston makes no connection, deceived by the 18th century spelling of the street name, and pronouncing it in one syllable instead of two. But the ruined fort and the shaded street under Beacon Hill are all that visibly remain to remind the world of a lesson it ought not to forget. In an exploit of extraordinary genius and daring the infant United States did for the great powers of the world what they were too small-minded and too insanely jealous of one another to do cooperatively for themselves. It took terrorism by the throat and shook the life out of it.

MR. WOLFE AND THE GENEROUS STRANGER

$\mathcal{T}$he labor of putting together pieces of the past in an attempt to make a whole out of time and the future is a puzzle for specialists. But the fun of picking up the pieces is open to anyone. This was the idea that animated the Reverend Jeremy Belknap when he organized a group of friends to found the Massachusetts Historical Society in 1790. "We intend to be an active, not a passive literary body; not waiting, like a bed of oysters for the tide of communications to flow in upon us, but to seek and find; not waiting at home for things to fall into the lap, but prowling about like a wolf for the prey."

Taking his own advice he wrote to his friend Paul Revere asking for a firsthand account of how the news got to Concord. Paul obliged. Jeremy printed it in the *Proceedings* of the Society and there Longfellow happened on it half a century later. Inspired, he wrote his great mythopoetic ballad. It was published just as the Confederacy reached its high tide at Gettysburg—"A voice in the darkness, a knock at the door, and a word that shall echo forevermore!" Who can measure the weight of the words of the poet in rolling back the tide and rebuilding the Union?

Another friend of Jeremy's began the solution of the Old South Meeting House mystery. In the tower of the church was stored the most valuable library in America. It had been assembled by the Reverend Thomas Prince, who had died not long before the Revolution. Among the many manuscripts were some in the handwriting of William Bradford, Governor of the Plymouth Colony, Pilgrim extraordinary, a contemporary of Shakespeare and the translators of the King James Bible and one whose prose attains to equal magnificence. The prize of all was Bradford's history *Of Plimoth Plantation.*

When the British military took over Boston in 1775 they needed a place to practice their horsemanship out of reach of winter ice. So the pews were taken out of the Old South and used for firewood and the floor made into a riding ring. Grooms and stablemen, as well as red coated officers, had the run of the library in the tower. When they left for Halifax, Nova Scotia, at the invitation of George Washington, sent by a cannonball from Dorchester Heights, the Bradford manuscripts and a good deal else had disappeared.

Some years later Jeremy's friend was prowling about Halifax. Like all Jeremy's friends, from that day to this, he was no oyster. Let us call him Mr. Wolfe. He stopped at a grocer's shop to buy a cake of soap. The grocer reached under the counter and whipped out a piece of paper to wrap it in. Mr. Wolfe's quick eye noticed something peculiar about the paper. "Do you have any more of that?" "Oh yes, quite a bundle." "Give it to me and I'll pay you twice for the soap."

Mr. Wolfe walked out, burning with excitement; outwardly calm and urbane as usual. At home he examined his discovery. It was one of the lost letterbooks of Governor Bradford! He sent it on to the Massachusetts Historical Society. It was the first inkling that anything of the Governor's writings might have survived, excepting only some of the early parts of his history long ago copied into the Plymouth church records. But the years passed, two generations of the Wolfe family passed away, and nothing more turned up. Then one day a young Mr. Wolfe was browsing among the bookstalls on Cornhill Street in Boston, just where the Sears block now faces the new City Hall Plaza. He picked up a famously dull work by Samuel, Lord Bishop of Oxford, known to his contemporaries as "Soapy Sam" Wilberforce.

Suddenly Mr. Wolfe's eyes almost started from his head. There in front of him was a passage, obviously quoted from the lost history, and the conscientious cleric gave the source as "from a manuscript in the library of the Bishop of London."

Mr. Wolfe and the Generous Stranger

Mr. Wolfe rushed to his friend, the editor of the Massachusetts Historical Society, who wrote to a friend in England. Sure enough, there it was, the priceless lost history, safe and sound in the Bishop's library, and nobody knew how it got there, least of all the Bishop! It took all the strength of the powerful arm of Senator Hoar of Massachusetts and an act of a special clerical court, meeting in St. Paul's Cathedral, to get it back to its rightful owners—but it is back—safe in a glass case in the vault of Boston State House for all the world to see and to admire.

Always there is the element of luck. That is what makes Mr. Wolfe's life interesting. The trained eye can pick up arrowheads in a plowed field. But when will the field be plowed? One day a still later Mr. Wolfe was in such a field. It was an unlikely place, a rather dingy restaurant somewhere under the Boston Stock Exchange, a building not long after pulled down to make way for the "New" Boston. Even Boston is made "new" every century or so. Mr. Wolfe was apparently no more lively than an oyster as he sat alone at a small table. He became aware of a well-dressed gentleman standing in front of him.

"You wrote something in the papers about the action between the Constitution and the Guerriere," said the gentleman, "and you got the date wrong." "Did I? I try to be accurate about dates." "Come with me," said the gentleman, "and I'll show you."

They went to his office. A safe was opened. A manuscript was put into Mr. Wolfe's hands, a whole great folio book, seventy pages or more. It was a log kept on board the U.S. Navy's most famous ship, the frigate *Constitution*, during the epochal summer of 1812! Suddenly Mr. Wolfe knew the meaning of Keats's famous sonnet. He felt a wild surmise "like some watcher of the skies when a new planet swims into his ken." The faded ink told a vivid story, the story of the great fight, as seen by Midshipman Frederick Baury and written the day of? the day after? Baury wrote the 20th of August. Other authorities say the 19th. It is a subject for scholars to argue about. Most extraordinary, as a quick search of the Massachusetts Historical Society discovered, the manuscript fitted like the last piece in a picture puzzle. Nearly a century before the Society had been given all the other volumes of the journal of Frederick Baury. But these, the most exciting pages, were not known to exist. Now these, too, were being offered by the generous stranger!

The mists of time are suddenly swept away, as when the late summer northwester sweeps out of Boston Harbor and sweeps all the Bay. We can see the terrific scene with new, young eyes, though it happened near two hundred years ago. We are cruising in the Frigate *Constitution* far out of sight of land off the Gulf of the St. Lawrence. The month is August. The wind is blowing fresh from the northwest, and there is a lively sea. "At 2 PM discovered a sail to the South'd. Made all sail in chase . . . ."

CONSTITUTION SHIP OF STATE

*A*ugust is *Constitution* month—the frigate *Constitution*. The heavy foliage and the hot, long days, relieved by the sudden sea breeze, recall each year a moment peculiar to New England for excitement and jubilation; epochal in the annals of the United States. On the second day of August 1812 the *Constitution* sailed from Boston and disappeared over the edge of the sea to eastward. On the nineteenth, her guns heard only by her own crew and those who received her shot, she fought the battle that makes her the most famous ship in American history. On the thirtieth the lookout at Boston Light saw her topsails rising with the morning sun out of the eastern sea.

It was the Sabbath and the Puritan city lay silent. The bells rang to church. As the tall ship beat up to land, the offshore breeze carried the sound of their ringing even from Watertown and Cambridge. But as the folk came from church, the surprising bells pealed boisterously. There was shouting in the streets. Not even the Puritan Sabbath could withstand the news brought by a boat from the *Constitution* just anchoring below the Castle.

The remnants of the crew of the British frigate *Guerriere* were prisoners of war below decks. The *Guerriere* was a shattered hulk lying some hundreds of miles offshore and forty fathom down. And the fight that sent her there had lasted just thirty minutes. In that half hour the action of the *Constitution* had raised the United States to the rank of a first class power in the world. It took a little longer than that, and the carnage was more considerable, for Athens to achieve the same status twenty-three hundred years earlier by sinking the Persian navy in the straits of Salamis.

In either case the significance of the event far exceeded the numbers involved. Athens went on to change the whole history of the Western world. What the United States did we hardly yet know. But we are still allowed to hope. The *Constitution*, an artifact created by the singular powers released by the events of 1776, proved in a conclusive trial its superiority over a similar artifact created by an ancient empire. Untouched by authoritarian tradition, untroubled by class distinctions, the American designed and built ship proved in a most practical way the value of that Constitution for which it was named, the frame of government for a new nation "concieved in liberty and dedicated to the proposition that all men are created equal."

The victory belonged to an administration that had been driven from office a dozen years before. It was the result of policies conceived when Washington was President, achieved in the term of John Adams. Then a navy had come into being, small, but bravely manned, technically superior. It was sufficient to teach the world how to manage Barbary Pirates. It was hardly imagined that it would challenge the huge armaments of England and France.

So when the Napoleonic wars turned hopeful change into world disaster, the response of the Jefferson administration was to depend on distance for defense and avoid trouble by an embargo on trade. The army was all but disbanded, the navy let rot. These policies were barely sufficient to deal with the Indians on the Western frontier. They were hopeless for the crisis of empires. And in 1812 the chickens came home to roost. The United States declared war on England and set out to conquer Canada. In a few weeks it had lost its army, and Detroit, Chicago and the Northwest Territory.

On sea things looked no better. A small American force, five ships, almost the entire navy, put out and promptly lost its chance to sink a lone British frigate by bad management and bad luck. The little fleet failed to close in before dark and an American gun blew up, crippling the attack. After that the ships went on a useless cruise of two months clear to the British

Isles, capturing no prizes and running great danger of being themselves captured.

That left the *Constitution* to cope with the British navy all by herself. She had been delayed in getting to sea by the need to ship a crew. The day she finally put out from Norfolk, Virginia, a British fleet sailed from Halifax, Nova Scotia. Isaac Hull, captain of the *Constitution*, looked to join his own compatriots, cruised north. Off the Jersey Capes, his lookout spied five sail. The number was right and he cheerfully sailed into the middle of a squadron of British seventy-fours, with support vessels. It was dark before he realized his mistake.

He put his ship about to escape. The wind was light and ahead. At dawn it fell flat calm. The whole British fleet was in sight, five and six miles astern. Then began a heroic chase. A stern chase is a long chase. This one lasted three days. And the British never doubted that they would win. When the Americans put out their boats to tow the *Constitution*, the British admiral summoned boats from his many vessels and with more oar power steadily gained on his quarry. But Isaac Hull knew a trick worth two of that. Bending on every rope in his ship he sent a kedge anchor nearly a mile ahead and dropped it in twenty-six fathom of water. The crew tallied onto the hawser and soon *Constitution* was warping through the silent seas with a small bone in her teeth.

For a while *Constitution* gained. But the British caught on and soon they too were kedging. Day and night the weary work continued. Twice British ships were close enough to try firing. But their shot fell short. And on the evening of the third day a heavy squall hit. With superb seamanship, risking spars and sails, Hull steered his ship through a night of wind and lightning to safety. Reaching Boston he lay in the outer harbor, taking on only essential supplies. The navy department had not sufficient money to provide them. A patriotic Boston citizen, William Gray, dug down into his own pocket to pay the bill.

Captain Hull and his crew and the ship they sailed were something new in the world. They expressed, in a single

Oldest known portrait of *Constitution*, attributed to Michel Felice Corne.

enterprise, the characteristics which, in the century that was to follow, would stamp every enterprise that the world would come to recognize as American. They could not wait on precedent. Captain Hull set sail again from Boston without orders. He had no positive orders not to sail. So he made his own decision.

His crew were equally independent. They accepted discipline as the necessity for survival on any vessel. But they were eager volunteers, fishermen trained in small family enterprises, seamen too long idled by Jefferson's Embargo, sharpshooters practiced on wild fowl and small game. Their officers were men risen from their own ranks. By contrast, the British navy, which outnumbered the American one hundred to one, depended on impressing its seamen by violence into its service and counted on political influence for the promotion of its officers.

The design of *Constitution* was a subtle refinement of existing models, her construction so strong and careful as to earn her the name of "Ironsides." Her rig was a bold evolution of all the experiments a race of seafarers from Quoddy Head to the Chesapeake had dared to try. She carried more sail, and could handle it faster, than any similar British frigate. The same was true of her guns. Her success was the success of an idea.

Laying a course to the eastward *Constitution* cruised for a week over empty seas. Then spoke a small trading vessel. Yes, the British frigate *Guerriere* was somewhere in the vicinity, spoiling for a fight. Her Captain Dacres had even entered a challenge on the trader's log daring any American ship of war to fight him. The British navy had absolute contempt for any power but its own. At the battle of the Nile it had frustrated the plans of Napoleon. At Trafalgar it had sunk his fleet. And for years it had been bullying and harrassing the merchantmen of all nations. It was said and believed among British captains that with a twenty-gun sloop it could beat an American frigate with forty.

The two ships sighted one another in the afternoon of the nineteenth of August. The British captain laid his main topsail aback and calmly waited. *Constitution* bore down before the wind, shortening sail, lashing the men's hammocks along the rail as an extra bulwark against small shot and boarders. The sharpshooters climbed into the rigging. Closing in the ships jockeyed for position for nearly two hours in a heavy sea, the wind coming hard from the northwest. At last, running before it side by side, the ships came close. The Britisher fired, his shot flying wild. Hull, on the quarter-deck, waited for the roll of the seas to level his ship. Suddenly he threw both arms up, squatted and shouted "Fire!" His tight breeches burst from stem to stern.

Now the terrific scene appears—from the faded ink of Midshipman Baury's close written page it springs to life—"At 5″ after 6 Pm hauled down the Jib and lay the Main Top Sail shivering and opened on him a heavy fire from all our Guns. At 15″ after 6 Pm the Enemy's Mizzen Mast fell over his Starboard Quarter on which our Crew gave three cheers." Then a fast account of the action, the maneuvering of the ships, an attempt to board "at which time Lieut. Charles Morris & Lieut. Wm S. Bush of the Marines fell off from the Taffenrail the former severely wounded & the latter killed. Filled away and shot clear of the Enemy when immediately (it being 30″ after 6) his Fore & Main Mast fell over on his Larbd Bow." Having no masts left to strike its flag the *Guerriere* "a complete wreck under a Sprit Sail, fired a gun in token of submission to Leeward. At ½ past 7 Pm hoisted out all the boats to take the prisoners out and bring them on board. At 8 Pm the boat returned which took on board Capn Dacurs formerly of His B M Ship Guerriere."

The British captain tendered his sword to Captain Hull, who promptly returned it to his severely wounded adversary. All that night was occupied taking the crew off the sinking British frigate, somehow crowding two hundred ninety-six more men aboard a vessel already filled with its complement of four hundred sailors and marines. The next day, it being impossible to save her, the *Guerriere* was set on fire. Ten minutes later she blew up and sank and with her sank the tradition, firm since the days of Queen Elizabeth, of Britain invincible on the seas.

Boston went wild with the news. No news that ever came to the city, not the news of any victory or relief from war, of

Gettysburg or Armistice, so stirred its heart. A child that day, a child of eight years, grandchild of John Adams, dying eighty years after, murmured as she died, "Thank God for Hull's victory."

Most anxiously the city had waited, feared, hoped, hardly expected. What if *Constitution* should tangle too closely with a couple of frigates? Boston, that had built the ship, whose pride it was, yet knew, as only salt water folk could know, the dangers, not of superior skill, but of more guns, more ships.

Then the tall sails had appeared off Boston light. The quiet Sabbath streets of the Puritan town had murmured like a hive of bees disturbed. A cutter had rowed in from sea bearing a smartly dressed lieutenant with dispatches to go overland to Washington. The news then was shouted from street to street.

Next day the ship itself came, its masts towering as high as the church spires—"At 9 Am stand into harbor. ¾ after shortened sail and came to off Long Wharf. Empd getting the prisoners of the Guerriere on shore. At 2 Pm unbent sails & sent them below."

The morning of the first of September 1812 was triumphant—"At 5 Am called all Hands to scrub hammocks and Bags. At 11 Am Capn Hull left the ship & on his arrival at the Wharf was saluted by a company of artillery which was answd by us . . ."

That salute still echoes.

Concord and Lexington and Bunker Hill had taught the world the dangers of trespassing on the ground of a free and independent people. That ground had now moved onto the face of the deep. For those with eyes to see, the future course of world history was suddenly revealed.

GHENT—A TREATY THAT ENDURED

*T*he treaty of Ghent, signed on Christmas Eve 1814, completed one of the most successful negotiations in American history. Yet it achieved no result but to end a war and leave unsettled all the questions the war had been fought about. It went even a little further. It opened to future question questions that had been presumed settled years before. Its triumph was to refer all disputes to time, the final negotiator, whose decision a vigorous and independent people could safely trust.

It proved that distrust, dislike and bad manners are no bar to a successful working arrangement. If there is common interest in getting on together and each party respects the power of the other to act for or against that interest, the apparently impossible can be accomplished. The sullen peace agreed to in the Netherlands between Britain and the United States has now lasted near two centuries and looks to last at least two centuries more.

Such an intelligent solution to human difficulties seemed unlikely, probably impossible, even as it was accomplished. The proclaimed reason for going to war in 1812 was to protect free trade and seamen's rights. This was mostly hokum. The only section that cared anything about seamen's rights was New England. And New England was perfectly willing to forget about those rights because it was making so much money as a neutral trading with both sides in the wars of Napoleon. The hawks in Congress were Westerners and Southerners who wanted to take over the remaining territory in North America still belonging to the Indians or the British.

It was the hawks' cheerful notion that Canadian resistance would crumble before an army of old men and boys. As for the

Signing the peace treaty at Ghent, Christmas Eve 1814. Copy of an oil sketch by Benjamin West, now in Old House Library, Quincy, Massachusetts.

British navy, ships cannot sail on land and the fleet of shallow draft gunboats built in Jefferson's administration—a much appreciated distribution of pork to politically important congressional districts—would protect the rivers and harbors. Unfortunately the gunboats sank, quite often even before the enemy got a chance to shoot at them. The ranks of the army could not be filled because men would not enlist. The credit of the government collapsed because the citizens would not subscribe to loans. The militia ran away. And after just two months of war the army that was supposed to conquer Canada had surrendered and the northern frontier was wide open to invasion.

Only the navy, or what was left of it after the neglect that followed the administrations of Washington and Adams, saved the United States. The frigate *Constitution* shattered the tradition of British sovereignty of the seas. Naval officers Perry on Lake Erie and MacDonough on Lake Champlain built fleets and fought them so successfully as to deter the British advance from Canada.

But when the peace commissioners began their talks, the situation could hardly have been worse. A British fleet was marauding in Chesapeake Bay. The government had been obliged to flee from Washington. Baltimore was being bombed—with the interesting effect of inspiring Francis Scott Key to write the national anthem against a background of "bombs bursting in air." The most powerful army ever to invade America was marching down the western shore of Lake Champlain.

British arrogance ran out of bounds. The *Times* wrote "Having disposed of all our enemies in Europe let us have no cant of moderation, no peace with James Madison. We shall demand indemnity. We shall insist on security for Canada. There is no public feeling in the country stronger than that of indignation against the Americans—conduct so base, so loathesome, so hateful. With Madison and his perjured set no treaty can be made, for no oath can bind them."

At the first meeting of the negotiators it was evident they had nothing to talk about. The British were forbidden by their instructions to discuss the impressment of seamen; the Americans were forbidden to discuss anything else, unless impressment was conceded in advance. The British made clear that they expected the cession of territory; at least half of Maine, Vermont and New Hampshire and so westward, with the sole right to maintain a navy on the Great Lakes!

The position of commissioner J.Q. Adams was peculiarly difficult, as representing New England, which was agitating secession from the United States. Fortunately he did not know that the Governor of Massachusetts was actually engaged in talks with the enemy. But commissioner Henry Clay made the assumption of treason and was quite ready to trade off new England for concessions in the West. Tension between the two men was personal as well as sectional, for puritan J.Q., as he lit his fire in the dark before dawn, was troubled to hear genial Harry staggering up to bed after a night of poker and whiskey.

But the poker had its uses. When even steady Albert Gallatin was ready to pack up and go home, the gambler assured his fellows that the British were only bluffing, "playing the game of brag." It turned out he was right. News came to the British Cabinet that its expedition down Lake Champlain had turned back because of MacDonough's extraordinary feat of sinking the British ships. And the Duke of Wellington, offered the command in America, turned it down, "That which appears to me to be wanting in America is not a general, but a naval superiority on the Lakes."

Suddenly all the pieces fell in place. The British dropped their extravagant demands. The Madison administration, eager to save anything from the wreck of its mismanaged war, was ready to settle for the status *ante bellum.* A treaty was written omitting everything that had caused the dispute. But it set up a method by which later commissions might discuss problems into an indefinite future. Adams wrote in his diary on Christmas Eve, "I cannot close the record of this day without an humble offering to God for the conclusion to which it has pleased him to bring the negotiations for peace at this place, and a fervent prayer that its results may be propitious to the welfare, the best interests, and the union of my country."

The prayer has been answered affirmatively. Acceptable relations with Britain survived even the shock of the Civil War. Gradually they became cooperation and alliance. A similar wisdom must guide the United States in negotiating with Russia to curb the suicidal nuclear arms race. The principle is the same—continued future discussion. The common interest exists. It is essential for the two superpowers to stop threatening each other. The real danger to world peace is of the proliferation of nuclear weapons among numerous unstable nations. Final settlement of all points that may come under dispute is never possible. They are best left to time, the final negotiator.

THE WAY TO PEACE

*T*hat man must be blind to the indications of the future who cannot see we are destined to have war after war with Great Britain," said Henry Clay, addressing the 14th Congress in January 1816. Henry Clay should have known, if anybody did, what to expect from destiny and Great Britain. He was one of the hawks who had brought on the disastrous war of 1812 and he had come from Ghent where he had helped put an end to the fighting; but not the hostility. The war was over; but not its causes nor its rhetoric.

The Treaty of Ghent settled nothing the war had been fought about. It left those subjects for time to resolve, with provision for future discussion and arbitration. Naval armaments on the Great Lakes were not mentioned. But they were serious enough to trouble cooler heads than that of young Henry Clay. President Madison had the strongest personal reasons for viewing with alarm naval encroachments. Very recently a naval task force had come up the Chesapeake, landed, eaten the dinner his cooks had prepared for him in the White House, and then after dinner burned the house down.

Now both nations had armed vessels on the Lakes. The possibility of a clash was ever present. Worse, each was building two seventy-four gun line-of-battle ships such as Nelson had commanded at Trafalgar. And the British engineers, eager to exploit the possibilities of a new element in warfare, the calmer surface of a fresh water lake, had on the stocks a real leviathan. It was something strange and terrible, a floating fortress, a ship mounting the unprecedented armament of one hundred ten guns!

Madison had a superior legal mind. He could assess a situation and imagine its possibilities. He could architect the Constitution. But he was weak at making it work, as the recent troubles had demonstrated. Now again, as at the Constitutional Convention, he had an opportunity to serve his country and posterity that suited his intellect. The prospect of a naval race on the Lakes struck him not only as dangerous, but silly. He instructed his Secretary of State to write to his Minister in London to feel out the British on the possibility of reciprocal disarmament on the Lakes. Lord Castlereagh, the most successful diplomat Britain ever bred, was Foreign Secretary. Fresh from triumph against Napoleon, he had the wisdom not to brandish his power but to make friends wherever he could. The American Minister was J.Q. Adams, recently a colleague of Henry Clay at Ghent.

Thus it happened that in the winter of 1816, even as Henry Clay was raising the bugaboo of war in the Congress of the United States, the American Minister, under instructions from his government, was preparing to lay the ghost in London. At precisely half past eleven o'clock one morning, tightly buttoned into a frock coat, he presented himself at the door of Lord Castlereagh's house in St. James's Square. After waiting barely five minutes in an anteroom, he was ushered into the private library of one of the most intelligent and, after the Duke of Wellington, the most powerful men in Europe. "His manner was cold, but not absolutely repulsive; his person handsome."

The etiquette of that time forbade the carrying of a briefcase, even reference to notes. A morning visit between gentlemen was elaborately casual, correctly informal. So the American had armed himself against forgetfulness with care. He had prepared a minute of ten subjects he wished to discuss. These he had arranged in such order that their first letters made a single word. By recollecting the word he would not lose track of his objectives however the conversation might ramble.

The talk, which would last two hours, began with banalities; the foulness of the weather and the progress of the Prince Regent's gout. Then it got down to business. Was His Majesty's government ready to discuss some of the disputes unresolved by the Treaty of Ghent? Castlereagh answered, "Yes. I remember, we thought it best to get along as far as we could at that time agree, and to postpone everything else. What are the subjects . . . " The first was the impressment of seamen. The answer was a polite and slightly evasive no. Several more subjects were discussed and then, somewhat casually introduced, the problems of Canada, Indians, border violations and perhaps mutual disarmament.

Castlereagh said, "Does your government mean to include in this proposition the destruction of the ships already existing there? As to keeping a number of armed vessels parading about the Lakes in time of peace, it would be absurd. The proposition you make is very fair and, I assure you, will meet with the sincerest reciprocal dispositions of this government."

That was it. In five minutes of seemingly casual conversation, the principle of total disarmament between the United States and Canada was settled. The details took a little longer. But within two years an agreement was signed in Washington, which still holds, limiting armaments to a few harmless Coast Guard cutters. It is an extraordinary instance of a great power being represented at a critical moment by a man of intellect and judgment equal to his responsibility. While the rest of the British Cabinet and the British people and press were still fighting the American Revolution, Castlereagh was weighing the balance of power in Europe and calculating means by which peace might be extended into the next century.

Castlereagh knew, out of his vast experience, that a treaty between nations spoiling for a fight wrestles as best it can with immediate problems. It does not attempt to settle the unsettlable. The essence of a good contract is its capacity to change. Such was the Treaty of Ghent. It stands to this day. The longest unfortified border in the world is its testament. Once that border was bristling with arms and the two opposing countries, animated the one by the thrust of empire, the other by the painful growth of democracy, could discover a quarrel in any conversation.

The interests of the two systems seemed totally opposed. What the one had the other wanted. Security for the populations of either seemed an impossibility. Britain controlled the sea. The United States was the stronger on land, but pathologically nervous and irritable because of fear of wandering tribes of Indians, trappers and prospectors in its territories too vast to control, even to measure.

Time eventually resolved these difficulties with the peaceable settlement of the empty lands. The countries found they could get on perfectly well together. There was room for both. Picking fights on every occasion had been a mere waste of time. The solution had been to remove the threat of sudden attack. Thus a temporary peace became permanent. The millennium does not arrive all at once in a single package.

HOW DISARMAMENT SAVED THE PEACE

*T*he Strategic Arms Limitation Treaty of 1816 between Great Britain and the United States scrapped their formidable navies on the Great Lakes. It prevented the building of any new armed ships capable of a serious strike. The only armaments allowed were a few one-gun revenue cutters.

There was nothing in the treaty to prevent the building of forts or military roads or the maintenance of standing armies. The British proceeded to spend a great deal of money to make strong defenses at Niagara and along the St. Lawrence and kept a garrison of five thousand redcoats on duty. The Americans were too busy exploiting the new land opened in the Northwest Territory to bother with military preparedness. They relied on a skeleton force of regular army troops barely sufficient, with the help of the squirrel rifles of the pioneers, to prevent Indian raids.

The treaty was strictly observed because it was to the advantage of both sides to do so. The Americans wanted to go about their business of getting rich as fast as possible. The British Colonial Office, which had learned very little from the American Revolution, was chiefly concerned with Canada as a place to send surplus population and how to keep it in order when it got there. All enjoyed, with a deep sense of relief, the fact that without warships on the Lakes a serious, sudden and secret first strike was impossible.

The calm lasted till 1837. Then the lid blew off in Canada. Nothing much had changed in Quebec since the days of Louis XIV. The same old regime was in charge, stirred and prodded and made uncomfortable by an occasional Scotsman or Irishman. With these, a liberal French gentleman of the old school,

Louis Papineau, rallying some of his own compatriots, started a revolution. But he was no George Washington. The revolution misfired, for it lacked both popular support and the backing of the clergy. The British garrison was put to work. The rebels, having no stomach either to be martyrs or fighters, as at Lexington and Concord, immediately dispersed in the general direction of the United States.

And then the trouble began. Refugees poured across the border. The populations on the American side were sympathetic. That perhaps is too mild a word. In spite of neutrality proclamations by President Van Buren and the governors of the several states, they were enthusiastic to help. The old illusion of the peaceful occupation of Canada by a friendly army of democratic republicans awoke in full force. There was very shortly a government in exile established on American soil with a secret army known as the Frères Chasseurs, or Hunters' Lodges.

These were presently joined by refugees from another abortive revolution in the Province of Ontario. There a hot Scotsman named Mackenzie, now best remembered as the grandfather of Canada's longtime premier Mackenzie King, had made his try. But his organization was worse than weak. His army, on the march to Toronto, was met by twenty-seven riflemen behind a rail fence. A single volley turned the rebels back and a few days later what remained of the embattled farmers was routed in a brief encounter with loyal militia.

President Van Buren, intent on preserving strict neutrality, sent a small force of Regulars to disarm the refugees. But his means were insufficient and the sympathies of the population entirely contrary. As fast as arms were confiscated, new arms were supplied. Mackenzie fled to Buffalo, recruited among unemployed bargemen and local toughs and the Hunters' Lodges and soon was established on Navy Island in the Niagara River. Then a dozen or more raids were directed into Canada.

To abate this nuisance, which the American government was too weak to control, the British in Canada decided on a drastic step. A commando force rowed across the Niagara River one night to the American shore, cut loose the little paddle wheel steamer *Caroline* which was being used to supply the rebels and sank it.

In the ruckus an American named Amos Durfee was killed. Then almost all hell broke loose. Fortunately there were no rival navies on the Lakes so hell was kept under wraps. Newspapers shouted for revenge. The *Rochester Democrat* wanted it "not by simpering diplomacy but by blood."

Van Buren sensibly preferred diplomacy. He got the whisper of an apology from the British government. He put Mackenzie in jail and managed to disarm his cohorts. And then he retired from office, having been defeated at the polls by old "Tippecanoe" Harrison.

All would have been well but for an outburst of human folly. The apologetic British government was thrown out and the pugnacious Lord Palmerston became Foreign Secretary. Cartoonists liked to draw him as an ugly small boy in short pants, with a straw in his mouth, waiting at a street corner to pick a fight. Queen Victoria wrote, "We had, God knows, terrible trouble with him about foreign affairs." He was the complete bully and he made bullying the cornerstone of British foreign policy. Events fell to his hand when a drunk Canadian in a New York barroom boasted of having fired the shot that killed Amos Durfee.

McLeod, the Canadian, was arrested and indicted for murder. Palmerston, claiming that the Niagara raid was a legal act of war, demanded extradition of the prisoner. Governor Seward of New York State, hearing the angry voices of his voters, refused. He claimed state's rights and threatened secession if the national government interfered. The execution of McLeod, Palmerston thundered, "would produce war, war immediate and frightful."

Luckily there was no British fleet on the Great Lakes to mobilize. So the British government had to content itself by sending out an order to alert the British Channel fleet, some three thousand miles away. Meanwhile Daniel Webster, now Secretary of State, went to work. Daniel was a very great lawyer, and a great man, though his methods, especially his private finances, were boldly devious. Helpless to release the person of McLeod, he went about thoughtfully to protect it. A change of venue was managed for the trial. And McLeod, now sobered up, remembered, with the help of an able lawyer provided by Webster, that he had an alibi. Some Canadians were brought over the border to attest to it. McLeod was acquitted, returned to a hero's welcome in Montreal and disappeared into the obscurity which was his natural environment.

Thus ended in farce the *Caroline* affair which involved at once a question of peace and war with Great Britain and of civil war and the existence of the Union. At Sarajevo in 1914, when every neighbor was armed to the teeth, such another affair ended in world tragedy.

THE FLOWER THAT MEANS SHARK

*T*he plant known to botanists as *Poinsettia pulcherrima*—Poinsettia most beautiful—evokes in the minds of North Americans the image of Christmas. Set on the windowsill against its background of snow in the darkest season of the year it is as much a part of the winter festival as sleigh bells, reindeer, the decorated tree, almost as Santa Claus himself.

The name Poinsett evokes in the minds of South Americans the image of *Carcharadon*—the great white shark. To diplomats of North America it ought forever to bring to mind a warning red light flashing at the Rio Grande.

Joel Roberts Poinsett, whose name is now most often found in dictionaries attached to the lovely plant he brought back from Mexico in 1828, was among the most favored of Americans born in any age. He came into the world just after the Revolution had established the first great democratic experiment. He was rich for his time as any Vanderbilt or Rockefeller. It was a matter of course for him to travel north from his native Charleston for education, thence to Europe and at last Asia. By the time he was thirty he had probably seen more of the world than any living American. He had studied law in the United States, medicine in Scotland, military management and tactics in England and Napoleon's France, and he had become a personal friend of the Tsar of Russia and for him had carried out an extensive mission of study and exploration across the Steppes. Commercial interests had taken him to South America and he spoke fluent Spanish and at least five other languages.

Some remarkable combination of genes, from his father French, his mother English, created in him a personality ardent, brilliant, curious and utterly charming that made him

145

shine even among such stars of the Old South as Henry Clay and John C. Calhoun. He lacked only one thing—judgment—either moral or practical. According to the peculiar lights of the Southern slaveholder he was an apostle of freedom, a torch sent directly from heaven to lighten the dark places of earth. It is unfortunate that torches drop sparks as well as shedding light and sparks start forest fires. The fires started by this particular torch are still burning.

Poinsett was the first Minister of the United States to the newly independent state of Mexico. Before that he was a special agent of the United States, with the title of Consul General, empowered to make commercial treaties among all the emerging nations of South America. He made some treaties, but their ratification was refused or long delayed. He became involved in the politics of each country through which he passed. His fault was a fascination with activity and a belief that a noble end should be pursued fairly as long as possible and after that by any convenient means. He is remembered in Chile for his part in its first failed revolution; in Mexico as the harbinger of war and the loss of Texas. He left both countries as *persona non grata*. He is the very perfect picture of an un-diplomat.

Yet all his troubles came on him, as so often since they have come on his countrymen, because he was a highly motivated, high-minded gentleman trying to do good in a hurry. Talleyrand, the consummate diplomat who put Europe together again after the Napoleonic wars, came up with the classic commentary on hurry, "Je n'ai jamais manqué une occasion d'aller au cabinet," a phrase too crudely rendered by the flat-footed Anglo-Saxon "I never miss a chance to slip out to the lavatory."

Consider Poinsett's behavior in Chile, a preview of Chile's tragedy in the Nixon era. His instructions were "to diffuse the impression that the United States cherish the sincerest good will towards the people of Spanish America as neighbors and whatever may be their internal system no interference of any sort is pretended." But the despotic rule of Spain was not to the taste of the young republican and a change might work to the commerical advantage of the United States. So he set about to encourage change. He became involved in the internal feuds of the dominant Carrera family and its feuds with other power families and with Spain. He became the unofficial quartermaster general of a rebel army and later chief of intelligence and strategy. As "advisor" he took part in a shooting war that ended in a pitched battle. His side lost, the opposing factions made a deal with Spain, and in the ultimate tragedy his friend Miguel Carrera, first President of Chile, was betrayed by his own men and shot.

Poinsett's "advice" may or may not have been good. The fact is that conditions in Chile were so rickety that no "advice" could make much difference. As a nation it had to find itself in its own bloody way. And Poinsett had to scramble out of South America as best he could, for the War of 1812 was in full swing and the British had command of the seas. He climbed over the Andes, secretly left Brazil in disguise and finally got home by way of the Madeira Islands. His own well-colored account and slow news from South America made him something of a hero; a bold Jack the Giant Killer. South Carolina sent him to Washington as congressman.

Ten years later he was chosen for the mission to Mexico, newly a republic. Mexicans were suspicious of their neighbors north of the Rio Grande. General Guadaloupe Victoria, presently by a coup d'etat to become President, had in a public speech described the citizens of the United States as "an ambitious people always ready to encroach and without a spark of good faith." Poinsett immediately proceeded to make good the allegation.

In no time at all he was embroiled in Mexican politics. And he appeared to be successful. He organized secret societies and achieved a cabinet reorganization favorable to American interests. In the process he got himself hated by everybody. But the Mexican method of election then in vogue, by bullets, proved too much for him. His life was endangered, though he showed much personal bravery, defying an armed mob. His friends won the election. But popular feeling was running too high against the meddling representative of Big Brother to the north. He was obliged to leave the country at the urgent request of the government he had helped hoist to power.

He lived to be Secretary of War in Van Buren's cabinet, performing efficiently. It fell to his lot to remove the Indian tribes to west of the Mississippi. A contemporary stepped into a church in Washington and observed this scene:

"Mr. Poinsett was investing the chiefs one after another with a large silver medal, which he hung over the shoulders of each of them, suspended by a blue silk ribbon. He expressed his pleasure at the conclusion of the treaties with them; and he promised that the engagements stipulated with them should all be faithfully performed. Two interpreters explained what he had said."

Indian treaties explained by interpreters are notoriously leaky documents. They sank long ago and efforts to make them float since have not been very successful or very creditable to the honor of the United States. But the bad start Poinsett gave inter-American diplomacy has continued too long. Gestures of friendly good will have too often turned out to be interference and betrayal. The Poinsettia is too lovely a plant to bear such a stigma to the end of time.

THE FIGHT FOR THE FIRST AMENDMENT

*J*efferson's smug remark about the blood of tyrants being the natural manure of the tree of liberty is not often quoted even by his ardent admirers. The world has had too much bitter experience since he made it. Poor fat Louis XVI was no tyrant. He inherited a tyrannical system which had run out of grease. Napoleon oiled it up, slipped in a few new parts and made it work beautifully, so beautifully that the French tyranny nearly took over the world. The world in the 20th century is trying uneasily to cope with the ancient tsarist system of coercion brought up to date by the application of modern technology to thought control.

The mere removal of the head of a tyranny does not kill the beast. Rather it is an encouragement for other heads to grow. Jefferson was closer to the mark when he suggested that, if ever a choice must be made between a free press and the forms of democracy, it is better to choose a free press.

The only force that can cope with the problem of some human beings claiming property rights in other human beings is freedom of speech. If those exploited have the right to speak, they will eventually find a voice. That is why the First Amendment to the Constitution is the most important and the hardest to maintain.

That is why the American Civil War, tragic and unnecessary as in retrospect it may seem, became inevitable when the United States ran out of great men capable of making and keeping political compromises. It is useless to say that the cost of buying all the slaves and freeing them would have been a lot cheaper than the cost of the war. Of course it would have been, by a factor of one to ten or maybe one to a hundred or even ten thousand. But the Civil War was not fought to free the slaves.

It was fought to preserve the Union, for only by preserving the Union could the First Amendment be saved. Self-government requires that all the people may be heard. Legal slavery required that they should not. It was therefore a battle to the death. It was a battle that was bound to be fought because slavery is only one of many subjects on which major power groups would gladly shut off debate. The free press is always in danger. The murder in 1978 of Pedro Chamorro, the very brave editor of the nearest thing to a free newspaper in Nicaragua, set off a necessary revolution. The Nazi mobsters murdered the free press and Hitler took over Germany. Free speech and arbitrary rule cannot live together.

It was the hope of the great men of the American Revolution that slavery would die a natural death by starvation. Instead Eli Whitney's invention made cotton a king. The prosperity of the South depended on cotton and the only known method of growing and picking cotton profitably was by the use of slaves. So cotton growing in the deep South and slave breeding in the border states became the economic foundation of Southern life.

To protect this foundation the ruling group that controlled the wealth and the politics of the South was ready to go to any lengths. In Congress in 1836 it imposed a gag that forbade the presentation of any petition on the subject of slavery. The first step was thus taken towards dictatorship. Furiously J.Q. Adams fought this fatal first step. His bitter rhetoric and extreme skill as a parliamentarian reduced his adversaries to rage, even speechlessness, the braggart bully's last stage of frustration. But for nearly a decade the gag held.

At the same time a crisis was beginning to crackle like a prairie fire through the Western states. The idea of freedom was carried out of New England by many young people seeking a larger life. From a very small farm in Albion, Maine, came to St. Louis one Elijah Lovejoy to learn the newspaper trade. Heeding a call to the ministry, he trained at the Princeton Theological School. Then he returned to St. Louis as the editor of a religious paper *The Observer*. He brought with him some strong convictions. At the farmhouse in Maine Garrison's

Liberator had been regular reading. Lovejoy's mother would clench her left fist, shake it, and holding the *Liberator* in her right, would exclaim aloud, "Right, Mr. Garrison! Right!"

Quickly there was trouble. In a frightful incident of mob brutality in St. Louis a free black man, who had attempted to escape from arrest after a street fight, was chained to a tree and burned alive. Lovejoy had the nerve to protest and concluded with the prophetic words, "We must stand by the Constitution and the laws or all is gone." Hoodlums began to throw stones through the office windows. A grand jury was called to investigate the lynching. The judge, appropriately named Lawless, in his charge condoned the crime. Again Lovejoy protested. That night about twenty roughs broke into the *Observer* shop, smashed press and type.

Lovejoy decided to move from slave Missouri across the river to Alton in the free state of Illinois. But it happened that the repaired press and new type were landed on the dock late on a Saturday. Lovejoy, a conservative churchman, refused to desecrate the Sabbath by either guarding or removing his property to a safe place. While he was in church it was thrown into the river. A public appeal brought funds for a new press. This too went into the river after a mass meeting declared that Lovejoy's attacks on slavery were ruining the commerce of Alton. Then came a personal attack by a crowd intent on tarring and feathering him. With great courage he faced it, spoke so firmly that its leader said, "Boys, I cannot lay my hands on so brave and defenseless a man as this."

But much worse was to come. While visiting his wife's mother in Missouri, a drunken mob broke into the house and the Lovejoys escaped barely with their lives to the doubtful refuge of Alton on the other side of the river. Celia Ann, with her infant son, lived in terror, became sick with terror. One night, while her husband was out to get her some medicine, a mob broke into the house. He returned just in time, drove the ruffians out. Then it was that he made up his mind that he must abandon non-resistance and take up arms in her defense. He sent to Maine for help. It came and soon he was able to write, "a loaded musket is standing by my bedside while my two brothers in an adjoining room have three others, together with pistols, cartridges, etc. And this is the way we live in Alton!"

The materials for another press arrived and were stored in a warehouse. Lovejoy appealed to the civil authorities for help. He was informed by Mayor Krum, like Judge Lawless appropriately named, that he could expect no protection. At a mass meeting, supposedly of his supporters but packed by a slavery mob, resolutions were passed urging him "as a Christian, even as St. Paul had fled from Damascus" he should leave town and take his press with him for his own good and the town's good.

Lovejoy faced the hostile gathering, rose to speak. With an extraordinary eloquence he silenced the shuffling feet, the coughing, the sound of spitting and the sneers. "I do not admit that it is the business of this assembly whether I shall or shall not publish a newspaper in this city. I have the right to do it. This right is solemnly guaranteed to me by the Constitution of the United States." His powerful presence and great voice dominated the crowd. He described the sufferings of his wife and child. His soon-to-be murderers were moved to tears. And he ended greatly, "It is because I fear God that I am not afraid of all who oppose me in this city. The contest has been commenced here and it must be finished here. Before God, and you all, I here pledge myself to continue it, if need be, till death. If I fall, my grave shall be made in Alton."

Four days later, November 7, 1837, Lovejoy was killed as he tried to prevent the burning of the warehouse that held his press and type. He was cowardly shot by an unknown assailant from behind a pile of lumber. "The first American martyr to the Freedom of the press, and the slave," wrote J.Q. Adams. "It sent a shock as of an earthquake throughout this continent." Civil war became a nightmare possibility. Suddenly the issue was made clear; minority rule through force and violence, or democracy under law, protected by a free press.

FATE FRUSTRATES COMPROMISE

*W*isdom lurks in the mind of all the people. The problem is to find it. The easy way is to choose a peerless leader and turn him loose to do his stuff. The hard way is to choose representatives and cheer them on to fight furiously for truth and enlightenment, for partisan opinion and advantage, till some sort of passable path is discovered.

But leaders without peer do not exist and nations that insist on having them end up with Hitlers and Stalins. The representatives bungle and hunt and end up with compromises. So the people, whose grain of wisdom insists that every problem has a solution, and want a quick one, cannot help turning with eager longing to the leader for the time being, the President. And the people are apt to be sorry later.

The greatest compromise of all, the one that made the most gigantic effort to solve the unsolvable, was the Missouri Compromise of 1820. It worked for a whole generation and that is good going for a major unsolution. It might have worked indefinitely but for the machinations of a President neither wise nor scrupulous nor prudent who came in by the back door.

If it had been allowed to work out its natural course, the problem which it sought to postpone might have simmered for yet another generation till it cooled with its own breath. Instead America had the Civil War.

Thomas Jefferson was still alive when the crisis of 1820 came and passed. He wrote, "This momentous question, like a fire bell in the night, awakened and filled me with terror." And J.Q. Adams wrote in his diary, "I take it for granted the present question is a mere preamble—a title page to a great tragic history."

The territory of Missouri had asked for admission as a slave state. And then an amendment had been proposed which would have made children born of slave parents free in twenty-five years and prohibited the importation of more slaves. It was an ingenious idea, one of many current at the time, for the gradual elimination of the curse. But the slave power would have none of it. Terrific oratory erupted in both houses of Congress and eventually, by the defection of a scattering of Northern members, "doughfaces" according to bitter John Randolph, the amendment was defeated and a compromise reached. It was agreed to let Missouri enter the Union with its slaves, but henceforth all future states carved out of territory north of the 36th parallel would be free. The next year, by tacit agreement, Maine came in as a free state.

The immediate advantage appeared to lie with the slave power. But soon began the great emigration from Europe into the Northern states and territories. Free men would not go into the South, there to compete with forced labor. The manufacturing North waxed busy and prosperous; the agricultural South fat on the profits of cotton growing, with all the wealth in the hands of the planter class. And as the population of the Northern states grew and the free settlers moved vigorously into the Northwest Territory, the slavocracy began to consider that it might have drawn the short end of the Missouri Compromise.

The first great guns were fired over the tariff question. According to Southern theory, of every hundred bales of cotton grown, forty went North as tribute to bankers and manufacturers. Unless this unfair discrimination between the sections was redressed by tariff adjustments, the Southern states should secede. It was then that Daniel Webster rose in the Senate for Massachusetts and spoke for the nation on the 26th of January 1830 in his famous reply to Hayne of South Carolina, the greatest burst of eloquence ever heard in the Senate of the United States, "Liberty and Union, now and forever, one and inseparable."

It was sometimes said by envious contemporaries that nobody could be as great as the godlike Daniel appeared. No doubt this was true. Unceasing overwork turned him too often to the bottle and he was careless about debts. But the logic and reasoning of this speech, after more than a century, is still magnificent, untarnished by the rhetoric. It impressed the President, Andrew Jackson, a state's rights man and slaveholder, but first of all a patriot. So when the Satan of the South, John C. Calhoun, brought the question of disunion to a showdown, Jackson made it quite clear that he was ready to try him for high treason and hang him if necessary. A compromise was worked out and the specter of secession was laid for a few more years.

Then came a sudden and violent agitation in the 1840's over the annexation of Texas. The Republic of Mexico freed all slaves and declared all its land free land. But in the Mexican province of Texas, settled almost entirely by immigrants from the southern United States, nearly every fifth human being was a black chattel. When the Mexican government tried to enforce its emancipation laws, the Texans revolted and set up their own republic.

It was an uncomfortable situation. Americans were streaming across the border from Louisiana and enlisting in the Texas army in obvious violation of the neutrality of the United States. There was a state of war between the new Republic of Texas and its mother country to the southward. Sam Houston sent envoys to Washington to discuss possible annexation, with its conveniences of military protection and assumption of the Texas national debt.

The idea was popular in the South. The prospect of acquiring a huge new territory for slavery fairly made the mouth of Calhoun water. But there was powerful agitation against annexation in the North. And Union sentiment was still strong among the cooler heads in the South. So when a bill was introduced into the House for annexation, there was furious debate. John Quincy Adams from Massachusetts made a speech that lasted three weeks. The session ended and the bill died.

The Awful Question was still where the Continental Congress had put it, where the Missouri Compromise had left it, in the hands of the states. There it simmered and sizzled, spitting and steaming like a covered pot on the edge of a hot stove.

Then the whole country took part in the great debate as it went about its quadrennial business of electing a President in 1840. The Democrats nominated the incumbent, Martin Van Buren, opposed to slavery and the annexation. The Whigs nominated for President old Indian fighter William Henry Harrison of Ohio, a free soil man content to let slavery alone where it existed, but against its extension. To run on the same ticket they nominated John Tyler of Virginia for Vice President. Tyler was an owner of slaves and a breeder of slaves that he sometimes sold "down the river" to the deep South and the brutality of the cotton plantations. No slaveholder was more convinced than he of the necessity and beneficence of the "peculiar institution." Its extension into Texas and beyond seemed to him a very desirable objective.

To achieve their compromise the Whigs passed over the eminent and qualified Henry Clay, famous, like Webster, for his efforts to hold the Union together. They preferred the pastiche of a President from one side of the fence and a Vice President from the other. Then to glue it together they ran a political campaign still remembered for its inanity and its slogans of log cabin, hard cider and "Tippecanoe and Tyler, too." Van Buren could not rid himself of the incubus of economic depression that had shadowed the first years of his term. Neither could his propagandists counter the Whig barrage. Their campaign song about their Vice Presidential nominee, "Rumpsey dumpsey, rumpsey dumpsey, General Johnson killed Tecumseh," simply did not catch on. Tip and Ty won by 234 to 60 in the electoral college; but by the barest majority of the popular vote.

On the 4th of March 1841 "the inauguration of President Harrison was celebrated with demonstrations of popular feeling unexampled since that of Washington in 1789," noted J.Q. Adams in his diary. Just one month later he wrote, on the morning of the death of Harrison, "The influence of this event upon the condition and history of the country can scarcely be foreseen. It makes John Tyler of Virginia Acting President. Tyler is a political sectarian, of the slave driving, Virginian,

Jeffersonian school, principled against all improvement, with all the interests and passions and vices of slavery rooted in his moral and political constitution. This brings to the test that provision of the Constitution which places in the Executive chair a man never thought of for it by anybody. This day was in every sense gloomy—rain the whole day."

How gloomy the day, time would show.

THE DANGEROUS OFFICE

*W*hen the Republic was founded one rotten stone was built into the foundation. The Constitutional Convention created the office of Vice President in a rare moment of absence of mind. The need for an immediate successor to the President was obvious. What a special standby should do if not needed was an enigma. It still is. No duty could be invented that would not impinge on the prerogatives of the President. So it was resolved that this unfortunate individual should be a political eunuch and preside over the Senate.

The first victim, John Adams, described it as the most superfluous office ever invented by the mind of man. Mr. Dooley remarked a hundred years later that it was not exactly a crime to be elected Vice President. At best the office wastes the service and sours the character of a good man. At worst it may elevate a criminal or a boob to the Presidency, whose shortcomings probably would have been detected had he been exposed individually to the full primary and electoral process. In no case does it represent the considered opinion of the electorate. The choice of a President is tough enough. The choice of a President, second class, at the same time is beyond the strength of any convention or the imagination of any electorate. So the President nominate makes his decision and the delegates, exhausted and bored, go along.

The plan for the election of Vice President was so badly conceived that it had to be scrapped and redrawn within twenty years. The Founding Fathers could and did make mistakes. The most recent repair job was committed in 1965 and incorporated in the Constitution as the 25th Amendment. By its machinery, Gerald Ford became Vice President by appointment of Richard Nixon. Vice President Agnew had been forced from office when he pleaded no contest to a charge of filing a false and fraudulent income tax return. Nixon later resigned rather than face impeachment charges of lying, obstructing justice and breaching the constitutional rights of citizens. Ford then appointed Nelson Rockefeller Vice President. He also made a travesty of democracy and justice by pardoning Nixon for all federal crimes he "committed or may have committed or taken part in" while President.

Thus for the first time in American history the people had no part whatsoever in the election of their President and Vice President. Power passed directly from individual to individual, by what private agreements will probably never be known, but certainly will be long suspected. Secret goings on in the palace abruptly gave the nation a new chief. The danger of such arrangements is obvious. The transition of power from Hindenberg to Hitler is a recent memory. No event, in an age frequently shattered by appalling events, so shook the faith of Americans in their system of politics and justice as the trickery by which Richard Nixon escaped prosecution, and the full record of his crimes was hidden.

The office of Vice President had become superfluous by the middle of the 20th century. As the century approached its end it had become a positive danger. It ought to be eliminated. It was invented to cover a contingency which no longer exists. In 1787 it required the better part of a year to elect a President and get him to the capital. Now jet travel has compressed into three hours what once was a year's journey. In case of need a new President could be nominated and elected by the people within six weeks. In the interim Congress could take over, with a caretaker government headed by the Speaker of the House, to be confirmed within twenty-four hours in temporary office, or replaced by another member of Congress by majority vote. Congress represents the people. In an emergency it can act for the people. The palace guard cannot.

The extreme peril that lies in the Vice Presidential system of succession was made plain the first time it operated. The warning has been repeated since. The trouble originates in the politi-

cal advantage of a "balanced ticket." A law of opposite oper-
ates. The ticket of free soiler Harrison with slaveholder Tyler
turned out to be a first class ticket to disaster. Harrison, sixty-
seven years old, lasted just one month as President. His Cabinet,
excepting only Daniel Webster, resigned. Tyler began to fill
their places with Southern men. Webster left in 1842. To take
his place as Secretary of State Tyler appointed Abel Upshur of
Virginia and set him to work secretly to negotiate a treaty for
the annexation of Texas. The effect of this would be to extend
slavery into a vast new territory and bring on war with Mexico.

But Upshur was not fated to complete the deal. A huge new
naval gun called "Peacemaker" was to be demonstrated. A gay
Presidential party set off down the Potomac. On board were
Tyler, other politicians and their wives. Tyler had no wife. But
before the voyage ended he was tragically provided with one.
"Peacemaker" blew up. The lovely Julia Gardner was thrown
into the arms of the President. Her father, a state senator, was
killed, and so was Upshur. Tyler seized his opportunities. He
married Julia and on a plea of emergency persuaded the reluctant John C. Calhoun to take over as Secretary of State. Calhoun was the towering personality, the great brain of the
Southern Confederacy.

Calhoun hurried to a conclusion the negotiation with Texas,
and in the spring of 1844 presented it to the Senate for ratification. Thanks to a tremendous speech by Thomas Hart Benton,
it was defeated by a vote of 35 to 26. But the reprieve was brief.
The conspirators had another card up their sleeve. Pretending
that the election of James Polk in November, although by a
narrow margin, was a national mandate for annexation, Tyler
presented a joint resolution to Congress. The maneuver was
probably unconstitutional. But the lame duck session passed it
and the accomplished fact was irreversible. Just three days before his own retirement from office, Tyler signed it into law.
The nation was on its way to Mexican war, extension of slavery, then civil war.

J.Q. Adams wrote in his diary, "The day passes, and leaves
scarcely a distinct trace upon the memory of anything, and

precisely because, among numberless other objects of comparative insignificance, the heaviest calamity that ever befell myself and my country was this day consummated."

He was right. The rotten stone in the foundation had slipped. A crack was opening across the face of the whole edifice of the Republic. The accidental Executive had outwitted the Founding Fathers. A secessionist minority, by the workings of mortal chance and the Vice Presidential machinery, had seized control of federal power. They used it to wreck the house.

A STRONG RED LINE ON A MAP

*T*he experience of the disastrous War of 1812 taught the generation that fought it wisdom. The peace treaty developed a method of continued discussion that allowed solutions to develop as circumstances might permit. It provided latitude for the bluster of politicians and bought time for the world to consider the consequences of rash acts. Its success has shown that the method can prosper even though administered by human beings whose motives may range from honor and decency to evil and folly.

First came the epochal agreement to scrap the fresh water navies of Britain and the United States. Suddenly a ribbon of peace was run the length of the Great Lakes. Further to east and west it stretched precariously. And at either end, in Maine and Oregon, it was lost in uncharted wilderness and the swamps of diplomacy. These swamps were made dismal by angry clashes between pioneers armed with bare fists, axes and shotguns loaded for bear. During the dangerous Canadian uprisings of the 1830's some voyageurs took possession of a valuable acreage of tall pines. The sound of chopping aroused the neighbors. A state senator from Maine walked over to investigate. He was captured. His friends returned home with the news and bloody noses. The governor called out the militia and effected a rescue.

The " 'Roostook war" was headlined across the United States. The House of Commons was awakened from its accustomed sleep by the roaring of England's bull in a china shop, Lord Palmerston. General Scott, dispatched by the "red fox of Kinderhook," President Van Buren, arranged a truce. A lucky turn of English politics put Palmerston out of the foreign office. The seething pot was pushed to the back burner just in time.

There Daniel Webster found it, still bubbling and hissing, when he took over as Secretary of State in the Harrison-Tyler administration.

Daniel was a genuine genius with a few troublesome failings. He was compulsively ambitious, and this ambition was driven by an energy which required the dual stimulants of strong drink and public acclaim to sustain it. Over all ruled a grand and expansive nature which had to express itself in hospitality and expense that would have taxed the revenues of Louis XIV and far exceeded the fees even of the most brilliant lawyer in the United States.

Among those fees was the retainer from the great English banking firm of Baring Brothers, and others from rich men in Boston. Such conflict of interest caused some shaking of heads, but Webster went on his way grandly and his state elected him senator whenever he was not serving in some President's Cabinet. He was a broad-minded statesman who could see no motive for aggravating the ancient grudge between England and the United States. He wanted to be President and a diplomatic triumph would do no harm. And he needed money.

So when Alexander Baring, Lord Ashburton, was appointed by the new British government in 1842 a special commissioner to settle the Northeast Boundary dispute, Webster jumped at the chance. The nagging cause of the argument was the vague definition of boundaries in the treaty that had settled the Revolution. A key point was "the highlands between the St. Lawrence and the Atlantic Ocean," but no map showed their location. Since they did not exist this would have been difficult. But the record of the negotiations referred to a lost map with a strong red line drawn on it by Benjamin Franklin.

For half a century efforts had been made to survey that line. The arguments about it filled not just a shelf of books but the wing of a library. Eventually the King of the Netherlands, called on as arbiter, declared the task impossible and drew a new line splitting the difference between the rival claims. The United States, needled by the disgruntled State of Maine, rejected this compromise, growling that the King of the Netherlands was cousin to the king of England and even an honorary general in his army! There the dispute uneasily rested when Lord Ashburton stepped off a British warship at Annapolis with a bag of British gold in his trunk.

Just exactly what happened thereafter nobody knows. Webster produced an old map with a strong red line on it that purported to be Franklin's duplicate of a map handed to the Count of Vergennes. Jared Sparks, the historian and friend of Webster, remembered having seen a similar map in the French archives. This map and the line on it firmly supported the British claim. With the map, and Lord Ashburton's bag of gold for "expenses," Sparks went to Maine to persuade the clamoring politicians to calm down. They did, rather abruptly. A compromise agreement was reached, the President signed it, the Senate ratified and Webster retired from office in a cloud of glory.

The treaty cost the United States some three million acres of Maine land. Few people have seriously regretted the loss. It settled a nasty situation that could have been blown into war by a puff from Lord Palmerston or Tyler's successor, James Polk. But Her Majesty's Loyal Opposition claimed the Crown had been cheated and forced a debate. Then an astonishing fact came out. In British archives, known to the British Cabinet all along, was the actual map used by George III when he agreed to the peace of 1783. On it was a strong red line that proved the claim of the United States to the whole disputed territory! It was further brought out that the French map, which Sparks had found "while mousing around in the papers of the old Juggler Vergennes," as J.Q. Adams noted in his diary, had never been seen by Franklin. And now modern research has revealed that Sparks, while blowing up his imposture for the benefit of the Maine legislators, was aware of the existence of George III's map! These latter discoveries have not restored the acres to the United States; neither have they caused a war.

Thus by an act of skulduggery the ribbon of peace was extended from the Great Lakes to the Atlantic. Necessity provided the incentive to extend it to the Pacific. The saturnine

Polk, agent of slavery and Satan, having bitten off all he could chew by provoking war with Mexico, was in no position to take on Britain, too. So in 1846 he was glad to settle the long-vexed Oregon question by agreeing to extend the border to the Pacific on the 49th Parallel. Stiff talk about a "clear and unquestionable" title to the whole Oregon Territory up to "54′40″ or fight" was quietly dropped.

The ribbon of peace now stretched from the Atlantic to the Pacific. Without tanks, submarines, machine guns or atomic weapons confronting across it, now it is perhaps the strongest barrier in the world. It is protected by a century of developed self-interest, which has taught both parties the advantage of reasonable tolerance of the government of the other.

A THIRD PARTY AND THE CIVIL WAR

*E*xcept only Independence, the most important question ever debated in the United States was Union. Sixteen years before the actual outbreak of civil war the decision was made in free and open election to resolve the question by violence. The decision turned on the vote of an almost invisible fraction of the electorate that chose to throw away its ballots on the candidate of a third party. The result was the election of a man pledged to do everything the third party most abhorred. He immediately proceeded to do it. The country was split, as it turned out, irrevocably. No statesmanship, no eloquence, not even Webster's, could deflect an evil fate. It is the fate that originates in the human mind, that rejects moderation and demands an immediate answer to questions that have no answer, but that time may resolve if the patience of mankind can be persuaded to wait a long season.

In May of 1844 the Democratic Convention met at Baltimore. A majority wanted Martin Van Buren, experienced, moderate in his views, an ex-President. But the extreme pro-slavery wing of the party, led by delegates from the deep South, put over the two-thirds rule. Congressman James Polk, little known except to professional politicians, a dark horse from the ample stable of the aging and irascible Andrew Jackson, won the nomination. He immediately came out for the annexation of Texas, cost what it might—war with Mexico, the extension of slavery, even civil war.

The Whigs, a conservative-based coalition party, were in the mire. Their team of one old spavined thoroughbred matched with a bucking bronco had come to grief. Harrison was dead and Tyler had run clean off the reservation. Their wagon was stuck in the mud of slavery and the Texas question. There was nothing for them to do but to do what they ought to have done four years before—hitch it to a star.

Henry Clay was a man of transcendent abilities. He had been Senator, Congressman, Secretary of State, Speaker of the House, Peace Negotiator abroad. He was known across the whole nation as a chief architect of the Missouri Compromise that had saved the Union in 1820. He also had been, and to some extent still was, a gambler—especially good at poker playing—a duelist and fond of good whiskey—though he preferred good wine—and a Southern grandee who loved to raise and race horses. Like Washington and Jefferson, he was a slaveholder who deplored the institution of slavery but could think of no way of getting rid of it. Instead he devoted his great abilities to the effort to contain it, limit it and trust to time and the prosperity of free institutions to eliminate it. Along the road he acquired a great host of admirers and friends—and for every friend a detractor and enemy.

It was Clay who said, "I'd rather be right than be President." He had his wish. Among the enemies he made would be one quite unexpected, whose path at first ran parallel to Clay's. His name was James Birney. He was younger than Clay, but like him belonged to the planter class, was a Kentuckian and owned slaves. The men were on friendly terms and worked together for a while on an impractical scheme to return freed slaves to Africa, the American Colonization Society. It got nowhere. Birney, religiously moved, freed his slaves and left the South, settling in the free state of Ohio. There he joined the Abolition cause, but in opposition to the Garrison wing that advocated separation of the North from the United States and believed the Constitution a compact with the devil. Birney wanted to move politically, within the framework of the Constitution, and free the slaves at once. Like many converts he was intransigent in his opinions.

He joined the Liberty Party and became its nominee for President in 1840. The party polled about 7000 votes and was vigorously opposed by abolitionists who considered its platform too reasonable. Another peculiarity of the campaign was that

Birney, from May through November of the election year, was on a lecture tour in England. Naturally enough, his fellow citizens in America were barely aware of his existence, being better amused drinking hard cider and watching Harrison-Tyler torchlight processions.

But the Liberty Party and its nominee, which had been a joke in 1840, became a deadly serious matter four years later. At stake was the annexation of Texas and the whole future of the slave power in the United States. It was the culmination of the proposition clearly stated by a resolution of the Alabama legislature, "It needs but a glance at the map to satisfy the superficial observer that an overbalance is produced by the extreme northeast, which as regards territory would be happily counterbalanced by the annexation of Texas." Whatever arguments might be used to persuade voters of the advantages of acquiring Texas—its potential wealth, sympathy for the fellow citizens settled there in danger from Mexican retaliation—the real reason was plain, the extension of slavery.

Yet as the campaign progressed the abolition groups concentrated their attacks, not on Polk and the Democrats but on Clay. Birney and his partisans maligned Clay as a gambler, a profane swearer and a slaveholder. By implication, the strict sabbatarian Polk, who refrained from swearing, though also a slaveholder, was by comparison saintly. The abolitionists thus persuaded themselves that two courses only were open to men of conscience, either to stay away from the polls altogether or to vote for Birney. Either course would assist the election of Polk, almost certainly bring on war with Mexico and suddenly and perilously extend the slave power.

The litmus test of abolition was applied in strange places. The Liberty Party in Massachusetts put up a candidate for Congress against the most famous champion of civil rights in the nation, J.Q. Adams, because he refused to come out for instant emancipation. The single issue fever was virulent and on its way to being fatal. Whether the election of Clay would have staved off a showdown long enough to prevent the Civil War nobody can ever know. But it is certainly a strong probability that the man who negotiated the Compromise of 1820 and invented the Compromise of 1850, which Franklin Pierce managed afterwards to wreck, would have found a way to avoid war with Mexico. Had there been no war with Mexico, no sudden extension of slavery by violent means, there would have been no Civil War—at least not in 1860.

It was not to be. Clay lost New York by 5080 votes. The vote for Birney in New York was 15,812. Less than half the votes cast for Birney, not to mention the votes that were not cast at all, would have comfortably carried the state for Clay and made him President. The psychology of crisis is not easily explained. It is like the monkey in the fable with his fist in the narrownecked jar. He would not take it out half empty. He could not take it out full. Some people prefer sudden death to making a choice between relative imperfections.

POLK'S WAR BREEDS CIVIL WAR

*G*reat tragedies are moved on small wheels. Rosencrantz and Guildenstern are a common species of intelligent and unimaginative mediocrity and might just as well be called Guildencrantz and Rosenstern. But they did their part to do in the noble Hamlet. Such a mediocrity was hard working, narrow, humorless, conventionally religious James Knox Polk who beat the radiant Henry Clay in the Presidential election of 1844 by a margin thin as an onionskin.

At stake were foreign war, civil war; the lives of a generation of boys then living or about to be born; millions of acres. James Polk's hand was eager to grasp the acres. His mind could not grasp that that same hand was sowing dragon's teeth. His imagination extended not beyond real property. So with unseemly haste, on taking over the Presidency, he consummated the shotgun marriage of Texas to the United States, performed in the last minutes of the Tyler administration, by sending in federal troops in preparation for a planned invasion of Mexico.

It was manifest destiny, so the cry went up, for the United States to extend its borders from the Atlantic to the Pacific, from the Tropic to the Arctic. To Polk it probably mattered little that Texas, which had been free under Mexico had been annexed as a slave state. Although himself the owner of slaves, he was not dogmatic on the subject of the extension of slavery into new territories. What he wanted was territory. The slave question he felt would take care of itself. Whether the result would be a grand extension of the principles of the Declaration of Independence or a new empire over subject people on the Napoleonic model was a question which did not trouble his mind.

So he arrogantly set about to buy California and all the land between it and Texas from the feeble government of Mexico. When that government refused to sell, he cold-bloodedly set to work to arrange a war. Perhaps he used less finesse than Bismark on a similar enterprise. He could hardly have used less scruple.

A strict Sabbatarian, he noted in his diary for Sunday, the 10th of May, 1846, that the urgency of preparing a special message to Congress had obliged him to profane the day with labor. On Monday, by his message, Congress was informed that Mexican troops had invaded American territory and spilled American blood on American soil. "War exists," it said, "and not withstanding all our efforts to avoid it, exists by the act of Mexico herself." He asked Congress for a formal declaration of war, and men and money to prosecute it. Within two hours, having closed off debate, the administration-controlled House voted war and the following day the Senate did likewise.

Massachusetts, with customary perversity, dissented. In the House five out of seven of its voting representatives, led by the aged J.Q. Adams, voted nay. In the Senate there were only two dissents and one of them was "Honest John" Davis of Massachusetts. It was a preview of the similarly lopsided and stampeded vote in 1964 for the notorious Tonkin Bay Resolution, an act based on a lie concerning an incident that never occurred.

The action of the President and Congress was greeted with fury in Massachusetts. The preamble to the military supply bill "War exists by the act of Mexico," according to the *Boston Whig*, was an outright lie. In fact the war had been precipitated by an American invasion of Mexican territory and the blockading of the Rio Grande. Charles Sumner drove home the point in a series of letters signed "Boston."

He began rather mildly, politely pointing out to Charles Winthrop, the congressman from Boston who had voted for the measure, that he had made himself a party to a lie. In the next letter he said that Winthrop had voted for "an unjust war and a national falsehood in the cause of slavery." In his third letter he really got down to business, proclaimed Winthrop a modern

General Scott's army landing at Vera Cruz 1848.

Pontius Pilate and his vote "wrong by the law of nations and the higher law of God. It cannot be forgotten on earth; it must be remembered in heaven. Blood! Blood! is on the hands of the representative from Boston. Not all great Neptune's ocean can wash them clean."

The doors of Boston society closed to Sumner. Winthrop replied with the argument that Congress had to support the army in the field whether the war was right or wrong—an argument not successfully contradicted till 1972 and the ending of the Vietnam War by act of Congress in denying further military support to the Executive. Now in 1846 feeling rose and rose in Massachusetts against the war. The dominant political party in the state began to break apart—into Conscience Whigs in violent opposition and Cotton Whigs, whose living depended on the continuous flow of cotton to northern mills, in timid support.

Meanwhile the national war machine rolled on. The better trained, better supplied and better commanded American armies won brilliant victories against the brave, disorganized and much more numerous Mexicans. Two future Presidents were made in the glamour and the shouting, Zachary Taylor and Franklin Pierce. And Mexico, disastrously defeated, American armies occupying its capital city, was, at gun point, robbed of all its northern territories, one third of its real estate.

While all these big guns were going off one other shot was fired from Concord. Very few heard it at the time. It was by no means the musket shot heard round the world. Rather it was the thin whistle of an arrow into the clear sky, an arrow which has not landed yet. Utterly disgusted by the actions of his government, Henry Thoreau wrote an essay which he called *Civil Disobedience*. "When oppression and robbery are organized I say let us not have such a machine any longer. This people must cease to hold slaves, and to make war on Mexico, though it cost them their existence as a people."

Years later, as the practical materialism of the 19th century turned into the disaster of the 20th, all the actors in the old American political drama being dead and most the survivors of its result, the great national tragedy, the Civil War, Thoreau's work fell into the hands of Mohandas Gandhi, the Indian Elijah. Gandhi read it and underlined certain passages. Today the British Empire is extinct and India is free. *Civil Disobedience* translated into many languages, is the best known work of American literature in Asia and in Africa and it is forbidden reading in totalitarian countries. And America celebrates a day for Martin Luther King.

Civilization has not yet discovered solutions to all the contradictory demands of mankind. If it had, education would be more successful than it is. But the approach to solutions suggested by Thoreau, now, after a further century of experiment, seems more likely to succeed in inter-American relations, or in fact world relations, then that so enthusiastically prosecuted by Polk.

THE 7TH OF MARCH AND DANIEL WEBSTER

*W*e, the people of the United States . . . " as the Constitution defines us, are still the people of the *United* States. But it took a civil war and something very close to ruin to keep us united. And on the 7th of March 1850 it was a close thing whether ruin would not get the better of union once and for all.

On that day Daniel Webster rose in the Senate theatrically dressed, as always, in blue coat with shining brass buttons, high stock and buff waistcoat to make his last great speech. Had he failed in his effort, or not made it, the odds are heavy that secession would have happened almost at once and the Union been broken, not to be restored. The slow tides of industry and population were rising to favor the North. Webster's speech gave those tides ten more years to rise.

For a week it had been known that the Demosthenes of Massachusetts was going to make a speech. It was not known what he would say. For thirty years he had championed the cause of Liberty. But he had been equally the champion of Union. So early on the morning of the 7th of March, a glorious morning of Southern spring, the avenues were filled with well-dressed men and women, all moving towards the Capitol. By noon there was barely breathing space in the Senate Chamber. The galleries were packed and the corridors overflowing. Even the steps around the Vice President's chair were covered with a bouquet of beribboned and crinolined ladies.

Henry Clay had put before the Senate a package of bills to cool the seething caldron of discontent the Mexican War had brought to a rolling boil. John C. Calhoun had snarled at the package; as it were, rent it with his teeth and spat it out for South Carolina and the slavocracy. President Zachary Taylor

176

Daniel Webster on his farm at Marshfield, Massachusetts.

had promised immediate war if secession passed one inch beyond the threat stage. And a convention had been called of slave states, shortly to take place in Nashville, Tennessee.

The temperature had risen because California was applying for admission to the Union as a free state. Texas was already in as a slave state and might be cut up into several more. And there were all the empty territories in between. What would become of them?

Both sides were terrified of losing an advantage. At stake was control of Congress. Each new state meant at once two new senators to shift the balance of power. And since population, by the old rule of the Constitution, was counted as all the whites and three-fifths of the slaves, slave owners could move their human property into empty lands and pick up votes in the House, too. So the North demanded no extension of slavery and the South clamored for it. And both sides were ready to go to war at the drop of Daniel Webster's hat.

Daniel Webster's hat was the biggest in the Senate and his great head contained the greatest brain. His voice was big, too, and his presence, but what raised him above every other man was his extraordinary power in argument. No other, then or ever in this country, has been able to marshall facts and present them with his force, his precision and his success. When he came to Concord to argue in the Middlesex court, the philosopher Emerson dropped everything to listen and was so shattered by the impact of his personality that he could get no work done for a week after. He experienced Webster as a natural force, like Niagara Falls or a bolt of lightning, "His words are like the blows of an axe, in his splendid wrath his eyes become fires."

Webster was the highest paid lawyer in the nation in private cases. He was also a great advocate employed in politics. His employers were the "solid" men of Massachusetts. When he needed money—and he often did—he borrowed it from bankers who later cancelled his notes; or received it in great wads directly from admirers. He was a prince, a genius, who lived by no rules of ordinary mortals. He could drink tumblers full of brandy and never turn a hair. He could live without sleep. When he rose to speak the Court, or the Senate, or the World fell silent.

On this 7th of March 1850 he began, "I speak today not as a Massachusetts man, not as a Northern man, but as an American . . . " That was a stopper. Feelings had got to such a pitch that there were only Southerners and Northerners. Webster brought them up short as Americans. And then he laid down point by point what had to be done. California must come in as a free state. The territories must be left to nature and time, the domestic slave trade must be banned in the District of Columbia and a tougher Fugitive Slave Law passed.

He made a terrible prophecy, "Secession! Peaceable secession! Your eyes and mine are never destined to see that miracle. Secession must produce war!" And he ended with an exhortation and a promise as powerful now as then it was. "Let us raise our conceptions to the magnitude and the importance of the duties that devolve upon us; let our comprehension be as broad as the country for which we act, our aspirations as high as its certain destiny; let us not be pygmies in a case that calls for men."

It was a horrible dose that he prescribed. Nobody but Webster wielding the long-handled spoon could have induced the country to swallow it. The slavers cried furiously that the prohibition of the trade in the capital city was unconstitutional and undermined the moral sanction of slavery derived from ancient precedents in Greece and Rome, the Bible and the acts and words of the Founding Fathers. The Abolitionists clawed the air in fury and anger, denounced the Constitution as "a covenant with death and an agreement with hell." The more rational Free Soil partisans regarded the open-ended territorial compromise with keen suspicion and the Fugitive Slave Law with disgust. Emerson expressed in his journal the mind of a great minority concerning that law. "I will not obey it, by God!"

It cost Webster a large chunk of his reputation then and thereafter. He began to recover it late in the 20th century. To him was attributed every vile motive from overweening ambition to outright dishonesty.

Perhaps he saw with perfect vision. He compared the uncertain present with a future bright with good possibilities or blackened, charred and ruined by a preventable, total war. His keen mind determined accurately the limits each side would accept. And by force of his genius he persuaded acceptance. The compromise saved the Union then. Something better than the three third-rate Presidents that followed might have saved it indefinitely. He saw, as the world needs to see again as it considers means for strategic arms limitation, that any reasonable alternative is better than mass murder. For below the surface of politics move forces beyond the comprehension of contemporary man.

FRANKLIN PIERCE — THE AWFUL MISTAKE

$\mathcal{S}$uddenly, in 1852, all the giants were dead. There was a little giant, Stephen Douglas of Illinois, and a broken heart in the worn-out body of Daniel Webster. But the giants who had made the Union and made the principles of the Declaration of Independence the light of the world were a race extinct. The annexation of Texas and the trumped-up war with Mexico had opened up far lands to slavery. Gold had been discovered in California. The West could not break enough sod or grow enough wheat to satisfy the European market. The country was on a binge of exploitation, expansion and greed.

The threat of secession, so nearly become a fact two years before, had been put to rest by the combined effort for compromise of the great Webster and the brave and patriotic Clay. The effort killed Clay physically and killed Webster politically. By common consent the divisive issue of slavery was no more to be talked of. A way had been found to put the monster to sleep. And so the two major parties set to work to discover standard-bearers. The flag that could attract the biggest army would then march on Washington. There the army would enjoy the spoils of office, while the bearer of the standard relaxed and took his ease in the White House.

The Democratic convention met in Baltimore and passed the two-thirds rule. That effectively killed off Stephen Douglas, the idol of Illinois, the hope of "young America." It killed off all the other candidates of whom anybody had ever heard. Then the supporters of wily James Buchanan, machine politician from Pennsylvania, determined on a bold and risky strategy. They divided their forces in two parts, one to hold staunchly to Buchanan, the other to switch rapidly from one candidate to another, at each move picking up support, till at just the right moment they would return to Buchanan and nominate him in a rush. It was a good strategy. It worked just a little too well. On the forty-seventh ballot it was decided to push an unknown candidate and prove he could not win, pick up his votes and go on from there. Franklin Pierce of New Hampshire was trotted out. There was a little talk behind the scenes. On the next ballot he picked up more votes. And then there was an avalanche. The talk had determined that Pierce was "safe." North Carolina, then the whole South, came to him with a rush. On the forty-ninth ballot not a single vote was left with Buchanan!

The Whig party moved in to Baltimore as the Democrats moved out and with something less than enthusiasm nominated Winfield Scott. The magnificent Webster could never muster more than thirty-two votes. The Whigs' real best bet, their incumbent in the White House, former Vice President Fillmore, could not quite make it. The Whigs felt they must have a general to win. They dared not change the prescription. General Scott was a very good general. But he proved less successful in conquering the hearts of his countrymen than conquering Mexico.

Being a precise type of military man he soon got the nickname of "fuss and feathers." His innocent remark that "soldiers had a greater dread of fire upon the rear than the most formidable enemy in front" delighted the ribald Irish, who declined to take in good part his well-meant compliments on their "rich brogue." The Germans did not like his remarks on their "foreign accent."

Franklin Pierce was a well-handled dark horse and stayed in the shade of the elms around his comfortable New Hampshire home. His only excursion was to the Isles of Shoals to visit his college and intimate friend, Nathaniel Hawthorne. In fact his best claim to posthumous fame is that after he became President he appointed Hawthorne to the lucrative post of Consul at Liverpool, so becoming the godfather of the great writer's European novel *The Marble Fawn*. But even Hawthorne could not make Pierce exciting. He used up 140 pages of a campaign biography to tell of the father's Revolutionary service, the son's patriotism, good looks and devotion to wife and family. An old note of J.Q. Adams in his diary is more interesting, "The bill was opposed by Franklin Pierce, a new member and young man from New Hampshire, who spoke for half an hour very handsomely against it."

There was the whole of Franklin Pierce. He was handsome and he spoke handsomely. Being elected President, he stood bareheaded in a snowstorm and spoke extempore his inaugural address without notes, a landmark performance. He enjoyed greatly the panoply of office. He offered Cabinet positions as if they were crumbs from the rich man's table. He could not learn to say no. Sometimes he offered the same job to two people. To satisfy his Southern support he proposed to add Cuba as a slave state "by purchase if possible, or by other means."

He brought into his Cabinet the unscrupulous Caleb Cushing of Massachusetts, a copperhead, the slang term for sympathizer with slavery. From the deep South in Mississippi he brought Jefferson Davis, arch secessionist, to be his Secretary of War. By the time the first session of the first Congress of his administration was over, it was plain he could not control it. Conspiracies ripened like mildew in a warm closet. Then his rival for the last—and the next—nomination for the Presidency, Stephen Douglas, charismatic orator but superficial thinker, brought out his Kansas-Nebraska bill, the infernal machine that blew up the Union.

Idiotically, Pierce supported it. This bill was a bomb with a short fuse. It took out of the hands of Congress the option of deciding whether slavery could be extended into a territory and placed the decision in the hands of those settlers who should first move into it. As finally passed, it repealed the Missouri Compromise of 1820, opening Northern territory to the possibility of government dominated by slaveholders that had been closed "forever" against such possibility. It undid in a single stroke all the statesmanship of the previous thirty years, it calcinated in a hot fire the cement of the Union. Of it Charles Sumner, the conscience of Massachusetts, said, "It annuls all past compromises with slavery, and makes all future compromises impossible. It puts freedom and slavery face to face and bids them grapple. Who can doubt the result?"

The result for Franklin Pierce was total annihilation. Such a little man should never have been President. A better political system, even so imperfect a system as the marathon campaign for delegates that superseded the smoke-filled room, might have prevented it. A few direct primaries, even a primary in his own New Hampshire, might have smoked out so weak a character. Then it is just possible—and such possibilities take on enormous importance in the age of the hydrogen bomb—that the Civil War might have been prevented. A strong and upright man in the Presidency could have blocked the Kansas-Nebraska Bill. The nominating machinery is the key to the future of democratic government. Doubtless it will never be perfect. But its improvement is a ceaseless task, made necessary by constantly changing social and technical conditions. It is the most important task of legislators.

THE DAY THE BRAINS RAN OUT

*T*here is a question mankind would ask of history. On the answer the future depends. Or no future. Were the irrepressible conflicts of the past repressible?

The great American tragedy is the Civil War. Its cause was slavery. The best brains and the strongest wills in the nation wrestled with the problem for three-quarters of a century and kept it down. Then government ran out of brains and will power. There was an eruption that physically destroyed half the country and left the other half morally and intellectually bankrupt. In an atomic age nothing at all might have been left.

It had been the hope of Washington and Jefferson that slavery would wither away, being unfit and unable to compete with free labor. Unfortunately it proved profitable for cotton growing. A great crisis occurred in 1820 when Missouri applied for admission to the Union as a slave state. It was like the point of a spear driving into the free North. A compromise saved the situation. Slave Missouri was balanced by free Maine and Congress passed an act that henceforth slavery was "forever" prohibited north of the parallel 36°.

If slavery could be contained there was still hope that it might perish of economic starvation. But then came the annexation of Texas and the Mexican war. There was again a crisis in 1850, resolved by another compromise, which traded off free California against slave Texas. This left the old compromise of 1820 intact, reaffirming the duty of Congress to settle each question concerning slavery as it came up. Neither abolitionists nor Southern fire-eaters were satisfied. But Clay and Webster, champions of union, could die knowing that the nation was still at peace and had a reasonable chance of remaining so. The future would still depend on damping down the question till

time, with changing economic conditions and moral perceptions and population densities, could quietly settle the matter.

When the dark horse Franklin Pierce won the Presidential
race of 1852 in a hand gallop, most people were content. They
were glad to let the slavery issue rest where Clay and Webster
had buried it. But horribly it was exhumed. Suddenly it became
inexorably entangled with the route of the transcontinental
railroad to the Pacific. Where should that route be, north, central or south?

The fate of the United States, the lives of its young men, the
decision for war or peace, would turn on this question. There
were strong and good reasons for all three routes. And there
were also sordid and bad reasons. The young senator from
Illinois, Stephen Douglas, who had done yeoman's service in
pushing through both houses of Congress the most recent slavery compromise, was a heavy speculator in Western lands. He
and friends were in a good position to profit by the central
railroad development. He needed Southern votes for railroad
schemes and political schemes.

Douglas had been an early favorite in the race that Pierce
had won. He was favored to win the next race. He was the most
popular figure in the great Northwest, a powerful manipulator
in the Senate, a telling speaker. If he could unite Northwest
and South, he could be sure of the Democratic nomination over
Pierce, whose lamentable weakness was already, after less than
a year in office, making him an object of contempt. And for
such purposes he was in an advantageous position. He was
Chairman of the Senate Committee on Territories. His word
there was law. The dazzle of his career blinded his admirers to
his most conspicuous fault. Quick as were his thoughts, his
actions were quicker. He thought as he ran and the speed of his
running determined his next turning. On slavery he had no
moral conviction. He believed it was suitable in the South
where it paid; unsuitable in the North where it didn't.

Great pressure was building up to organize the huge Nebraska Territory, move out the Indian tribes, open it for settlement
and run the central railroad to the West. So in the winter of

1853 friends of Douglas in the lower house entered a bill for this purpose. Based on the Missouri Compromise, it assumed the exclusion of slavery. It passed by a majority of two to one. Douglas reported the bill to the Senate. But it did not come up till the last day of the session. It then failed, primarily for lack of time, but only by five votes.

One speech was made in the Senate of great significance. Atchison of Missouri, a fierce slave advocate, said, "There is no remedy for the Missouri Compromise. We must submit to it. We may as well agree to the admission of this Territory now." Abraham Lincoln thereafter maintained, and others have agreed with him, that a determined effort in the next session would have carried through the bill unchanged. The effort was not made. And tragedy resulted. The slavery issue, like a drowsy tiger, stretched, bared its claws, rolled itself awake and crouched ready to spring. And in the White House Franklin Pierce did not take down the big game rifle that hangs over the mantelpiece and is available to all Presidents.

Every person in a position of power must be judged by the effect of his use of it. Pierce was not a bad man, but the evil that he did as President of the United States tops the record. When a word from him might have saved the Union, he took pen in hand and, writing down what others dictated or suggested, signed the warrant for its dissolution.

This is what happened. The bill for organizing the Nebraska Territory, that had barely failed in the last session, was brought in unchanged in the next and was referred to the Committee on Territories, dominated by Douglas. After consultation with slaveholders, Douglas produced a completely new bill that eventually would be known to infamy as the Kansas-Nebraska Bill, with a report calling into question the constitutionality of the Missouri Compromise that had been basic law since 1820. But this was not enough. Under pressure, Douglas discovered a "clerical error" and a clause was added to the bill transferring the power to decide on the slavery question from Congress to the people in the Territory. Still not enough. Sharp-eyed Senator Dixon of Kentucky noted a flaw. No slaveholder could immigrate to the Territory, with his slaves, till after the people living in it had voted the question up or down. Explicitly the Missouri Compromise must be repealed. Douglas was aghast. Things were getting out of hand. He asked Dixon to take a ride in his carriage. Returning from the ride he exclaimed, "By God, Sir, you are right and I will incorporate it in my bill, though I know it will raise the hell of a storm."

The final, fatal step was taken on a Sunday morning. A group of senators, Douglas at their head, called at the White House. Like a pirate crew tipping their captain the black spot, they made it clear to Pierce that he must go along or lose the support of the Senate for his foreign policy. He resisted, then caved in. As a final humiliation Douglas obliged him to sit down and write out in his own hand the amendments to the bill. Now, lashed to the wheel of fate, he must go whither it rolled. The bill had become the administration's bill and every resource of patronage was used to drive it through the House, where it passed at last by a dozen votes.

The hell of a storm washed Franklin Pierce right out of the White House. It washed out Stephen Douglas's road to it. As he ruefully admitted himself, he could have traveled by night from Boston to Chicago by the light of the bonfires where he was burned in effigy. More serious, it closed the way for compromise. Time was clipped short. Time that alone might—just might—have found a better way than wholesale murder.

DISCUSSION CEASES, WAR COMES.

*T*he infamous Kansas-Nebraska Bill passed the Senate at 4:45 in the morning of the 4th of March 1854 after a bitter, vituperative, savage speech by Stephen Douglas. It thrust the slavery question out of Washington, into the territories, into the streets of the great cities. Bowie knives and guns, brickbats and paving stones, would now take up the argument. It was the bully boy's challenge to his neighbor across the fence, "Come on over and fight."

Charles Sumner and Salmon Chase, Free Soil senators, walked together down the Capitol steps in the thinning dark. Cannon were booming salutes as the slavocracy celebrated its triumph. "They celebrate a present victory," said Chase, "but the echoes they awake will never rest till slavery itself shall die." And in far-off Illinois, Abraham Lincoln, hearing the news while attending court in the Springfield circuit, talked far into the night with Judge Dickey, with whom he was sharing a hotel room. In the morning Dickey woke and saw his friend sitting up in bed, his eyes fixed on the opposite wall. As if still continuing the discussion of the night Lincoln spoke, "I tell you, Dickey, this nation cannot exist half slave and half free."

Seven years later Lincoln was taking the oath of office as President of the United States, from which already seven states of the deep South had seceded. Within forty days Fort Sumter was fired on. Let Walt Whitman tell it. "Beat! beat! drums!—blow! bugles! blow! Leave not the bridegroom quiet—no happiness must he have now with his bride, nor the peaceful farmer any peace, ploughing his field or gathering his grain. So fierce you whirr and pound you drums—so shrill you bugles blow." It was war. War to the finish.

This was the awful result of Douglas's Kansas-Nebraska Bill.

It broke the dams which statesmanship and common sense had been building and patching for three generations. It loosed a flood of passions that no feeble politics could ever after control. It hurts us still. It demonstrates the ways of unwisdom. The new law, which struck down the 1820 Compromise, transferred the decision when to use violence as the arbiter of disputes, from a body at least capable of considering the consequences, to mobs and guerrilla bands which understand nothing but continuous violence.

A Southern visitor in Boston wrote, "If the Kansas-Nebraska bill should be passed, the Fugitive Slave Law is a dead letter throughout New England. As easily could a law prohibiting the eating of codfish and pumpkin pie be enforced." On the day after President Pierce signed the act violence did indeed break out in Boston. An attempt was made to release a recaptured slave from the courthouse. A mob, armed with a huge beam and led by clergymen, broke down the main door. A federal marshal's deputy was killed. The attack failed. The slave was hidden and after a week of legal battling returned to slavery.

But what a return! Anthony Burns, the slave, was a pitiable sight, one hand broken, the other marked with a brand, a brand on his cheek. The streets were hung with black. The church bells tolled. Great crowds pressed against the barriered way to the harbor. "I saw," wrote one witness, "the cavalry, artillery, marines and police, a thousand strong, escorting with shotted guns one trembling colored man to the vessel which was to carry him to slavery. I heard the curses poured on these soldiers. The crowd yelled at them 'Kidnappers! Kidnappers!' " A hard-boiled State Street lawyer wrote, "When it was all over, and I was left alone in my office, I put my face in my hands and wept."

No other attempt was ever made to return a slave from Boston. And in one of Boston's great houses, the Lawrence house facing on Park Street, now the Union Club, plans were being made and subscriptions raised to send free men into the Kansas Territory. The New England Emigrant Aid Society, in the first year after the opening of the Territory, sent about a thousand men, armed with the tools of agriculture and the tools of war—"Rifles are as important as Bibles," spoke Henry Beecher from his pulpit, and thereafter Sharps rifles, the favored make, were known as "Beecher's Bibles." They built a village on the prairie and called it Lawrence.

The slaveholders of Missouri, too, were active. Led by their Senator Atchison, friend of Senator Douglas and one of the hawks who had forced through the Kansas-Nebraska act, they organized groups to cross the Missouri River and push into the new territory, taking with them their human property. Their propaganda was aggressive. Their actual settlement was less so. The country was not suitable for cotton growing. In fact, most of the settlers who really came to stay were from the Midwest, were neither pro-slavery nor abolitionists.

But the great national question, which ought to have been kept in Washington and there decided by those responsible for the welfare of the whole nation, was dropped on their heads. The local solution was instant violence. When a territorial representative was to be chosen, a small army of Missouri men crossed over for the day, stuffed the ballot boxes, and elected a slaveholder. A year later the same farce was repeated, on a grander scale, to elect a legislature. This time the army marched with brass bands, flags and a small train of cannon. It did not keep step, because along with the cannon were steadily diminishing wagonloads of whiskey. And the legislature which it elected immediately passed a law making even discussion of the slavery question a crime, punishable by ten years in jail.

Anyone who protested these methods was threatened with hanging or shooting. But two sides can play at that game. The Free Soil advocates were soon augmented by a grim-faced, cold-eyed old man, a prophet sent directly by God—or so he believed—to exterminate slavery. John Brown and his sons were armed with Sharps rifles and they knew how to use them. Within two years Kansas had acquired two separate governments and they were both illegal. And it had acquired an adjective before its name and it was well deserved—Bleeding.

When Charles Sumner made a speech in the Senate, "The

John Brown.

Crime Against Kansas," he was physically attacked. Representative Brooks of South Carolina entered the chamber at the end of a day's session. Finding Sumner bending over his desk writing, he hit him with a club and beat him senseless while Senator Douglas looked on. The Congress having abdicated its duty to the frontier, now the law of the frontier took over civilized government.

War could have been prevented if Congress and the Executive had done their job of maintaining the old Compromise till the question could cool. They shirked their responsibility, let the matter drift, turned the deciding over to the border ruffians, let armed brigands take over. World questions are the same. Sneak work by the Central Intelligence Agency stirring up trouble along borders, arms traffic, blustering, are no substitute for negotiation between powers. They are small men's methods of begging the question.

There is a reluctance by demagogues and hardline militarists openly to discuss the alternative to rational negotiation and intelligent compromise. For anyone who suggests nuclear war as a solution to human problems is apt to reveal himself as a very cheap politician, a great fool or an insane person.

A DECENT RESPECT FOR THE OPINION
OF WOMANKIND

A decent respect for the opinion of mankind is the granite of which the American democracy is built. Contempt for the opinion of mankind is the steel frame of arbitrary government. Since empires can rise very suddenly and seem to overshadow the earth, it is hard sometimes for democrats not to hanker after similar building material, although it is the common fate of skyscrapers to rust and be torn down. The system of slave labor that existed in the southern part of the United States before and long after the Declaration of Independence appeared to produce very satisfactory results. Every crack of the whip put money in the pockets of the masters of the cotton kingdom and the cotton it exported seemed as necessary as oil is in the 20th Century to keep the world's machinery running.

"Cotton is king," shouted Representative Hammond of South Carolina. "You dare not make war on cotton. No power on earth dares to make war on cotton." And when civil war broke out, a merchant on a wharf in Charleston, South Carolina, pointed to some bales of cotton and said to a reporter from the *Times* of London, "There is the key to John Bull's strongbox." Lord Palmerston, the British Prime Minister, said, "We do not like slavery but we want cotton." The English novelist, Anthony Trollope, visiting Boston, and asked what he thought would be the outcome of the war answered, "Why, secession certainly. The North may beat the South. But that will not prevent secession."

The one necessity for Confederate success was a supply of manufactured goods, especially powder and shot. There was almost no manufacture in the South. Even the two changes of cotton clothing commonly doled out to the slaves each year were made of cloth spun in Northern mills. But raw cotton provided plenty of rich exchange to secure every necessity. Provided only that it could be got to market. President Lincoln had declared a blockade of Southern ports. But it would not last long if Britain declared for the South.

Nassau in the Bahamas was the center for blockade runners. Its harbor was filled with swift ships, its waterfront with swaggering crews. Overnight it became a boom town. On the docks in Nassau the agents of British cotton mills were waiting with bags of gold to buy the contraband cotton. The fibers of cotton spun the thread that held the British Empire together. On them depended British industry. From them came the wealth that supported the British ruling class. It was the confident belief of the slavocracy that a few weeks of cotton famine in Lancashire would cause a revolt of the workers. An army of the unemployed would march on London, the terrified government would dispatch the British navy, and the game would be in the bag.

It did not turn out that way. In the emotional and highly charged atmosphere that preceded the Civil War certain aspects of genius were revealed, especially among women. Politics was the province of men. Politics had made the Mexican War and extended slavery, and the result was the Civil War. But opinion was the province of women. No man and no politics could control it then, or ever has. And on the subject of slavery it broke out suddenly and with force that changed the world.

About the time the *Constitution* was busy with the *Guerriere* off the Atlantic coast, a few miles inland, in Litchfield, Connecticut, a sort of human great stud, a clergyman named Lyman Beecher, was siring, on three wives, as one contemporary said, "more brains than any other man in America." Most of his thirteen children were famous in their time and two still are; Henry Beecher, "the greatest preacher since St. Paul," and his sister Harriet. It was Harriet's fate to meet and marry a man named Stowe, like her father a clergyman and even less rich in this world's goods. They lived in Cincinnati, separated from the

A New Nation

world of slavery only by the Ohio River. There Harriet learned the meaning of the Fugitive Slave Law, saw and smelt and felt the curse at first hand.

Then her husband got a job at Bowdoin College. In Maine, looking back on her Western and Southern experience, Harriet began a serial story she called "Uncle Tom's Cabin; or, Life Among the Lowly." It ran in an anti-slavery paper published in Washington, D.C., and by the time the last installment came out Harriet and most of the nation, even including many people in the South, were in tears. Published as a book it swept the country. But its greatest impact was abroad. Translated into twenty-five languages it sold in the millions of copies. It was much read by the God-fearing people of Lancashire in England. There it almost displaced the Bible and the *Pilgrim's Progress.* And so it came about that when the supply of cotton was cut off to the Lancashire mills there was no march on London, no threat of revolution. Tragic unemployment was endured, acute suffering. But when C.F. Adams, the American Minister to the Court of St. James's, was cold-shouldered by the British aristocracy, faced with the threat of war by the British Cabinet, he found support among the working people, and in Parliament from their great advocate, John Bright. Uncle Tom, the martyr slave, had done his work.

From a quite different background came another remarkable woman. Daughter of a New York banker, Julia Ward developed her bright soprano voice with the best teachers. She married the romantic Boston doctor Samuel Howe, fighter for Greek independence and founder of the Perkins Institute for the Blind. In Washington, at the beginning of the Civil War, her carriage was caught in a traffic jam as a regiment of soldiers swung by to the tune of "John Brown's Body." She stood up and sang with them and as they passed, the men shouted, "Good for you, Lady!"

The tune was singing in her ears that night as she fell asleep. Waking before dawn she saw clearly words written on the tablet of her mind. In the dark she found pen and paper and wrote them down, went back to bed and fell asleep. When she woke again she had forgotten the words. But on the table were all the lines that begin "Mine eyes have seen the glory . . ." As the "Battle Hymn of the Republic" it was published in the *Atlantic Monthly*. A young chaplain in the Union Army, happening on a copy and moved by the magnificence of its imagery, memorized it. Not long after he was captured and sent south to Richmond, where he was confined in Libby Prison, formerly a tobacco warehouse. There, one day, a black orderly whispered the news of the Union victory at Gettysburg. Suddenly the prison gloom was shattered, the blank walls seemed to fall away like the walls of Jericho, as in imagination the ragged, half-starved prisoners escaped, carried forth on the grand cadences they were singing in chorus, to the astonishment of sentries and Confederate officials, "He has sounded forth the trumpet that shall never call retreat — He is sifting out the hearts of men before his judgment seat — Be swift my soul to answer him, be jubilant my feet."

Ideas rule the world. What turned the tide in the Civil War could turn the tide in Asia, in Russia and in the Middle East. The opinion of mankind requires respect. And mankind's opinion usually reflects the woman's.

ONCE THE UNITED STATES HELD HOSTAGES

*I*t is hard to choose the darkest moment of the Civil War. There is so much darkness. Whether a nation conceived in liberty could live was the question. The South said no and seceded with its slaves. The onlookers, officially represented by the governments of the British and French Empires, tended to agree with the South. The Southern idea of a very narrow ruling class deciding the fate of all the remaining millions was one to which they were sympathetic. And from a practical empire point of view the Monroe Doctrine was a nuisance. Without it, and the Union to enforce it, the American continents seemed to offer a pleasant playground.

The key to the situation was Britain. Britain had the navy that could rule the seas. Without British cooperation, or at least non-intervention, no one else could move. And the British press spoke loudly and stridently for the British upper class. It chose the symbolic figure of Pharaoh as suitable for Abraham Lincoln and asked him again and again why did he not let that people go?

But the British government proclaimed neutrality. The cynical Lord Palmerston was Prime Minister. He had, in his opinion, two prime duties; to make the Empire stronger and to maintain his majority in Parliament. If necessary, he would risk war to keep that majority. The Parliament was made up of members representative of less than five per cent of the population. Property qualifications excluded most of the people from voting. Eighty per cent of the House of Commons and still more of the House of Lords were sympathetic with the Confederacy. There was one major exception. Prince Albert, the Queen's consort, deplored slavery and favored the North. The people, who feared and detested slavery, had no vote.

The military conduct of the war was no help to the friends of the United States abroad. There was the rout of Bull Run at the very beginning and then the long stalemate while the army of General McClellan did nothing before Richmond. And then the *Trent* affair. In absurdity, flagrant violation of international law, wanton trouble seeking and popular madness it equaled or perhaps exceeded the antics of the Ayatollah Khomeini and his Iranians. Its consequence could have been the extinguishment of the United States. Fortunately the Americans had for their leader Abraham Lincoln and for their representative in London a cool diplomat, C.F. Adams.

The British mail steamer *Trent* was stopped in the Bahama channel by the American man-of-war *San Jacinto*. Captain Wilkes, on his own initiative and without orders, sent marines on board and took prisoner two Confederate agents, Mason and Slidell. These two had successfully run the blockade from Charleston to Havana and were legitimate passengers under the protection of the British flag. They were taken to Fort Warren in Boston Harbor.

Boston proceeded to go mad. It carried on as if a great victory had been won on the battlefield. The City gave a splendid banquet to Wilkes, and Governor Andrew and the Chief Justice of the Supreme Judicial Court of Massachusetts made fulsome speeches. The Saturday Club, which should have known better, for it was made up of the best educated men in the nation, invited him to dinner.

From Washington the House of Representatives sent Wilkes an expression of thanks and voted him a gold medal. It requested the President to confine Mason as a convicted felon. There had already been a nasty exchange of threats between North and South. For North had captured some Southern privateers and suggested treating them as pirates. Whereupon South had selected by lot fourteen federal officers, prisoners of war, to be hanged in retaliation, and for safekeeping thrown them into a filthy county jail. Now North jubilated at the prospect of doing in some really important hostages, if the hanging should really begin.

Secretary of the Navy Welles sent a letter of congratulation to Wilkes. With the single exception of Postmaster General Blair, the rest of the Cabinet shared his joy. President Lincoln, untrained in international law, nevertheless sensed great danger from abroad, and being equally concerned how to control the popular clamor at home, remarked that he feared the hostages "would prove to be white elephants." Secretary of State Seward, gone temporarily crazy, was for declaring war on everybody at once, beginning with England but not forgetting France. Charles Sumner, Senator from Massachusetts, who had many English friends, did some useful work cooling him down. The upshot was that the Confederate Commissioners were kept locked up in Boston and the American Minister in England was told that he might inform the British government that Wilkes had acted "without any instructions from the government."

But long before this dispatch could reach England—there was in those days no Atlantic cable—the news of the *Trent* outrage was splashed across the headlines of every London paper. The British Cabinet met and decided that the British flag had been dishonored and that a peremptory demand should be made for the release of the prisoners, and an apology. Adams, calling on Lord Russell, the Foreign Minister, could say only that he was completely uninformed in the matter. The next weeks were purgatory. As dispatches came in it was his job to interpret them, soften and explain them whenever he could. Above all keep silent when silence was better than talk. "Rule Britannia" was sung in the streets. In Liverpool, hot for war because of its dependence on the cotton trade, there were angry mass meetings. The government prepared to dispatch troops for the defense of Canada. The navy was readied to break the blockade of Southern ports.

At this point Prince Albert, on his death bed in the grip of typhoid fever, intervened. He persuaded the Ministry to refrain from an ultimatum, and to insert in its note a suggestion of a hope that Wilkes had acted without authority. And with this in his briefcase a Queen's messenger took the first steamer to New York and at midnight on 18 December 1861 delivered it to the British Minister in Washington.

Lord Lyons was a careful diplomat and next day called on Seward and conveyed to him the substance of the British note; but allowed time for its consideration. On Christmas Day Lincoln called a Cabinet meeting. He had made up his mind what to do. An elaborate reply was prepared, full of legalism and reference to Britain's former insistence on its right of search on the high seas. This so the President could save face and calm down the public and the hawks in Congress. But its substance was simple. The prisoners would be released.

The trouble was settled very quietly in the end. A British steamer called at Provincetown. Mason and Slidell were slipped on board and carried off to London and Paris to perform as best they could their mission of trying to embroil England and France in the American war. But they never came nearly as close to success as free agents as they did as hostages in Fort Warren.

ABRAHAM LINCOLN AND SELF-EVIDENT TRUTH

*D*uring the American Civil War the future existence of the United States depended on public opinion in Great Britain. It was public opinion that restrained the hostile British government from interference. But public opinion did not have much clout in the day-to-day operation of the Empire. Mass meetings and marches, and in extreme cases riots, were the only way the people, unrepresented in Parliament, could directly influence government. The press, even in such great manufacturing towns as Manchester and Birmingham, spoke mostly for the ruling class, the very rich and the owners of vast amounts of inherited landed property. Only one Briton in twenty-three had a right to vote. Elections were controlled by a very small self-perpetuating group. At its head was Lord Palmerston, the Prime Minister.

His laugh was famous. "Ha!—Ha!—Ha!" slow, deliberate, like a wooden nutcracker. It was the laugh of the Waterloo generation, an echo of the Congress of Vienna, when he had been a young chargé d'affaires. His Foreign Secretary, Lord Russell, was of the same vintage. Their idea of foreign relations was the idea of Talleyrand and Metternich. It began with power at home. It must follow, therefore, as a natural corollary, that any decrease of power of a rival abroad was an increase of the power of Britain. For this was reserved the Palmerston laugh. In theory they were anti-slavery. But Britain had been buying cotton from the slave states for a long time. And commercial transactions were not concerned with the domestic affairs of foreign nations. So when the South seceded, the British government proclaimed neutrality, recognized the Confederacy as a belligerent and concentrated on the problem of cotton. It was confidently predicted that when the supply of cotton ran out it would be necessary for Britain to intervene. And then there would be one less rival.

It was not expected the waiting would be long. If nine or ten million people, acting in concert, wanted to go off by themselves and march to their own music, nothing could stop them. The Confederacy had promptly won the battle of Bull Run. The only puzzle was why it had not gone right on and captured Washington.

The *Trent* affair had caused a terrific stir. The English were excited by the scene on the deck of the *Trent* as described by Commander Williams at a dinner of the Royal Western Yacht Club. The brutal American marines advanced on Miss Slidell, daughter of one of the Confederate agents, their bayonets pointed at her breast. Only the action of the brave commander who thrust himself between and shouted "Back you damned cowardly poltroons!" prevented them from drawing blood. And there was Thackeray. He told the story in the drawing rooms of London, his eyes filled with tears, of his friend Mrs. Hampton, whom he had immortalized as Ethel Newcombe, a character in one of his novels. As she lay dying of consumption in South Carolina, her parents and sister had been cruelly refused permission to pass through the lines to see her.

No denial, no stack of affidavits, would persuade London society to abate one jot of its belief in these stories. Lincoln was a brute who encouraged atrocities, especially against women. With the news of General Butler's famous order that the women of New Orleans would be treated as women of the streets if they continued to insult Union soldiers, the British aristocracy declared war on the American Legation in London. The Prime Minister symbolically spat at the American Minister.

C.F. Adams, returning from an afternoon walk in London, opened a note lying on his desk. He said quietly, "Palmerston wants a quarrel." There can be no doubt Palmerston did. His note was abusive. Probably he hoped for an indiscreet reply out of which he could make political capital in Parliament. Adams foiled him by answering with a question, "Was the note an official communication or merely an expression of personal opinion?"

Palmerston never did answer that. Having overstepped the bounds of diplomatic propriety he found himself in an embarrassing position with his own Foreign Secretary, Lord Russell. For Russell was playing the game of intervention, with France as an ally, and he did not want Palmerston jumping the gun. To make matters worse the Secretary of the Exchequer, Gladstone, in a public speech declared that Jefferson Davis had made of the South a nation. These indiscretions forced Russell to tell lies to the American Minister and the honor of Great Britain got badly mixed up with the honor of the Foreign Secretary.

Indecision in the British Cabinet brought delay and delay brought its own solution. Beneath the surface warfare lay one strong current. The storm between sea and sky could not change the fact, though it hid it, that the whole ocean was moving in one direction—towards the recognition of human rights—towards democracy. Abraham Lincoln, whose perceptions of the deeps of human feeling were acute, called his Cabinet together one day, not any longer to ask their advice on the question of emancipation, but to tell them of his intention to proclaim it. The battle of Antietam, which had turned back the Confederate advance in September 1862, gave him the opportunity for which he had been waiting, a Union victory. On the first of January 1863, under the war powers of the Constitution, the emancipation of the slaves in the Confederacy became a fact.

The power of the blow can be measured by the violence of the reaction in England. The *Times* saw it as a dastardly attempt to raise up a slave insurrection. "When blood begins to flow and when shrieks come piercing through the darkness, Mr. Lincoln will rub his hands and think that revenge is sweet." The people, who had neither votes in Parliament nor great newspapers to speak for them, seemed to take a deep breath. Then the silence began to break. A trickle of resolutions approving emancipation began to come in to the American Legation. Then came a huge meeting at Exeter Hall in London. The crowd was so great that it overflowed into the Strand and stopped traffic. Ten thousand people tried to crowd in— among whom was just one member of Parliament. The *Times* called it "a carnival of cant" and the audience "good honest simpletons."

The carping of the media made no difference. There were meetings all over England, a great, restrained outburst of feeling. The feeling ran strong, even in Liverpool, the very hotbed of Southern sympathy because of the cotton trade. Observing a mass meeting there a reporter wrote, "As long as the Proclamation is in existence public opinion in England will never permit our government to take any action in favor of the South."

Certain events are like that. They change the course of government within and without. For ideas are more dangerous than any traffic in arms. They cross frontiers without passports. Of such was the Emancipation Proclamation of Abraham Lincoln. Of such in effect, though by intent contrary, was the edict of the old men in the Kremlin that banished Sakharov, and with him the cause of human rights, into the silent, but still beating heart of Russia.

TWO-THIRDS REQUIRED—AND
A MAN FROM MAINE

*W*hen a great issue is decided in the Senate by the single vote that makes or unmakes a necessary two-thirds, the normal reaction in the country is abundant rage. Teeth are gnashed. Reprisals are talked of. But the gnashers and reprisers are usually wrong. Whether the issue is a Panama Canal, the packing of the Supreme Court or the impeachment of a President, time usually proves the greater wisdom of the framers of the Constitution.

Once, when the two-thirds rule was circumvented by an unwise President and a slippery Congress, civil war resulted. That was the unconstitutional annexation of Texas. The passions raised by the Civil War then nearly caused the destruction of the balance of power principle by which the American democracy has survived and prospered. A runaway Congress made an almost successful attempt to destroy the Executive as an effective force by impeaching Andrew Johnson.

This famous impeachment trial was resolved, as all political matters are resolved, by such complicated interplay of unknown forces that science is baffled. No theory of history can accurately account for the effect of Charles Sumner's unhappy marriage on the result. Neither can anyone know just how impotent Sumner was in that marriage, for his impotence was rather mental than physical, and had its origin in the domination of a mother. On the other side of the question was Senator Fessenden of Maine. His vote was crucial to the outcome. The fact that he was technically a bastard may have made his vote certain to fall as it did.

President Johnson was impeached not because he had committed any crime but because he disagreed with much more

206

than a majority in both houses of Congress. Disagreement is not a crime under the Constitution. It is a crime in Russia and in all totalitarian countries. If the impeachment of Andrew Johnson had succeeded, the way would have been opened for the United States to slide into the same abyss.

The case against Johnson was trivial and absurd. Because Congress could not drive the Executive branch to carry out extreme measures of reprisal against the white majority in the South, it decided to reduce the President to a mere cipher in the scheme of American government. Congress passed a law, over the President's veto, forbidding him to fire certain of his appointees without consent of the Senate. This Tenure of Office Act was obviously unconstitutional. Meaning merely to test the act by a court case, Johnson fired Stanton, his disloyal Secretary of War.

But Andrew Johnson was born under an evil star. Rising from extreme poverty by very great abilities, courage and tragic chance to the highest office, he had neither tact nor judgment. If there was a way of fouling up a situation, he fouled it up. At his inauguration as Vice President he was weak with some intestinal illness. He took a stiff drink of whiskey. It almost knocked him over. Ever after he was accused of being a drunkard. On the Congressional circuit, trying to help the election of his own supporters at midterm—a tactic that almost never works—he responded to hecklers with violent abuse and resoundingly lost the election.

So when he laid himself open to attack by firing Stanton and the House happily impeached him, the country cheered. Charles Sumner was ecstatic. The most doctrinaire of abolitionists, he saw the person of Andrew Johnson as the sole obstacle to the instant acceptance of the newly freed men of the South to a position of complete equality, even superiority, to their recent masters. The proper place for Johnson, he said, would be a straitjacket. That he would find pleasure in putting him there, there can be little doubt. At this moment in his life Sumner was about as miserable as a man can be. He was publicly disgraced by the desertion of a young and beautiful wife and for a cause which, true or not, no man likes to admit. It is unlikely that he was indulging in much human sympathy for others, especially for another whom he considered the chief enemy of the human race.

Impeachment, Sumner declared, was "a political proceeding before a political body with a political purpose." He was, in effect, prepared to declare, along with a temporary majority of his countrymen, that the Constitution was a scrap of paper not worth the reading. But quietly, inevitably, appeared on the other side of the question a man from Maine, a fellow Republican with Sumner, a man whom Lincoln had deeply trusted, Senator Fessenden.

Fessenden possessed one of the most brilliant minds in the Senate and very probably the mind the most rigorously trained. He was sensitive in matters of conscience to a very rare degree. The question uppermost in his mind was always the question of right, of strict honesty in all affairs. His own birth, in the eye of the law and in the Argus-eyed puritan morality, had not been honest. His whole life, from earliest consciousness, seems to have been a sustained effort to repudiate by excellence of achievement this one irremediable fact.

His father, one of the handsomest men of his generation, while yet in college, had fallen in love with a beautiful and sensitive girl of a most respectable family. She became pregnant. Unquestionably they intended to marry. Such unions were a common fact of early New England as the frequency of seven-month first babies testifies in the church records. But for some reason they did not; perhaps the bitter opposition of the unfortunate girl's family. And at the age of a few days the infant Pitt Fessenden was taken from his own mother and delivered into the hands of his father's mother living in Fryeburg, Maine. Later his father married another woman who took the child and brought him up as the elder brother of her own children.

From infancy Pitt was precocious. When not quite thirteen years old he was admitted to Bowdoin College. At twenty-one, the earliest permissible age, he was admitted to the bar and within a few years was Maine's most noted lawyer and was soon a congressman, then senator. All his life he was firm for the Union, serving Lincoln briefly as Secretary of the Treasury. After the assassination he returned to the Senate.

Never an abolitionist, though believing firmly in the rights of man and in the emancipation Lincoln had enunciated, he could not go along with the extremist Sumner. In a private letter he wrote, "If I could cut the throats of about half a dozen Republican Senators, Sumner would be the first victim as by far the greatest fool of the lot." To Fessenden the association of Sumner, the professional moralist and pompous orator, with such men as "Beast" Butler and the vindictive Thaddeus Stevens in the impeachment was an indecency.

The impeachment failed because Chief Justice Chase, who presided, and a mere seven Republican senators who deserted their party, insisted that it was a trial under the Constitution for committed crime, the only legal ground, not a political condemnation of the style of the French Revolution. It was to Fessenden the other senators turned for guidance. In language a Maine jury could understand and all future generations ought to understand, he spoke, "If the President was impeached for general cussedness, there would be no difficulty in the case. That, however, is not the case. Whatever I may think and feel as a politician, I cannot and will not violate my oath."

Fessenden's life was threatened. Mass meetings were held in Maine and he was bombarded with letters from constituents promising everlasting hate and political death. By the accident of alphabet he was the first of the Republican senators called who might refuse to vote with the majority. "Mr. Senator Fessenden, how say you? Is the respondent, Andrew Johnson, President of the United States, guilty or not guilty of the high misdemeanor as charged in this article?"

When Fessenden, leader of the recalcitrant minority, rose and spoke in a high, clear voice "Not guilty," it was all up with the impeachment.

POWER SHIFT

*I*n 1876 hardly anyone thought the election would be close. It was time for the Republicans to go. General Grant was completing the most scandalous administration in American history—till then. He would gladly have accepted a third term. But the Republican party dared not take the risk. Grant was captain of a disabled pirate ship. The Credit Mobilier had involved more than one congressman in bribery charges. Jay Gould and Jim Fisk, perpetrators of the Gold Conspiracy, had bribed Cabinet officers. The great railroads, stretching their tracks endlessly over new country, fighting like wildcats for rate advantages, were routinely paying off legislators.

So in 1876 the pirate crew made the captain walk the plank. Almost literally they took him down to the dock and dumped him in the harbor. Even as his successor entered the White House General Grant sailed for Europe, there to stay for several years, out of reach of questioners.

General Grant was a total embarrassment to the Republican party. Something drastic had to be done to make the party acceptable to the respectable middle class of voters—but not too drastic. The powers within the party, the money interests and the elected officials they backed, had no intention of letting go the reins.

So Rutherford B. Hayes was picked. Even his name inspired confidence. He was no Tom, Dick or Harry. Rutherford, a sound family name, coupled with Hayes, another, appealed to the Victorian sense of propriety. And Hayes was a proper man. No breath of scandal had ever stirred a hair of his head. In the back rooms they called him "Old Granny." "Lemonade Lucy"

was his wife, a teetotaler. Prayers and cold water were the
family fare in the midst of a gilded age.

Rutherford may have been henpecked. But henpecked men
are notoriously reliable. In addition he had been a brave soldier
of the Civil War, a general, a congressman and a governor of
Ohio. His public record was clean, his views liberal and high-
minded and he had an excellent reputation for running the
machinery of politics and accepting sensibly its less than perfect
product.

To oppose him the Democrats chose Samuel Tilden, a lion of
reform. Every paragraph of their platform began with the
words "Reform is necessary." Tilden was Governor of New
York, and he was indeed a lion who had cleaned up Tammany
Hall and sent Boss Tweed to jail—and incidentally made enemies among the less law-abiding classes, not just Bowery
roughs but a good many men who wore tall silk hats to work.
The only trouble with Tilden was that he was a tired lion. His
political hide was full of the holes and scars of many battles. He
had been a shrewd, as well as honest, corporation lawyer and
accumulated a large fortune. At the age of sixty-two, loaded
with credits, with honors, with money, he was a calm candidate.

Tilden was like a lion roaring in a forest populated by nothing but small animals. The big ones were in jail or about to
take the boat. When he roared of reform and reminded people
of the innumerable scandals of the administration, they hurried
on about their own money business or just paused to yawn.
And for the last time, with effect, the Republicans waved the
bloody shirt, "Every man that shot Union soldiers was a
Democrat."

The public was indifferent, the lion was tired, but yet he
roared to some purpose. When the votes were counted Tilden
had 250,000 more than Hayes and more than enough electoral
votes, assuming that the disputed electoral votes of four states
went to him. If they went the other way, Hayes would win by
one electoral vote. The dispute was settled by a lopsided Elec-

toral Commission set up by the Congress, eight Republicans and five Democrats.

So Hayes became President, although there is no doubt that Tilden was elected. Just what deals were made is not completely known. An essential part of the deal was an agreement that no further serious attempt would be made to enforce the 14th and 15th amendments that guaranteed civil rights to all Americans.

Which of the two men actually became President probably made little difference. The country was set on a course of shameless exploitation of natural resources and of the human resources of a great tide of immigration. No President would be strong enough and no electorate would want the executive arm to be strong enough to alter this condition to any substantial degree for nearly two generations.

What changed in 1876 was the balance of power in the United States. Congress would take over the management of the nation. A seat in the Senate, held for a lifetime, would be of more value, reckoned in terms of money and power, than the White House. The Speaker of the House would become more powerful than the President. The same process began again in 1976 with the election of Jimmy Carter. When the shouting died it was discovered that it made little difference which party was in power, the Democrats or the Republicans. The will of the nation was in paralysis, pulled to a standstill by contrary special interests, each striving for more than its share of the national wealth.

TRANSITIONS

*W*ars begin with a shock, a moment of unbelief followed by exhausting effort sustained by heroism and despair. Peace happens silently, unknown to the dead, unnoticed by the living as they move from the necessities of shared peril towards the options of individual choice.

In the United States these transitions are measured by elections. Elections are little wars. In time of great wars the little wars become very little indeed. Change of government is too big a risk. But when military tensions relax, domestic and local tensions increase. The measure of the peace can be gauged by the quality of the elections.

After the Civil War federal troops were active in the South for a dozen years. The deal that made Hayes president required the end of the effort by the North forcefully to persuade the South to change its ways. The bitter price for the practical political reunion of the nation was the sacrifice of the civil rights of the former slaves.

But what the country wanted or where it intended to go or how it intended to travel were not readily apparent. Mrs. Lightfoot Lee, heroine of *Democracy*, Henry Adams' anonymously published novel that caused a sensation in the 1880's, went to Washington to find out. She never did, although she professed pleasure in watching the wheels go round, driven by a rank steam of corruption. We who come later have a clearer view.

The Hayes' administration had been upright, almost prissy in its uprightness; dull, unpleasant smelling brass compared to the gilded, fetid corruption of Grant's. But Hayes' was not popular and the chicanery which had been so marked in the executive department moved quietly into the legislative. Hayes'

213

adminstration is memorable for no positive act of statesmanship. Socially it was remarkable—and utterly discouraging—as the first when prohibition came to the White House.

After Hayes the Republicans fell back on the inevitable magnet to attract the necessary votes to keep them in power, a general—Garfield. To charge the magnet with practical juice they chose for Vice President a notorious political boss, Chester Arthur, Collector of the Port of New York whom Hayes had removed from office. Arthur was a skillful and accomplished spoilsman. A job in the Custom House meant a regular percentage of pay contributed to the party. To outraged liberals the nomination of Arthur was the nomination of Satan, impeccably dressed, his cloven hoof hidden in a highly polished boot.

When Garfield was shot in 1881 by the mad office seeker Guiteau, President Arthur fooled everybody, especially the people who had pushed him into office. His character did not change. Rather it emerged from under the scum that had covered it, polished and urbane, even honest. Like the rising sun on a misty morning, Arthur shone slowly, in contrast to such men as Teddy Roosevelt or Lyndon Johnson who, having been put away for the duration, suddenly burst like rockets in the night from the closet of vice presidential obscurity.

Arthur shone, all 6'2" and more than 220 pounds of him, tightly got up in black frock coat, gray waistcoat and trousers, and tall silk hat. His carriage was painted dark green with fine relieving lines of red. It was drawn by two perfectly matched bay horses in silver mounted harness. At state dinners seven or eight wine glasses were set at every place. The specter of prohibition fled gibbering from the White House.

And then, to the confusion of moralists and the extreme annoyance of his supporters, Arthur gave the country at least the shadow of a reform administration. The Civil Service Act became a reality. He courageously vetoed an immense pork barrel rivers and harbors bill. And as a natural consequence, his party refused him renomination.

For twenty years after Grant's second term no President succeeded himself. It is probably much more than coincidence that federal troops withdrew from the South at the beginning of this period and the military phase of the Civil War ended. A rather similar condition began to be apparent after the Second World War. Total military involvement finally ended with the withdrawal of troops from Vietnam. Civil life resumed, unconcerned with military considerations.

There was no absolute assurance that the condition of peace that descended over America was there to stay. But there were indications. There was plenty of talk of armaments, there were ructions and troubles and interferences by great powers all over the globe. But no American soldiers were fighting.

America began to do what it had done before. It quarreled and bickered and tried to find itself. It would not let any President control its destiny without argument. Gone were the days of crisis and easy acquiescence. The aspirations and the problems of so many individuals, of so many groups, were too diverse to be solved to the satisfaction of a real majority. The post war age would be dominated by well-heeled minorities unabashed by the silent disgust of citizens too indifferent or too disillusioned to bother to vote. Special interests would fight like jackals for a share of the spoils. The democratic method would proceed on its wasteful way, only less wasteful, in the long run, than any other method.

Jimmy Carter came to office less powerful than any President since Hoover. Peace is a frame of mind unfriendly to executive power. Ambitious change, social reform, were out of fashion. He could not, nor probably would his successors for some time to come, command a real majority of the nation on any issue requiring a moral judgment as opposed to a selfish or a sectional one. Success, if any was to be achieved, would depend on the manipulative skill by which a competent Executive outwits a rambunctious Congress to achieve the impossible compromise called government for the people. The people had been fooled quite often in recent years and their mood was skeptical. The young and the old and the honest had been almost pressed to death by inflation. The individuals who seemed to ride the bubble successfully were the fast buck artists, the operators in high finance, the real estate speculators, the political wheeler-dealers. All the people had been shaken and disillusioned by the Watergate disaster and the still unexplored shadows within that melodrama. Missile gaps, missile build-ups, great societies, threats and promises, had seemed to achieve neither security nor prosperity. It would be a smart President indeed, or perhaps a very lucky one, who deserved and secured a second term in office.

WE DON'T WANT TO FIGHT
BUT BY JINGO IF WE DO

A domestic quarrel may break some china. A quarrel with the neighbors may break some heads. And quarrels usually begin with words. For this reason nations invented the language of diplomacy. Straight talk is risky.

The foreign policy of Grover Cleveland's second administration was cautious and correct. It was intended to keep the United States clear of the foreign entanglements against which George Washington had warned. Yet it was in this administration that the United States suddenly, for the first time, exercised its muscle as a world power and, escaping from the bitter financial depression of the 1890's, rushed headlong into the exuberant imperialism of the new century.

The cause was a diplomatic mistake. The result was not intended. No one, apparently, was more surprised than President Cleveland. The perpetrator of the mistake was a hard-boiled Boston lawyer not generally considered naive. The most reasonable explanation of the Venezuelan crisis of 1895, the long shadow thrown ahead of the First World War, is that it came about through an almost subconscious need to distract the nation from financial panic, foreclosure of loans and the desperate Pullman strike.

Whatever the explanation, the Venezuelan crisis of Cleveland's second term remains one of the finest examples on record of how not to conduct foreign relations. A war impossible to justify between natural allies was avoided by inches. Germany was encouraged to hasten on a disaster course. The wise and equitable Monroe Doctrine was stretched into an imperialist umbrella. South America was alarmed by the distant thunder of gunboat diplomacy. And the merchants of prejudice, jingo politicians and jingo press, takers-up of the white man's burden, were shown a glorious field for operations.

By accident of the death of the incumbent, Richard Olney had become Secretary of State, moving from the office of Attorney General. He was reputed to be "the worst tempered man in Boston." That probably was going too far. When his temper was under control he was urbane, highly intelligent, a good talker and host. But an unfortunate cow that walked on his tennis court was summarily shot and he indulged in a lifelong quarrel with one of his children whose marriage displeased him. Domestic tyranny was rather fashionable in those days.

Olney shared a pervasive intellectual error of his age, Social Darwinism. This simple theory held that the perfection of mankind was to be achieved by the survival of the "fittest." Since sharks and black ants were good at survival, their ways were worth studying, perhaps imitating. Anyway, combat was the key. Olney was a scrapper by nature, by training and by conviction. He was a "strict constructionist." He took the lead in breaking the Pullman strike, almost inventing capital's new weapon, the injunction.

Foreign relations had gone into eclipse since the Civil War. The nation, hurrying westward, had forgotten about Europe except to borrow money there. Europe was our banker and about as popular as bankers usually are when debts are pressing. And Olney was probably no worse prepared for his new job than most of his recent predecessors. He spoke no foreign language, his preferred reading was the *Boston Transcript* and he had, twenty years before, made a short vacation trip to the British Isles and had once gone to Paris for a few days on business.

On his desk when he came into office as Secretary of State was the Venezuelan boundary dispute which had lain simmering for half a century. He checked the map to be sure where Venezuela was, and also Guiana, a good chunk of which Venezuela's current dictator was claiming from Britain. Then he sat down and wrote a note to the British Foreign Minister in London. It was perhaps the most remarkable note in American diplomatic history, very probably the worst phrased and worst reasoned. For Olney, except for the ugly temper it revealed, it was not characteristic. A good lawyer even with a strong case does not use loose language. Perhaps it was the heat of Washington in July and the threat of populism and free silver that drove his pen.

He began by breaking the first rule of diplomacy. He began with an ultimatum. The note must be answered by a certain date or else! That "else!" is all very well if you are Bismarck armed to the teeth doctoring a telegram with the deliberate purpose of provoking war. But the United States was completely unprepared and its fleet was no match for the British. Neither did it have any real conflicting interest with the British.

Then Olney sounded forth on a tin trumpet. "Today the United States is practically sovereign on this continent and its fiat is law upon the subjects to which it confines its interposition." The rest of the note was twelve thousand words of bad history, bad law, bombastic language and bad manners. Cleveland, honest, forthright, stubborn, not a man noted for considering the ultimate consequences of any action, applauded. "It's the best thing of the kind I have ever read."

The British government yawned and failed to reply within the stated time. When it did, it flatly rejected the American position. Cleveland and Olney were furious. They were not prepared to acknowledge any part of a blunder. They had to choose between temporizing, which, events having gone already so far, would certainly lose the Democrats the next election, or rushing headlong into the breakers. They chose to rush, strapping on a life jacket as they went.

A message to Congress was written, almost but not quite asking for a declaration of war. It suggested, however, a loophole, that useful way out, a commission to investigate. Wall Street panicked. Teddy Roosevelt cheered, "If there is a muss I shall try to have a hand in it myself. They'll have to employ a lot of men just as green as I am for the conquest of Canada." And the Kaiser sent off a friendly telegram to the Boers in

South Africa which was a sharp warning to the world of the insane ambitions of imperial Germany.

When the British government woke up to what was happening, that the big boy on the other side of the water was on the brink and about to tumble in, and that Germany was shaking a mailed fist, it drew back. Fortunately the British Ambassador in Washington, Sir Julian Pauncefote, was as ept as his opposite number in London, American Ambassador Bayard, was inept. With Talleyrand skill, he flattered the principals and smoothed the issues.

Teddy Roosevelt had to wait three years for his war and be content to charge up a hill in Cuba instead of conquering Canada. Cleveland, a man of strong character, though of limited view, managed to control Congress in spite of that new force in politics, "yellow" journalism. The direction of foreign policy would not be taken over by popular clamor and headlines till the advent of the amiable and prayerful McKinley with the jellyfish spine.

Since, the world has been obliged to live with confrontation and disaster. There is no cheaper way to buy votes than by tough talk in the international theater. But the careful language of diplomacy, often forgotten, then painfully relearned, is the language of civilization. In Cleveland's day nations had only navies to throw at one another. Now they have atomic bombs.

REMEMBER THE MAINE

*I*f enough trouble is stored in one box, it needs not even Pandora to open it. It will blow off its own lid. When the battleship *Maine* steamed into Havana harbor in 1898 it stuffed one box to bursting. Spontaneous combustion did the rest.

The political world was packed for an explosion. So were the coal bunkers of the *Maine*. It is now substantially proved that no evil conspiracy blew up the *Maine*. There is very little doubt that she blew up because of bad design and the negligence of her command. And the United States engaged in an unnecessary war for no reason at all. The consequence of that war was to veer the Great Republic off course and into the shoals and narrows of imperialism.

The island of Cuba had been in a state of revolution for three years. The empire of Spain had been in the process of dissolution for three hundred. The natural course of events indicated was the immediate establishment of an autonomous government for the island, attached to Spain but not controlled by it. Imagination suggested independence as the next probable and desirable step. Thereafter perhaps union with the United States might be arranged by common consent of both countries, for the advantage of both and for the promotion of peace and prosperity in the Caribbean.

Such a gradual solution might have been more comfortable for the world. It might have saved the United States from the Philippines adventure and the impossible task of reconciling the Declaration of Independence with American imperialism. It seemed the probable solution as the *Maine* resumed the custom of a winter courtesy call by the United States navy at the chief port of the Caribbean. At the same time the Spanish cruiser

Vizcaya was on its way across the Atlantic to pay a similar courtesy call at the port of New York.

Unknown to the world was a secret telegram sent off just previously by the American Consul in Havana, Fitzhugh Lee. Lee was a large man, always dressed in a white suit and wide-brimmed panama hat, who spoke no Spanish. He was an alumnus of Harvard, had been a Confederate cavalry general, Governor of Virginia and was a nephew of the famous Robert E. Lee. He was also short of funds and had a very strong interest in acquiring a franchise to build street railways in Havana.

Lee's telegram used a code word that signified help was needed, American lives and property were in danger. Why Lee sent his telegram when he sent it has not been satisfactorily explained. There had been a riot around a newspaper office that was advocating separation from Spain. But things had calmed down. The Spanish government in Madrid, moving with unaccustomed speed, was preparing to grant the demands of the insurgents. The Spanish general, "Butcher" Weyler, whose administration had been repugnant to Cubans and Americans alike, had been recalled. Good news filled the headlines. An armistice with the rebels was about to be signed. Concentration camp practices were all abandoned. And Lee had barely sent his telegram when he sent another urging delay in the *Maine*'s visit.

But the irreversible machinery of bureaucracy was in motion. The *Maine* was at sea. On the morning of January 25, 1898, she appeared at full speed off Havana streaming clouds of black smoke, the ensign of the United States hoisted at the peak, the Union Jack at the foremast head. This was the signal for a pilot. Soon the *Maine*, crew at general quarters in smart blue uniforms, the officers in frock coats, was passing old vine-grown Morro Castle. Crowds thronged wharves and buildings as she picked up a buoy in the anchorage reserved for vessels of war, between the Spanish cruiser *Alfonso XII* and the square-rigged German training ship *Gniesenau*.

For ten days the *Maine* lay quietly at anchor. Every precaution was taken to prevent incident. The crew was not permitted shore leave. And Captain Sigsbee made punctilious calls on Spanish officials and entertained representatives of the top Spanish society aboard his ship. Relations became more than courteous. They became friendly. Captain Sigsbee went to the bullfight with the Spanish commander. The officers began to make shore visits.

Then the *Maine* blew up. It was early in a hot dark night, no breath of air stirring. There was a bursting, rending and crashing roar of immense volume followed by a succession of heavy, ominous metallic sounds as the superstructure overturned and fell and the whole forward part of the vessel sank. The afterpart sank gradually to the muddy bottom leaving some of the deck above the water. Two-thirds of the crew, 255 men, were killed. The Captain and all but two of his officers, being in the aftersection of the ship, survived.

The whole world cried out "Why?" The Spanish authorities had everything to lose by such a disaster. The rebels could gain nothing but American intervention, which they did not want, any more than George Washington would have wanted the French to take over the American Revolution after Yorktown.

Theodore Roosevelt was sure he knew why. "The *Maine* was sunk by an act of dirty treachery," he wrote. The press was even more explicit, showing pictures of just how the job was done, complete with diagrams of the wiring of a submerged mine. An American seaman arrived in New York with a block of cement as tangible proof. Fitzhugh Lee was content to place responsibility on "unknown conspirators."

What the U.S. Navy had to lose was reputation. Who was negligent, American seamen or decadent Spaniards? The American court of inquiry concluded that the *Maine* was blown up from without, the Spanish court that she was destroyed from within. Admiral Rickover, in an exhaustive review of the evidence published by the Naval History Division of the U.S. Navy, agrees with the Spanish. The salient fact is that the coal bunkers of the *Maine* were divided from the powder magazines by one-half inch of sheet steel. Spontaneous combustion was a known hazard on coal-carrying vessels and to prevent it required a degree of attention greater than the ship's complement on the *Maine* was in the habit of giving.

Neither President McKinley nor his Cabinet nor the business interests that had put him in office wanted war. American demands were being met and McKinley knew it. But war fever was in the air and McKinley feared for his popularity and his re-election. Roosevelt, clamoring for war, burst out, "The President has no more backbone than a chocolate eclair." Roosevelt was right. McKinley had no backbone. So he gave in to the clamorers, after some weeks of squeezing, as a tube of toothpaste gives in, sending a long and soggy message to Congress made up of platitudes and half truths. Congress took over and war was declared.

The simple world of Theodore Roosevelt and William McKinley has disappeared in a heap of rubble. These honest Americans understood no more than the vainglorious Kaiser or the sophisticated French and English general staffs of the impersonal thrust of science, the force within the atom. But no longer can mankind plead ignorance. Two world wars have provided experience. Yet governments persist in the *Maine* mistake and stubbornly continue to place too much high explosive too close to too much heat.

DEFIANCE OF THE LAW OF GRAVITY

*G*eography determined that the destiny of Cuba should be closely tied to that of the United States; Old World imperialism that it should be separate and not equal.

The great object of American policy towards Cuba as far back as the first administration of Thomas Jefferson was to keep the island out of dangerous and unfriendly hands. In the second administration of Dwight Eisenhower the catastrophe avoided for nearly two centuries occurred. The island fell under the domination of the dangerous and unfriendly imperialism of Russia. Vesuvius erupted and the destruction of American policy was as complete as of Pompeii. Much can be learned by digging into the ruins.

The influence of North America was felt on the island of Cuba for the first time in 1762, the second year of the reign of the young and popular King George III. It was felt keenly and abruptly, much as an oyster feels the point of the opening knife. A British fleet arrived off Havana and after siege and assault subdued it. The leaders of the expedition, Lord Albemarle and his two brothers, immediately secured all the available treasure in gold, sugar and other portable goods, worth about 40 million in modern dollars. Their personal fair share, according to the customary method of division of loot in that age, was 10 million. Then they opened the harbor to general trade.

Within a year at least 700 merchant ships entered the harbor where before, under Spanish rule, the number had been never more than 15. The goods they carried were eagerly snapped up by the Spanish colonials and there was general satisfaction in the increase in the number of slaves for purchase.

A New Nation

The mood of triumphant Britain was exultant. Wolfe and Montcalm had fought their epic battle on the plains of Abraham. Canada was now part of the American colonies. Cuba, pearl of the Antilles, lay in the palm of Britain's hand. The way was opening to Spanish Florida and the Gulf.

Benjamin Franklin, the wisest man on two continents, wrote to his friend, the famous evangelical preacher George Whitefield, that reasonable peace was assured, "if John Bull does not get drunk with victory, double his Fists and bid all the world kiss his Arse."

John Bull did just that. The utter ineptitude of British home politics drove America to revolt. Cuba went back into the hands of Spain. But the Yankees stayed, as traders and carriers, too important to be eliminated by any effort to revive the old Spanish imperial system of closed monopoly. The economy of Cuba plunged profitably forward on a fatal course towards a single product, sugar. Any effort at diversification of crops was given up. Food was imported. By the 1820's when James Monroe was President and the Spanish Empire was beginning to break up and the liberation movement was rushing ahead in South America, Cuba had become the richest colony and the largest sugar producer in the world.

President Jefferson had tried unsuccessfully to buy Cuba. Thereafter the annexation of Cuba had been a topic of conversation at the White House, present at the breakfast table as regularly as sugar in the coffee. Now J.Q. Adams, Secretary of State to Monroe, wrote to the American Minister in Spain, "It is scarcely possible to resist the conviction that the annexation of Cuba to our Federal Republic will be indispensible to the continuance and integrity of the Union itself. There are laws of political as well as physical gravitation. Cuba, forcibly disjoined from its own unnatural connection with Spain, and incapable of self support, can gravitate only toward the North American Union which by the same law of nature cannot cast her off from its bosom."

But the politics of empire intervened. England, cured of its age-old habit of hating Spain by the necessities of the Napoleonic wars, had developed a keen distrust of France and Russia. And England's fleets dominated the oceans. So the Monroe administration settled for a very famous compromise, that later generations would know as the Monroe Doctrine. Calhoun, the Southern fire-eater and Secretary of War, was for taking Cuba by force, which he insisted was the policy recommended by Jefferson. But Adams was skeptical. England would object. Why not instead use the jealousy of England to ward off the ambitions in the new world of Russia and France? And in the background of everyone's mind was the dread question of slavery. If Cuba were annexed, it would be as a slave state.

So Cuba was left to suffer miserably in the death grasp of Spain. On an island occupied by more slaves than masters, independence was a dangerous course. The rest of Spanish America broke its ties with Europe, and they were never successfully rejoined. Revolution had its way. It was a great triumph for United States diplomacy. Without having anything like the military strength to enforce it, the United States established the principle that henceforth the Western hemisphere must be let alone by all foreign powers to find its own salvation by purgatories of its own choosing.

The plan worked. It saved the Americas from the more violent forms of exploitation. It shielded them from the two world wars that came after. But it required a sad sacrifice of the people of Cuba. Slavery continued there for a full generation after Lincoln proclaimed emancipation. Then contract labor, the importation of Chinese at low wages, perpetuated the evil. And independence at last from Spain brought even more dependence on the sugar industry. Political independence did not bring freedom from want, from ignorance, from a caste system as old as the Spanish Empire.

Neither American good intentions nor laissez-faire capitalism could make up the gap. The Second World War messed up Franklin Roosevelt's plans for a good neighborhood in the Caribbean. And capitalism has an unfortunate affinity for "strong" governments. Perhaps some of Ben Franklin's advice, had it been heeded in the 1940's by a nation drunk with victory, believing itself all powerful, as well as all enlightened, could have discovered a way to solve the Cuban dilemma.

It was not solved. Cuba fell under the influence of a foreign power not friendly to the United States. But the friendship of Russia left Cuba still in a state of dependency. The opportunity for the United States will always lie in restoring the balance, helping the Cuban people to achieve real equality with the people of the rest of the world and especially of the United States; letting bygones be bygones. It is imaginable that Cuba may yet become part of the North American Union. The courses of history are not inevitable. Geography is fixed, giving certain tendencies to the interests of peoples. History is fluid. Its direction can be changed by wise, even magnanimous policies. The natural state of relations between Cuba and the United States is friendly. Free trade has never failed to benefit both countries. So have friendly diplomatic exchanges.

OF RIGHT OUGHT TO BE FREE
AND INDEPENDENT

*C*uba and the United States were born to be friends. Friends are born, not made. Millions pass one another every day with a "good morning" or a "good night" and forever part as strangers. Then two strangers, perhaps strangers speaking not even the same language, drawn by invisible force, meet as friends and so remain. Nations do likewise. Interests in common, aspirations shared, are magnets which cannot be denied. The barriers men and circumstances impose are but temporary impediments which time sometimes violently, sometimes silently, dissolves. For a thousand years Scots and English fought savagely, then merged and became Great Britain by the unlikely expedient of England accepting as King the son of its late Queen's worst enemy.

Whether a grandson of Castro, having gone democratic, will some day be elected President of the United States, or whether there will be some other equally improbable conclusion of difficulties, is time's conundrum. But it is a probability that verges on certainty that the domination of the affairs of the beautiful demi-continent by remote Russia will end at last at the insistence of the Cuban people. Revolutions that import foreign masters lose popularity. The rest is best left to nature and nature's God. This is especially true when direct interference, as by the United States, in the affairs of its nearest neighbors, must inevitably be construed as a still worse, because closer at hand, sort of imperialism. So it was a wise policy that guided the action, and the inaction, of Secretary of State Seward and President Lincoln during the most serious crisis the United States has ever known. It is unfortunate that similar wisdom has not always guided their successors in office.

The crisis came in the winter of 1862-63. That monumental ox of stupidity, General Burnside, famous only for his whiskers, had managed to lose 13,000 men storming the impregnable Confederate position at Fredericksburg. "It is well that war is so terrible," said General Lee watching the slaughter, "or we should grow too fond of it."

Battle failure brought on an attempt by radical Republicans in the Senate, sparked by Charles Sumner, to forcibly change the administration by pulling down Lincoln and his Cabinet, beginning with Seward. Lincoln, "by great tact, shrewdness and ability," as an eyewitness observed, succeeded in splitting the hostile cabal. But deep scars remained. Soon after, Napoleon III, Emperor of the French, offered to mediate a peace, with the clear intention of establishing the Confederacy and furthering French ambitions in Mexico. The sky seemed dark indeed, but Seward perceived an opportunity. He believed Britain was suspicious of France, not too eager to go adventuring in such company. Without the British navy the French could not do much. So he took the risk of writing a blistering reply to Napoleon's offer, "Peace proposed at the cost of dissolution of the nation would be immediately, unreservedly, and indignantly rejected by the American people."

The result, with a little help from Editor Raymond of the *New York Times,* was to raise Seward's popularity and buck up the administration. But Napoleon III went right ahead with his plans. A month before the battle of Gettysburg, he landed French troops in Mexico. They met unexpected resistance. In Juarez, a full-blooded Indian, a true native son and the President of a legitimately elected government, the Mexicans were about to find a genuine patriot. But his troops were not a match for professionals on open ground. The French army, taking Mexico City and making collaborators of the minority Clerical party, issued a manifesto proclaiming Mexico an empire and began to feed supplies to the Confederacy.

An Emperor had been already picked. He was a decent man, but not very strong in the head, Maximilian, younger brother of Franz Josef, Emperor of Austria. He had qualms about tak-

ing the job. But being assured—falsely—of the great desire of
the Mexicans for his services, he accepted. He was strongly
urged to go by his ambitious and lovely wife, Carlotta, daughter of the King of the Belgians.

So this strange shipload of royal blood arrived out of the
medieval past to set back the new world clock. It was bristling-
ly surrounded by 30,000 French bayonets and solidly supported by many chests of French gold. It was an obvious threat to
the United States. It was a flagrant challenge to the Monroe
Doctrine. And the United States, in the midst of civil war, could
do nothing about it.

So Seward set about doing nothing with consummate skill.
He explained to the French government that friendship with
the people of France was the first desire of the American people
but. . . He pointed out that the United States could not look
with indifference on any armed intervention for political ends
in a country so close as Mexico. From Paris the American Minister wrote back, "Your dispatch on Mexico breaks no eggs. It
makes a record." A record was all that Seward dared to make.

Seward counted on the Mexican people. And he was right.
There is a natural tendency to resist foreign domination. It may
take a long time, but always it is there. Juarez represented the
true Mexico, the people who cared about independence in the
American sense. And the unfortunate Maximilian played into
his hands. He lost the support of the reactionaries by refusing
to restore their property. And the support of the people he
never had, except a few who thought he was the reincarnation
of an ancient Aztec god because he had a fair skin and a blonde
beard.

After Appomattox, the American press and the American
Congress were all for throwing Maximilian out bodily. Grant
gave his general, Schofield, a year's leave of absence with instructions to cross the border into Mexico, join Juarez and organize a foreign legion of discharged Union soldiers to march
south and fight the usurper.

Seward frustrated this scheme by an adroit coup. He managed a private meeting with General Schofield and persuaded

the tired veteran, with the help of good wine and cigars, that he was needed much more as a diplomat in Paris than as a soldier on campaign. He said with a perfectly straight face, "I want you to get your legs under Napoleon's dinner table and tell him he must get out of Mexico." After carefully arranged delays, Schofield did go to Paris and he did attend glittering diplomatic dinners. He had the impression of being immensely useful, even while others were talking French. Thus diplomacy was kept in the hands of diplomats and the General was kept out of trouble.

To persuade the French to leave Mexico, hints, not war, were all that were necessary. A fight was brewing in Europe between France and Germany. Suddenly word came that Napoleon was withdrawing his troops. Poor Maximilian was unbelieving. To the French commander he said, "Your Emperor, offering his hand as guarantee of his words, promised me his support for five years. I cannot believe that he has forgotten this." The Frenchman could only bow his head in silence.

Frantically Empress Carlotta took ship, rushed to France to plead with Napoleon. He gave her a cold refusal. She fled to the Pope. He could offer no help. She fell down insensible and never recovered her reason. The French troops left Mexico. The patriot army came down from the north. The sad Emperor was captured, tried by a court martial and summarily shot.

It is the frequent end of a foreign intrusion into a land whose people passionately desire independence.

OIL AND INDEPENDENCE

*I*t will help to understand the world energy crisis, which is the newest crisis in the independence of the United States, to invent a few words. They are all created from the Greek word *megas*, meaning great and customarily translated as one million.

The first word is megadrum. It means one million barrels of oil or equivalent energy. It may be imagined in the shape of the familiar black oil drum, but vast in size, forty feet higher than Boston's Bunker Hill Monument and five times as wide at the base. Or to use another simile, it is a cylinder whose base completely covers the skin diamond of a professional ball field and whose top towers some eighteen stories above the ground. This megadrum of energy is worth twenty megabucks—a megabuck is one million dollars—or thirty or forty, or whatever higher price the Arab states care to put on it.

The measure of the dependence of the United States on the good will or good nature of foreign nations is the number of megadrums of energy it must import each day. In 1979 it was ten. The future peace of the world depends, probably more than on any other factor, on whether that number rises or falls. The security of taking refuge behind a Maginot Line of atomic weapons shuffling through underground tunnels is an illusion. The cost of testing such a system, something on the order of one hundred million lives, would mark the end of civilization, possibly of human life.

The megalife is a statistic with which sane minds are unwilling to deal. Defense on such terms is suicide. It is better to approach the problem of continuing existence and the avoidance of war in a practical way. That way begins with development of sufficient energy to satisfy the needs of all nations. And the key to that development is the United States.

Peoples go to war when they think their life is threatened. The staff of life in the last quarter of the 20th Century is oil, without which bread cannot be made nor jobs be found for all the world's workers and their dependents. And so a cut-off of the supply of oil can bring the threat of war; if continued long enough it will bring war itself.

One of the major factors that made possible the long truce after the Second World War was the superfluity of oil; or at least the assumed superfluity of oil, that let Americans waste it profligately and kept down the price of the Arab product. Change was abrupt, as historic changes are apt to be. Suddenly America was short of oil. Soon the whole world was made aware of the shortage by oil's rising price.

Bewildered by statistics, people suspected a plot. The Arabs were engaged in a conspiracy; the oil tycoons were putting up the price by holding back supply; somewhere there must be a pool of oil or pool of gas—just dig deep enough and get it; dig coal and turn it into gas; strain sunlight through quartz crystals and turn it into electricity.

Actually the situation was fairly simple and very serious. The only thing really lacking was time. There may have been plots, but they were not important. Certainly there was greed and sharp practice. Always there is when the stakes are large. But these aberrations did not alter the main facts. Oil, coal, gas and uranium produced in the United States in 1979 supplied each day twenty-eight megadrums of energy. Ten more megadrums had to be imported, double the importation of only a few years previous. So that by 1979 the real independence of the United States had been reduced by about one-third from what it had been in the very recent past. There was a crisis and it had to be met boldly and courageously and by taking risks, in the certain knowledge that there was no risk so serious as loss of independence and the attempt to recover it by war or the threat of war.

The nation could not sacrifice any part of its existing means of energy supply. In fact it needed to increase its means by every possible method, because no method of increase then conceived was going to make much difference in less than five years, probably ten or more. Something could be done at once by economy. A drastic change in the attitude of the public towards gasoline waste and unnecessary driving could save several megadrums of energy a day. The violent rise in the price of gasoline during the next two years did indeed have this effect. But the danger was acute and it was immediate. For only as the United States cut back on its requirements of Middle East oil would world tensions lessen. The peace of the world depended on the United States recovering its independence.

There is a word that John Kennedy made popular and that the world turned into a cliché to explain and to condone such a state of affairs. It is interdependence. But no society can work satisfactorily for very long when it is in the control of and at the mercy of a potentially tyrannical power, either within the state or beyond it.

The trouble in 1776 had comparatively little to do with taxes and a great deal to do with monopoly and the limitation of choice. Stamp tax, tea tax and all the rest were only symptoms of the disease. The harmony between the old country and the new was destroyed when Britain undertook to enforce a theory of empire management that required the colonies to admit their status as second class citizens. The result, since distance and the age favored it, and the habit of independence acquired over long years of colonial self-sufficiency was not easily broken, was a quick transition from the forms of monarchy within an empire to practical self-government in a democratic republic.

Captain Preston, one of the veterans of Concord fight, when an old man, answered some questions as to why he did what he did. "Never saw a stamp in my life. Never paid a penny for one. Never heard of John Locke or the eternal principles of liberty. Never read nothin' but the Bible. Young man, what we meant by goin' for those redcoats was this; we always had governed ourselves and we always meant to. They didn't mean we should."

The day after Congress voted Independence in 1776, John Adams wrote to Abigail, his wife, "You will think me transported with enthusiasm. I am not. I am well aware of the toil and blood and treasure that it will cost us to maintain this Declaration, and support and defend these States. Yet through the gloom I can see the rays of ravishing light and glory. I can see that the end is worth more than all the means."

Fifty years later, on the anniversary of the famous Declaration, he was asked by his fellow townsmen in Quincy to give a toast for the day. He answered in two words. More than one hundred and fifty years have passed since. His words are still all the words needed on the 4th of July or any other day of the year—"Independence Forever."

PILGRIMS' WAY

$\mathcal{T}$he American people are addicted to extravagance. It is a vice natural to hungry folk who arrive in a land of plenty. For Americans are a nation of immigrants from many lands come to improve their lot. Fortunately, over the centuries they have learned to cope with the strict economy which extravagance sometimes makes necessary; then move energetically and intelligently to the next step, which is to discover new sources of supply and wealth.

It is a pattern which has been often repeated since the Pilgrims landed on Cape Cod. It has little to do with ethnic origins. It has molded and shaped imported beliefs to suit its own purposes. It is in the soil and in the climate.

It happened that toward the end of the decade of the 1970's Americans were in one of their periodic hangovers from too much extravagance. They were also in the first stage of recovery; the stage of self-doubt and questioning. The stage of self-doubt was observable on the roads; a real effort was being made to save gas, there was acceptance of slower speeds, a looking askance at those who jack-rabbited when the light turned green. The questioning was a general whisper, a rustling, as of leaves in a forest at the approach of a storm. The representatives of the people in positions of trust would hear it if they had ears to hear. If they did not they would lose their jobs. A great many Americans had already lost their jobs. The colossal blunder of the managers of the automobile industry in refusing to believe that there was an oil crisis had nearly shut down the industry. A lot of Americans were cold who had never been cold before. They were suddenly face to face with the very situation which their ancestors had faced when they made the great decision to leave the old country and come to the new.

They were uncomfortable and it was time to do something about it.

The first impression of the Pilgrims on rounding Cape Cod and dropping anchor in Provincetown Harbor was one of extreme dreariness. A forest of trees, hardwoods and pine, came down almost to the water's edge, surrounded them and seemed ready to swallow them up. The gloom of the great forest and November was such to make some of them wish they had never left home. The stage was set for the great American cycle to begin. The situation could hardly have been worse.

The men went ashore to explore. The women followed with a mountain of dirty clothes to wash. There was a brackish pond just back of the beach. They filled great iron pots with water and hung them on poles over small fires. Then they began to get warm. It was a luxury only a few rich Englishmen had known since the Conquest; that few Europeans know to this day. They were common people and they were comfortable in a cold climate.

There was so much firewood lying about, under the trees dead branches and driftwood along the beaches, that they hardly troubled to cut down any trees; just gathered the stuff up and heaped it on their bonfires. Some larger logs they took in their long boat back to the *Mayflower*. They observed that all over the Cape there was black soil, the accumulated humus of ages, a foot and more thick. Innocently, they began to destroy it, taking away the protective cover. Their descendants completed the process, cutting down the last trees to boil sea water to make salt.

The quantity of easy fuel encouraged extravagance. The New England house, on the principle of the Indian wigwam, soon evolved. It was built around a huge fireplace. The improvement the newcomers added was a chimney. This carried both smoke and heat out of the house far more effectively than the Indians' hole in the roof. The ancient style of the English cottage was quickly abandoned. After one mistake, when the Pilgrims built a hotter fire than they intended, they gave up thatch in favor of shingles. Sparks from the chimney landed on the grass roof of their first Common House, burning it down just as it was finished.

From that first day with the pots on the beach at Provincetown it became an accepted principle that the cure for cold was a bigger fire. This had the added useful effect of clearing the land for cultivation. It also cleared the land of Indians, who moved away as the wild game fled before the white man's axe.

It took barely a century to convert every river valley and level bit of upland in Massachusetts into cornfields and pasture. The Cape, stripped of trees, became a sand heap. By the time of the Revolution the Rev. William Emerson could stand at the window of the Old Manse and watch the fight at Concord Bridge. Between the village and the river no trees were standing. Another fifty years and the voracious fuel seekers were climbing the rocky south slopes of Walden Pond. "At least they can't cut down the clouds," wrote Henry Thoreau. To supply the fireplaces of the students at Harvard, benefactors willed tracts of woodlands in Maine. Wood schooners from the Penobscot were a common sight sailing up the Charles with the tide.

Necessity began to curb extravagance. Ingenuity began to contrive solutions. A country that had got used to the idea of being warm in winter was not going to give up the habit easily. Ben Franklin invented his stove. Now a lot less heat went up the chimney. Thin walls of wood were doubled; plaster was added for insulation. Storm windows were put up in winter. Then came the central furnace and imported coal, oil and gas. The cycle was complete. New England was dependent for its comfort on economy of resources and trading its manufactures and skills for heat. The grass, the bushes, the trees, began to grow again on Cape Cod. Perhaps in another thousand or two thousand years the black soil the Pilgrims found will have again accumulated.

By 1980 the country was dependent for its comfort, possibly for its life, on fuel brought in from beyond its borders. Time had to be captured to find new solutions. The American people had the future firmly under their right foot. If they pressed down on the accelerator the price of oil would rise, the skies would darken and there would be a storm brewing over the Middle East. If instead they let up a little on the right foot and threw out the clutch and coasted when they could, took the bus and shipped by train, the price of oil would fall. The standard of living would rise in the overpopulated and less prosperous parts of the world. Birth rates would fall and population would come into balance with the means of subsistence. And the United States would benefit as new markets opened up for its products.

The decision would be made by the American people, each as an individual. If he and she decided to become a nation of left-footed drivers, quick on the clutch and light on the gas, they would save a megadrum of oil tomorrow and within a year or two they would be saving two or three each day. They would insulate their houses, insulate their bodies with new and scientifically designed clothing suitable to cold weather, and save many a megadrum of oil formerly radiated to outer space.

Above all they would experiment and question and demand answers of their suppliers of the necessities and the comforts of life. The patter of the advertising man sounds hollow to the hearer bundled in blankets in front of the television. They would insist on driving gas-economical cars and would buy them abroad if they could not buy them domestically. They would remind their representatives in city halls, in statehouses and in Congress, at first gently with ballots, at last with marches and maybe rioting in the streets, to profit by the example of George III. One nation indivisible cannot tolerate a condition of freezing in the cities or of dying of thirst in the sunbelt; of roads choked with traffic because trains and busses do not run. War to capture or control the last pool of oil on a plundered planet is no solution. Neither is it a solution to waste the energy in the next to last drop of oil. Alternative ways are better and the American way is to find them.

PEOPLE CAN LEARN

*T*he nuclear accident at Three Mile Island may prove to have been one of the most fortunate accidents in human experience. The world was warned of danger. The rational advocates of nuclear power were put on their mettle to prove that it could be made safe. The rational opponents received their mandate to scrutinize and continue to scrutinize the quality of the proof.

Safety is always the second thought of mankind. The 19th Century played with the new energy resource of steam with reckless disregard of its social consequences. The 20th experimented more cautiously with nuclear power. Perhaps mankind had learned something. The cumulative frightfulness of railroad accidents makes later generations amazed that it took so long for public opinion to insist on obvious remedies. The passion for fast and cheap transportation ran far ahead of common sense.

The first railway in America was built in Quincy in 1826 to carry granite to Bunker Hill. It proved that one pair of horses could move a load of forty tons along rails. It also proved that railways could be dangerous. For the idea of using steam as a motive force having seized the imagination of the world, a party of men interested in a line from Boston to Providence came to inspect the granite road. At one end was a steep grade, up which cars were dragged by ropes. The ropes broke, the cars ran away, the passengers were hurled out and Mr. Gibson, a well-known Boston financier, was killed.

So the dishonor of the first American railway accident belongs to Massachusetts, as well as the honor of the first railway. Soon after, in South Carolina, there was proof that steam, too, could be dangerous. A strange contraption, called "Best

Friend," a locomotive with a vertical boiler looking like a gigantic bottle, was put on rails and made several trips. Then the fireman, annoyed by escaping steam from the safety valve, tightened it down and sat on it.

The interest of the general public in safety ranged from negligible to non-existent. But the death of Mr. Gibson impressed his fellow entrepreneurs. The way to Providence was made level across the famous stone viaduct at Canton and the principle of railroads at a uniform grade was universally adopted as a result of the accident.

The death of the fireman made less impression. The Emancipation Proclamation was far in the future and the loss of an expensive locomotive was more serious than the loss of a human chattel. But even in the North the safety of the worker was not much considered. Railroad passengers might sue for negligence and enough negligence in the hands of a shrewd lawyer could bankrupt a road. But a worker was expected to assume the risks of his job with the pay it gave him.

This concept was nailed down at the beginning of the railroad age by a famous decision of Massachusetts' Chief Justice Shaw. Nicholas Farwell, an engineer on the Boston and Worcester road, lost a hand because of the negligence of a switchman. The management was "distressed" and offered to pay his medical expenses and give him $500. Farwell sued and his suit was denied. Because, said the court, since safety depended on the good conduct of fellow employees, any neglect of duty would be most quickly noticed and corrected by those doing the work. "By these means, the safety of each will be much more effectually secured than could be done by a resort to the common employer for indemnity."

Such reasoning did not seem absurd to a generation that conceived of a railroad system as a train of stagecoaches pulled by an unusually strong horse. Cars were coupled together by the "death dealing link and pin." Brakes were operated by hand. On freights the brakemen ran along the tops of cars, in constant danger of bridges. The air brake began to reduce the hazards on passenger cars a decade after the Civil War. But it was more than sixty years after the opening of the granite road, when the cost of the new brake had dropped to fifty dollars per car, that public opinion demanded that "at such a price it is time to put an end to the human sacrifices due to the exposure of men upon the tops of freight cars."

The law dragged its feet. Legislatures stumbled. The first worry of management was to keep financially afloat. Safety was nobody's business. Trainmen and public took their chances. Till the Revere, Massachusetts, disaster.

It was a muggy August evening in 1871. Fog was drifting in over the marshes, thickening the dark. At Revere a long train of cars loaded with beach excursionists was just pulling out. In the last car a young man standing in the aisle was laughing and chatting with four girls. Suddenly the dim-lit car was filled with a fearful glare. The young man turned. The look of horror on his face was all that one of the surviving passengers remembered as the Portland Express plowed right through the car.

This accident ended the era of indifference. Several years earlier the Governor had appointed three intelligent men to study railroad problems, from financing to safety; "a sort of lens by which the otherwise scattered rays of public opinion could be brought to bear upon a given point." After the Revere disaster the Massachusetts Railroad Commission wrote a remarkable report. It opened a new epoch in railroading; that period when a person was safer in a railroad car than in a bathtub at home.

The public hearings were sensational. Wendell Phillips, somewhat out of a job since Emancipation had made abolitionist fervor unnecessary, urged a general indictment for murder. Fortunately the Commission kept cool and dug out the facts. No one person, no single group, could be held entirely responsible. The conductor had not looked at his watch. The dispatchers had lost all track of the trains. The guards made wrong signals with lanterns too dim. The Express had bad brakes. The cars were wood and telescoped. The kerosene lamps in the cars started fires. Fire, burst boilers and escaping steam killed or maimed nearly 100 people.

The remedies were all at hand; more responsible management, automatic air brakes, no more oil lamps, a block system of track control, telegraphic communication, powerful warning lights, steel cars so coupled they could not telescope, inspection that did not sleep. All that was required was to use them. Public indignation forced the issue. Legislatures acted. Elected executives forced compliance with laws. Railroad commissions, with careful and perceptive reports, showed the way.

During the twenty years that followed the Revere disaster an extraordinary reform in railroad management occurred. Safety became a major concern. The paying passengers were the first to benefit. The law has always favored those endowed with economic wallop. The workers of the system came next, with the concept that the safety of a brakeman on top of a moving car was more than a simple money transaction where a hired man staked his life against a day's wages. The apogee was reached when the misdemeanorly intruding public, trespassers on the railroad's right-of-way, were included. The report of the Massachusetts Railroad Commission for 1889 stated: "If there is a remedy for the slaughter—if people can be prevented from falling a victim to their own imprudence on railroad tracks— then to allow the slaughter to continue savors more of barbarism than civilization."

The age of steam began in thoughtless eagerness to exploit a source of seemingly unlimited power as fast as possible. The apparent benefits were enormous, plain to see. Let doubters stand aside or be run over! The atomic age began in fear; in a mushroom cloud that darkened the prospect of all future life. Yet as a civilization more and more dominated by science and industry hurried towards the 21st Century, the exhaustion of fossil fuels within forseeable time became a certainty. Alternatives must be found. Doubtless they would be, if mankind tried hard enough. If that alternative included nuclear power it must be made safe. That was the first obligation of government. No government could stand that did not place safety first.

THE SWITCH THAT WORKED
AND THE BRIDGE THAT BROKE

*T*he world was halfway through the age of steam before it realized that it was in the midst of a scene of carnage of its own making. The atomic age began with such a scene. But when man made his first grand effort to master the forces of nature, the terrors crept on him unawares.

Before that only those who had gone down to the sea in ships brought back a firsthand impression of what nature could do when it let loose on those brave enough to try to conquer it. Samson had demonstrated the possibilities of kinetic energy when he pulled down the pillars of the temple and the roof fell on the Philistines. And nobody knows who first burned his fingers to make fire the servant of man. But the generality of mankind never experienced the blind terror of man-released force till it met it at a railroad crossing. When the Portland Express tore into the rear of the train of cars loaded with summer excursionists at Revere in 1871, it began to dawn on people that they might be preparing their own funeral.

All at once the public interest began to do something about safety. The highly intelligent Massachusetts Railroad Commission pointed out that inventors had a great many answers to problems other inventors had made. The loose coupling of cars could be controlled by the use of Ezra Miller's ingenious device that applied both compression and tension to create a train that would not telescope if suddenly stopped. George Westinghouse's automatic air brakes were available. There were even possibilities, such as electricity and low pressure steam, which could eliminate the lethal oil lamp and fiery stove that turned any crashed car into a holocaust.

But the second stage of safety is the hardest. The first depends on the skill of engineers, the ingenuity of inventors; the second on the uncertainties of human reaction in a crisis; on careful training to do the right thing at the right time; on loyalty, on love of fellow human beings. Within a decade of the Revere disaster most of the important new mechanical improvements were in use. The machinery was in good running order. But the education of those who had the charge of it had yet some way to go.

A large party of sports fans were returning from a rowing match on the shore south of Boston in the evening of October 8, 1878. They were loaded aboard a very long special train of twenty-two cars pulled by two locomotives. And the special, being delayed by the hilarity of the fans, was running an hour late. Meanwhile a regular freight train had left Boston going south on the outward track. The crew of this freight, believing the special was already safe at the terminal in Boston, stopped at Wollaston to pick up some empty cars.

They calmly, against all rules of the road, disconnected the inward track in both directions and made use of it to shunt the freights off the siding and onto their train. It was already dark. Along came the special. Seeing its headlight the engineer of the freight, suddenly realizing his danger, put on full steam and just managed, by a split-second margin, to get his locomotive and cars off the inward track. That track, however, was broken in two places by the business of shunting. But the switches were of the newest safety pattern and all should have been well. Left alone they would have sprung automatically into place as the approaching special tripped the safety device.

It was a preview of the Three Mile Island mistake. The conductor of the freight, catching sight of the special just as his engineer was putting on steam to clear the track, jumped from his moving train and rushed heroically across the path of the rapidly approaching special—to do the wrong thing. He seized the lever of the siding switch, threw it and just at that instant, when it was set neither one way nor the other, the incoming locomotives flew by. They flew through thin air, landed on the ties, tore them up for a considerable distance, toppled over and made an insuperable barrier against which half a dozen cars were crushed before the rest of the train came to a stop.

The two firemen and two engineers of the wrecked locomotives were flung high into trees that lined the track. They descended through the branches as through a safety net. Keeping their senses and with courage undaunted they ran back to their engines and managed to put out their fires before they spread to the heaped-up debris of the cars. This rational behavior considerably reduced the consequences of the conductor's panicky mistake. Only nineteen passengers were killed.

A worse instance of human failing, because deliberate, was revealed by a disaster at Bussey Bridge over South Street between the Boston districts of Roslindale and Forest Hills in the winter of 1887. A locomotive pulling a train of nine cars loaded with some three hundred commuters was making its usual run. The bridge collapsed just after the locomotive had crossed and the cars piled up in a dreadful heap in the street. The engineer looked back and, after a first impulsive attempt to brake, put on all steam and with whistle screaming ran on to Forest Hills where he got help in a hurry. His quick thinking saved many lives, for fires were put out before they could consume the wreck.

But the inquest revealed some awful facts. The bridge had collapsed because of a design defect in a hanger. The hanger had been for a long time broken almost through, as anything but a most careless inspection would have shown. And the bridge had been built by an "agent" for a bridge company that did not exist. Very promptly Massachusetts enacted severe laws that thereafter insured sound bridge construction and honest inspection. And across the nation orders from worried railroad managements so jammed the bridge manufacturers that it was months before all needed reconstruction could be done.

The public began to learn that there was no permanent railroad. The process of rebuilding, re-equipping and reshaping for heavier loads and more traffic had to be continuous. Change would not stop. It never will. It is impossible that the world's appetite for energy can be satisfied with its limited supplies of fossil fuels. Neither is a mass migration to the sun belt practical. Even were this to occur in the United States and New England be left a sparsely populated national park, it is not an answer available to such industrial nations as Germany and Japan. The hardline solution of risking war to control the oil of the Middle East is not sensible. Even if war made any sense, this planet's supplies of fossil fuel just will not last indefinitely. There will be no profit in going to war for the last drop of oil.

As the horror of railroad accidents rose to crescendo, so did the public clamor to stop them; yet not to stop the trains. The search for energy solutions will probably follow the same course. But the atomic age has one great advantage over the age of steam. From the outset it has known the danger. The world knows what the atom can do. The requirement is to tame it. The solution lies in the genius of man; in the universities, the libraries and the educational institutions that allow that genius free play and opportunity to work.

HORSE SENSE AND HORSEPOWER

*A*mericans can learn a lesson from the horse. As they approach the 21st Century they are discovering what even a dull farm boy knew at the end of the nineteenth, the value of one horsepower. The designers and builders in the last great age of carriage making had brought their art to something very close to perfection. So if an ounce was added for steel to strengthen an axle or to smooth a sleigh runner, an equal ounce had to be shaved from some other part where strain was less and appearance might even be improved by the shaving.

The most stylish and expensive rig, just before the motorcar took over transportation, was exquisitely built of the lightest possible material to provide easy suspension and free wheeling for maximum comfort and safety and speed. With this behind a good horse a Gibson Girl in all her glory could cut past the slow-footed traffic of the world and display more style in sixty seconds than has been seen in any sixty years since the carriage became horseless.

It was practical, too. A horse can pull just so much weight. A good horse has always been a valuable animal and gradually it dawned on the human mind that it was foolish to waste that value dragging dead weight. Americans are famous for applying common, or horse, sense to everyday problems. Distances are greater than in the old countries and from the very beginning of settlement the people occupied their minds with how to get about.

The first horses arrived in Salem just one year before John Winthrop with his fleet arrived in the Bay to settle Boston. But since there were no roads the only use for a horse was to do farm work or carry a rider and such baggage as he could stuff into a saddlebag. Until after the Revolution the news and the mail were carried by post riders such as Paul Revere.

The first few clumsy vehicles, wheelbarrows, handcarts and such, began to appear almost as soon as streets were laid out. But the streets often were too narrow for horse traffic to pass and farm carts must stop at the edge of town. It took a while to make rutted tracks into roads and open up the towns, and there was no demand for any wheeled traffic but the heaviest drays, usually pulled by oxen at a mile or two an hour. The first coaches for passengers appeared in Boston in 1669 and there is note of some in Connecticut in 1686.

They were great heavy clumsy things, imported from England, liable to capsize and break apart in mud roads under the frantic pull of the horses, and were more dangerous to the passengers than an Indian raid. The second wave of immigrants to Boston, the French Huguenots, brought a more practical vehicle, the two-wheeled cabriolet. It soon developed into the chaise, or shay for short, drawn by one horse and able to take a terrific beating, rolling over boulders in a country road or sliding down the edge of a hill without tipping over, one wheel four feet higher than the other. It was capable, as O.W. Holmes claimed in his famous ballad of the wonderful one-hoss shay, of working perfectly for a hundred years and then all at once crumbling into a heap of dust.

One horse was the ideal power plant. Most Americans could afford one horse and the national economy was built on that economical principle. After the Revolution, when Bulfinch's State House was a new landmark on Boston's Beacon Hill, Federalist Governor Christopher Gore chose still to drive out to his beautiful country house in Waltham in a coach drawn by six horses. But that was merely for show. A dandy in a gig, as the improved shay began to be called, could make the trip with one horse, to Boston and back, while the Governor was going one way.

The genius of young America began to concentrate on improving transportation. The power plant could be improved somewhat by the slow process of horse breeding. But a new invention could improve a carriage or sleigh instantly. So every farm boy, blacksmith, mechanic and tinkerer from Maine to Carolina spent a good deal of time thinking how to do the job better and maybe get rich.

One such was Sam Bailey, born in Pittston, Maine, of the generation that would fight the Civil War. By the time he was eighteen he had invented some smart improvements in the sleighs that raced along the ice on the Kennebec, and was master of his own little company of half a dozen artisans. He moved to Bath and prospered mightily. He learned how to get patents for his inventions; new kinds of carriage springs, better runners for sleighs, new methods for bending wood for greater strength and beauty, new machines for turning shafts and whiffletrees.

In the gilded age of Grant and his successors business was booming, railroads building. The demand for carriages was enormous. Bailey moved to Amesbury, Massachusetts, and set up the twenty-fifth factory there engaged in carriage manufacture. Soon his Essex Trap and Whalebone Wagon was world famous. Buyers came from Europe and west as far as California to attend Amesbury's big annual event, the spring Carriage Opening where the new models were shown. The "Ghost Train" left town every night, twenty or more flatcars, each carrying five shiny new carriages to market, wrapped in white muslin sheets, an eerie sight as it rattled across the Essex County marshes.

The perfection achieved by the carriage and sleigh designers can be compared only to the design of the clipper ships; or the yachts, defenders of the America's Cup. A horsedrawn vehicle or a sailing vessel, to perfectly succeed, must respond to the slightest effort of steed or wind. There can be no waste of energy. The ultimate achievement of the Amesbury shops was Bailey's Whalebone Wagon with wire spoke wheels and pneumatic tires. A horse could whisk this along a good road, with a full payload, almost as fast as the same horse could trot with no load at all.

Then the gasoline motor appeared and changed all the rules.

Gasoline had been an unwanted product of the making of kerosene for lamps. The problem was not to save the stuff but to get rid of it. The automobile industry quickly showed the way. Great size, great weight and many cylinders could supply power unlimited and satisfy any amount of ambition for conspicuous spending, even though the task was still to move one or two people who, on average, weighed less than their grandparents.

Then Arab oil embargos and troubles unlimited in the Middle East succeeded where common sense had failed. By the 1970's America was back at the starting point, where Christopher Gore left off and American ingenuity and invention took over. The monumental goof of the motor industry creating cars the public did not want was apparent at last to the overpaid officials in the executive suite. The behemoth with the insatiable thirst for gas was wanted nowhere but in a junkyard. Inventors and designers were back at work. Sam Bailey reincarnate was at his old job of figuring out how, by saving weight and friction, one horsepower could do the work of six.

THE SACRED COD

*I*f people would go to a certain place to live, they must have a reason for their going and some livelihood when they get there. The reason for the Pilgrims' departure for "the Northern Parts of Virginia" is clear enough. They were seeking a place where they could think as they pleased and practice their religion unmolested. They were fugitives from superior force that would have prevented them, even to the point of extermination.

The same reason animated the great wave of Puritan migration ten years later into Boston Bay. It is the reason that has been uppermost in the minds of many millions of immigrants to the United States since. But the other reason, the means of livelihood, has never been far behind. Aboard the *Mayflower* the chief concern of about half the passengers was finding a more prosperous existence.

It was also the main reason the *Mayflower* company was allowed to sail at all. There was plenty of opposition in high places, but Sir Robert Naunton, Secretary of State to James I, was put up to the job of approaching the King by a Pilgrims' friend at court. He waited till the King was one day in good humor and then asked him if some poor emigrants might go to America "to enjoy their liberty of conscience under his gracious permission."

His Majesty sniffed a rat and answered that the proposition sounded all right but Naunton had better discuss it with the Archbishop of Canterbury. Sir Robert, who had not been born yesterday, quickly changed the subject to the great advantage the King would gain by getting his distant dominions settled by some people not otherwise useful, indeed a nuisance.

"What will they do for a living?" asked James. "Fish!" said

Sir Robert. Then the Monarch burst out, with his customary vehemence—James considered himself an authority on most subjects, including witchcraft—"So God have my soul 'tis an honest trade! 'Twas the Apostles' own calling!"

That settled it. The King's assent was assumed to be got and the Pilgrims were free to risk an Atlantic crossing and the perils of settlement in a barren country to set up in the fishing business. It was even possible to raise a little venture capital. For already for more than a century the wealth of the new world fisheries had been drawing like a magnet those who were willing to seek fortune in far places. Every January a fleet set out from Europe, three or four hundred sail, to fish the banks of Newfoundland. They carried out with them a quantity of salt. They carried back in May and June a rich cargo of dried and salted fish. There would be a real advantage gained if a fishing and salting station could be set up three thousand miles nearer the source of supply.

It was a profitable trade. Captain John Smith, he whom Pocahontas saved, gives figures. "Is it not a pretty sport to pull up two pence, six pence and twelve pence as fast as you can hale and vere a line. He is a very bad fisher indeed who cannot kill in one day one, two or three hundred cod." The Pilgrims, town bred, were not at first either good farmers or good fishers. But within a year, with the help of the friendly Indian Squanto, they had learned how to take shad from the brooks to fertilize their corn and how to catch the cod that followed the shad.

The pattern for living was set for future generations. Salted down and fried, codfish, with cornmeal cooked a dozen delicious ways, was breakfast, dinner and supper. It was also the foundation of trade and future wealth. The soil of Cape Cod, when the trees were cut down to make fuel and farms, blew into the sea. The farmers could only go west on foot to find new land, or follow the good soil down to the sea in ships. Most chose to follow. On the north shore of the Bay it was worse still. Gloucester, Beverly, Marblehead, never grew much else but rocks. Farming there was all sweat and no crops. So from the first the people followed the sea.

Water, salt and fresh, was—as it still is—the one great natural resource available to New Englanders. The energetic people made the most of it. Israel Thorndike's was a typical case, distinguished only from others like it by its more than average good luck, hard-fisted energy and sharpness of intellect. When Israel was six years old his father was lost at sea. His elder brother, the country still being a colony of England and subject to primogeniture law, inherited the family farm in Beverly, less the widow's third. Yet Israel, with no start but a grammar school education and half a dozen dollars, before he was seventeen years old, had learned the fisherman's trade, accumulated a small capital and was the owner of six little smacks amounting in all to 150 ton. Came the Revolution. He swapped his fishing boats for a share in a privateer and the opportunity to be its master. He had luck, good and bad, was commissioned an officer in the navy of Massachusetts. Towards the end of the war he stayed mostly ashore financing and fitting out the privateering expeditions of others. He made no great fortune, but he did not go broke as so many others did who ventured in this high-risk business.

War over, he tried his hand at a land venture, building a toll bridge from Beverly to Salem. That started him in politics. He got elected to the state convention and did his part to ratify the Federal Constitution, then was elected to the Massachusetts House of Representatives and worked, without success, to have the pay of state councilors cut from six to five shillings. All the while he was still engaged on the sea. He began to send small ships to the French and Spanish islands of the Caribbean. The staple of their out cargo was dried cod, with some lumber and manufactured goods. The cargo home was rum and molasses. He began to build a fortune. With more capital he built larger ships, began trade to the Mediterranean, then clear round the world to China. But Jefferson's Embargo Act turned his mind inland to freshwater rivers. Cheap power on the Charles at Waltham persuaded him and others to try cotton manufacturing. It prospered and in his old age he and his co-risktakers were beginning to operate mills on the Merrimac, still building on the profits of Massachusetts' sacred cod.

The image of the Sacred Cod, first hung over the Speaker's

desk in the Old State House two hundred years ago, hangs still before the eyes of the Massachusetts legislature in the New State House on Beacon Hill. It asks the same question King James asked. "What will they do for a living?" If energy costs go on rising many will emigrate to the sun belt. So oil drilling is planned on Georges Bank. The Cod may feel some concern about oil spills. The frantic search for a few more months of cheap oil may not make altogether good sense. There are alternatives. Nuclear power is probably a necessary interim expedient till science and ingenuity, so plentiful in the Northeast nerve center of the nation, can find a better way. There is also water power, wind power, wave power and sun power. And as for gasoline, Israel Thorndike, watching the last gas guzzlers roar by on their way to the scrap heap, would certainly quote what he learned from his hornbook with his first letters. "Waste not want not. Wilful waste makes woful want."

CALVIN COOLIDGE AND HONEST POLITICS

*C*alvin Coolidge was an envi-
ronmented man. A cruel selection operated to produce his peculiar species and him to represent it. As he was born and in
youth formed, so he remained unchanged by any later influence. Not many survived the burying winters and meager subsistence of the Vermont hills. His mother bore two children.
She did not outlive their childhood. His sister died when he was
a schoolboy. At his moment of triumph he was sad. Before his
inauguration as President of the United States, having won
election in his own right, he wrote a line to his father. His
second son had recently died. "You and John and I are all that
is left."

The religious inheritance, reflected in his name, that had
brought his ancestors to live in the narrow passes of the hills,
was severe. Certain habits of thought, confined for a long time
to special places, grown and winnowed in particular climates,
develop distinct types. To a Darwin arriving from outer space
in a celestial *Beagle* the peculiarities of the American bred in
the New England hill country as compared to one bred on the
plains of Georgia might suggest different species.

Whether individuals within a species have genius, or even
distinction as individuals, is another matter. Some escape from
their environment. Others remain environmented all their lives.
Calvin Coolidge went to college in Amherst. Emily Dickinson
lived and died there. Both grew up to the tunes and the meters
of the simplest hymn forms. One applied these forms to politics
and produced nothing but politics. The other applied them to
poetry and transcended the limits of time.

But politics, of its nature timely, not timeless, is the prelude
to action in a democracy. Few American Presidents have con-

tributed much to the philosophy of the state. Even fewer have said anything later generations care to read. But they have kept the ship afloat. Even the worst have not succeeded in sinking it. The record is better than that of hereditary kings or dictators. The reason is politics. An American President has to explain his actions all the time. The explanations are interesting even when the ideas are not.

Calvin Coolidge had a singularity, characteristic of his species and in him developed to the highest degree, of doing nothing with very great skill. Where a platitude would suffice he never substituted action. When the ladder of his ascent had as yet reached no higher than Lieutenant Governor of Massachusetts he remarked, "I don't think I could defeat myself if I tried. I don't know exactly why but I guess it is partly because I am not all the time doing foolish things."

He never did do foolish things. Gifted with a sense of humor rare among politicians, rare indeed among any group of individuals who are sifting themselves as fast as possible to the top of the human heap, he saw himself accurately as an oil can. A drop of oil here and there was his contribution to progress. The first time he met Frank Stearns, owner of a conspicuously successful Boston department store and, like Coolidge, a graduate of Amherst, he said quite casually, "Ever anything you want up on the hill come up and see me." Stearns did come up and see him, about nothing in particular, was impressed by what he saw, and never thereafter ceased to work for Coolidge till he was seated in the White House.

When an apple was ripe, Coolidge knew how to pick it. A mountainy man is always on the watch for frost. Coolidge was a male chauvinist. Soon after his marriage, he handed his attractive wife fifty socks to darn with the remark, "There's more where they came from." But he was not a male chauvinist pig. That title belonged to Levi Greenwood, President of the Massachusetts State Senate. Greenwood chose to confront the wave of the future in the chain mail of tradition. Grumpily he took on the whole attack of the suffragettes and lost. Within twenty-four hours Coolidge, who had cannily avoided the issue, had garnered pledges of support from a majority of his colleagues for the suddenly vacant office and emerged as one of the most powerful figures in the state.

He did a good job as President of the Senate. With an unemotional yes or no, in private conference, he settled the fate of bills due to come up on the Senate floor. He had no interest but in the job to do and doing it well for the power it gave him. His interest in money was to live within his income, at that time less than $2,000 a year. The fact of his honesty was as apparent as the quills on a porcupine and warned off trespassers. His idea of a good legislature was one that did not pass too many laws and gave administration a chance to catch up with legislation. He kept his Chamber in order. One day there was a furious battle between senators and one shouted to another to go to hell. The offended dignitary complained to the President, who settled the question, "Senator, I have examined the Constitution and the Senate rules and there is nothing that compels you to go."

Coolidge had just one hobby, which he succinctly expressed to a lady trying to make him talk at the dinner table, "Holdin' office." After holding a decent number, it came quite naturally for him to sit down in the Governor's chair. There luck favored him. In 1919 the Boston police struck, professional thieves converged on the city, mobs took possession of the streets. Coolidge waited till the very last moment, then called out the National Guard. Many critics thought he waited much too long. But his sense of timing was acute. And when he sent his famous telegram to the President of the American Federation of Labor, Samuel Gompers, "There is no right to strike against the public safety by anybody, anywhere, anytime," he electrified the country.

That made him Vice President of the United States. It might almost as easily have made him President. There was a power vacuum in the Republican party in 1920. The nominating convention, weary, deadlocked, bumbling in the heat, fell into the hands of a conspiracy of old guard senators. They agreed on one of their own, the amiable Harding, who would sign the

President Calvin Coolidge as an Indian Chief.

bills the Senate sent to him and not bother to send any bills of his own making to the Senate to be passed. That was put over. But the cabal's choice for Vice President was suddenly thrust aside. Someone shouted "Coolidge!" The convention exploded. Within two minutes it was impossible for any chairman, any number of bosses rushing frantically in from the wings, to stop the stampede for the man from Massachusetts.

He should, of course, have suffered political death. But luck favored him. After three years of doing nothing, apparently, but actually closely observing and learning, he took over the Harding Presidency, scandals, Cabinet and all. According to his own account he would not have managed nearly so successfully in the top office without that chance to watch and learn the game. He knew just what to do. He had built up much political capital as presiding officer of the Senate. He knew the men who got things done across the nation. He appointed a famous fixer with a fascinating name, C. Bascom Slemp, a Virginian, an ex-congressman, who knew everyone and everything below the Mason-Dixon line, his Secretary. After that everything was fixed—including his own nomination for the Presidency. Coolidge knew just how far his friends from Massachusetts could push him. And when more push was needed, he knew how to go out and get it. For he had taken the advance precaution of making friends beyond the border.

That is politics. It may not be the highest end of man. But without it the highest ends are seldom attained. When Jimmy Carter entered the White House there was for the first time since Coolidge a President shaped by a very distinct environment. It was a quite opposite environment. Instead of sharp rock chips in his shoes there was the sticky red clay of Georgia. A grin and promises replaced the downturned mouth and meager hope of honest Cal. It produced a television election victory but not the politics that keeps nations on course, even a middle course.

NO ARMISTICE FOR PRESIDENTS

*W*hoever sits at the desk in the White House oval office, Republican, Democrat, man or woman, there should be always one plain framed photograph in view—of Woodrow Wilson. Like the *memento mori*, the death's head on the work table of the medieval philosopher, it is the symbol of all symbols to remind American Presidents of the vanity of power. His was the saddest life. He held the greatest sway. He was the idol of the most millions all over the world. Those wonderful eyes looked out and saw so far. But they could not see his own feet. They were made of clay.

Under the picture should be a legend—"It can't be done alone." Every President has a partner. He is bound to the (Senate by rules as strong as words in the Constitution can make them, as custom and respect over centuries can strengthen rules. The House is his instrument—or his enemy—to carry out his purposes or its own as the electorate may demand. But the Senate is the great eccentric. It does what it damn well pleases. Most senators have been in office much longer than any President. By law, at least one third of them must stay in office at least two years longer than the term of the immediately elected President. In the war between the President and the senators, no armistice is binding, no battle is the last.

Professor Wilson of Princeton wrote, "The Senate is not immediately sensitive to public opinion and is apt to grow more stiff if pressure is brought to bear on it." President Wilson, being the same person, knew this. But at the supreme moment the nerve that controlled eye and hand failed. Like Casey at the bat, with two down and the bases loaded, he struck out. There has not been much joy in Mudville since.

President Wilson could have had his League of Nations right

after the First World War. If he had, it might have prevented the Second World War. There is no telling. It is a possible, even a reasonable conjecture. It was Wilson's idea that bad as the Versailles Treaty was, its mistakes and indecencies would be rectified by the League. The great material strength and the moral force of the United States, working within the League, would keep the world in balance and keep the peace. But with the United States out of the League, failure was certain. In that much he was right.

Speculation on what might have happened is not especially useful. History concentrates on what did happen and what to do better next time. That is why incumbent Presidents should look deep into the eyes of President Wilson and think a bit.

When Wilson was halfway through his first term, Senator Henry Cabot Lodge of Massachusetts still felt able to give him important support in carrying through an unpopular revision of the Panama Canal Treaty. But soon after Lodge was referring to Wilson as a liar and wrote, "I never expected to hate anyone in politics with the hatred I feel towards Wilson." Something went wrong. Wilson knew it. He never did anything to make it better. He did many unnecessary things to make it worse. Therein lies the tragedy. And for the tragic conflict of these two personalities the world paid a bitter price.

When the First World War abruptly and unexpectedly ended with the armistice of November 11, 1918, there was powerful sentiment for a new world order. It could be compared to the powerful feeling that swept the nation in 1976, when opinion united at the end of the Ford and the beginning of the Carter administrations in an emotional willingness to make whatever sacrifices might be necessary to make America independent of Arab oil. It was at such an emotional crisis that Wilson made his big mistake. He assumed the mantle of an Old Testament prophet about to straighten out mankind once and for all. He forgot how well he had run the politics of war. Forgot how he had held his country back till rage and frustration with the German submarine attack made further holding back impossible. Forgot how George Creel, a brilliant newspaperman, and his highly intelligent cohorts had organized public opinion in the first modern campaign of hate. Forgot all about hanging the Kaiser. Remembered only his own preaching of a new world order.

But Lodge remembered. "Give us the treaty of peace. Let it chain and fetter, impose reparations, build up the barrier states, put the monster where it cannot spring up again." And then Wilson sailed off across the Atlantic Ocean, taking nine days to make the trip, and basked in the cheers of starving Europe that hailed him as a savior and had not one vote to elect an American President. He had treated the Senate almost with contempt, feeling so very sure of the support of the whole people. The fact that he no longer had a majority in either house of Congress did not faze him. He was confident in his mission, confident that the terrific internal strains within the Republican party between progressives and conservatives would prevent any coalition. What if Borah, the perpetual windbag from Idaho, inveighed against entangling alliances? Neither a league of nations nor a league of senators could ever count on Borah's insecure support.

Like Louis XIV who informed the world that he was the state, Wilson made it perfectly clear that he was the American Peace Commission. There were others present, but they did not count. Unfortunately he was no match for the cruel wiles of old world diplomacy. He had much better have left the negotiating task to others and kept up his fences at home. So when he did come home he began to sense that the country was slipping away from him. Frantically he tried to save his treaty and his League of Nations. But the Machiavellian skill of Lodge was on a par with the diplomacy of old tiger Clemenceau of France. A speaking tour of the United States brought cheers from crowds and no votes in the Senate. It also brought on a stroke.

Even yet the League might have been saved. Senator Hitchcock, loyal worker for the cause, pleaded with the sick President for a little compromise. "Let Lodge compromise," grated the thin, tired voice. "But might we not hold out the olive branch?" "Let Lodge hold out the olive branch."

And that was the end of the League of Nations, an end before a beginning. The Senate voted down the Peace Treaty and the League, and the next election voted in "normalcy," Harding and the road to the Second World War. No doubt Wilson's hardening arteries and Lodge's stomach ulcer had some part in the debacle. But if President Wilson had listened to Professor Wilson, worked with the Senate instead of trying to browbeat it, he just might have saved the world a lot of trouble. He might have been remembered as very great. Instead he is remembered as the best example that "it can't be done alone."

THE CITY

*E*very man carries in his heart the image of a city. For Pericles it was Athens; for all the Caesars, Rome. For Haroun-al-Rashid it was Baghdad, where the slaves for sale in its market were as beautiful and various as the flowers in its perfumed gardens. For Thoreau it was Walden. For Augustine it was the City of God.

Whether a man's city is peopled with angels or with woodchucks with the souls of angels, whether it supplies all the delights of the flesh that the soul of man can desire; whether its streets pulse with trade and the tentacles of its power reach to the uttermost ends of the earth, or whether on its acropolis is born art worthy of the admiration of the gods, each generation leaves to its posterity the image in its heart. Each citizen, however vast his imagination or how petty, however generous his understanding or how mean, fixes his personality on the place of his being. The carelessly tossed paper, the broken bottle, are one person's monument; a graceful spire, an open space, an amazing sculpture, another's. Some create, some preserve, some destroy. The sum of all is the city.

The city of Boston bears the image of many generations. In this it is unique among American cities. For although it is the capital of a state and a region, both their commercial and intellectual heart, its fortunate topography and a certain stubborn quality that has endured among its people, have preserved much that was worth saving. It is also new. Some of the best architecture and city planning of the 20th Century have found their way there. Married by the Charles River to Cambridge, it breeds ideas. Worldly goods are symbolized by the carefully allocated skyscrapers in its financial district. And there is a ring of enterprise and lively accomplishment that surrounds it along its electronic Route 128. It is the nearest thing to an eternal city that America knows. Living into the future it remembers a long past.

Boston is the Most Beautiful City. Perhaps the Celestial City is better—that one the Pilgrim found at the end of his *Progress*—but till we reach the same destination Boston will do. And the best thing about Boston—since 1960 at least—is that it has kept on changing for the better. Almost without knowing how it got there, hardly aware itself of the road it was taking, Boston has returned to the place it occupied at the beginning of the 19th Century—the finest city in North America.

There is no other city that can equal it in the arrangement of its spaces or the distinction of its architecture. One must travel to St. Mark's Square in Venice and the Doge's Palace to find a public building as magnificent as Boston's New City Hall, looking westward towards America across its great plaza and eastward to the sea, past the Faneuil Hall of Smibert and Bulfinch and the strong and lively granite of the Quincy Market of Alexander Parris. Only a step away are the architectural gems, the Old State House, the honest Old South Meeting House, and Christ Church, that Old North, graceful as a clipper ship. The mind is raveled in their history; the eye entranced by their beauty. And who can stand on a winter day, the wind northwest, the sky all blue save for flying clouds, at Brimstone Corner on the Common and look up at Peter Banner's perfect spire of the Park Street Church and the golden dome rising above Bulfinch's State House without a moment of awe and wonder?

Boston has become what now it is by the everlasting war between art and civilization on the one side and greed and barbarism on the other. Suddenly in 1960, the balance tipped decisively in favor of civilization. It was a close thing. The shift of the weight of a hair could have moved the center of the city westward beyond the Common and left all its ancient beauties to the rats.

Boston, like most cities, has destroyed much of value, because neither planning nor contemporary taste at any given time is infallible. But some of its best buildings it has kept. And most important it has kept air to breathe and light by which to see. Happiness is still to walk in Boston. There is no happiness in walking down a tunnel between skyscrapers.

To some old Puritans goes the first credit. They bought from an eccentric clergyman named Blaxton, who had been living at peace with the Indians on the peninsula before they came, forty-four acres of land. This they set aside for a Common. Even the motorcar has not succeeded in invading it, though it has bored under it for a place to be out of sight and smell, at least for the time its occupants are free to roam the city on foot.

The rest of the city grew up as a wooden village along the waterfront. It had not much to recommend it as an example of urban planning, although its many wharves and steeples presented a busy and exciting scene when Captain John Bonner first drew a map of it in 1722. On Christmas day of that year, as on every Christmas day in old Boston, work was continuing as usual. With one exception. The richest citizen of Boston, Andrew Faneuil, with his nephew Peter, did no business. They attended the French Church on School Street, fragrantly decorated with pine boughs and holly, and then went home to feast on turkey and goose and drink Madeira wine.

Their Puritan neighbors looked at them askance. The celebration of Christmas was popery and trucking with the devil. But these French were undeniably Protestants of the strict school of John Calvin. They were accepted in Boston, as wave after wave of new citizens would be accepted and assimilated after them. Driven from the old world by the brainless persecution of Louis XIV, they came to enrich the new. And in due course some of their ways and customs which were cheerful and good, such as celebrating Christmas and drinking wine, would replace the severity of the Puritan Sabbath relieved only by a shot of rum.

Peter Faneuil not only celebrated Christmas but in 1742 gave Boston a great present. The citizens thanked him and have continued to mispronounce the name of his hall. They called it Funel for a long time, then they switched to Fanuel. But out of respect for the donor they kept the French spelling with its difficult diphthongs. In 1805 Charles Bulfinch doubled the hall's size while retaining and refining the style of its architecture. Then Mayor Quincy, as the city grew and its need for decent market space became imperative, filled in the edge of the harbor and added his granite buildings. While the harbor fed the commerce of the city and railroads carried commerce to and from the country, the Quincy Market served magnificently. For a century port and city prospered. Then came horrid decay.

By 1960 it was high time for another Christmas present. The last hurrah of the Curley era was a dying echo and it was dying over the ruins of a great city. In it were many buildings and monuments, gifts of citizens, of citizens' groups and of societies. But the greatest gift of all, a concerted effort by many diverse groups together, comes very seldom. Such a thing happened in 1960.

It was a miracle. When the Second World War ended, no buildings of real importance had been built for more than twenty years. Dozens of great stores had closed their doors, never again to open them. The tax rate had increased tenfold. The people who could afford it had fled the city. Business and enterprise were following.

The thing that happened was, in appearance, subconscious and spontaneous. It had been preparing consciously and deliberately in the minds of some leaders for a long time. It was accepted and enforced by the voters. It was a truce in the war between politics and business. Suddenly a lot of people realized that in civilization and order there was some hope; in unrestrained greed no future for either people or politicians.

Kevin White became Mayor in 1968 in time to move into the grandest city hall in America. The city over which he came to preside is the most beautiful, and he continued to work to make it more beautiful. It was the gift of his predecessors, political men like Mayors John Hynes and John Collins; of state and national politicians like Foster Furculo and John McCormack, who carried through Congress the decision to build a government center downtown, where city, state and nation could meet and prosper. It was the gift of private citizens like Harold Hodgkinson and Charles Coolidge, leaders of enterprise in the city. It was the gift of genius for city planning in Ed Logue; of genius in architecture of Pei, of Gropius, of Kallmann and McKinnell and of Rudolph.

Such things do not happen very often. There were such times in Florence, in Venice, in Paris, perhaps once or twice, or even three times in a thousand years. Boston, now in its fourth century, in its rebirth in beauty and usefulness, gives hope once again of the redemption of the values of civilization.

TRUMPET THAT SHALL NEVER
CALL RETREAT

A great work of art ennobles the beholder. When the inspiration for that work of art is the highest moment of the place of its origin, the whole world is ennobled. The riders on the frieze of the Parthenon carry the joy of ancient Athens into the dullest reaches of man's latest century. The reverent kings and queens that stand in granite majesty in the west portals of Chartres Cathedral bring the contemplation of the peace of God into the distressed atomic age. So it is on the crest of Beacon Hill before the State House in Boston where Colonel Robert Gould Shaw forever advances with the 54th regiment of Massachusetts infantry that can never break step.

There, caught in bronze, is the moment that explains the Civil War, that proves, as in a fire, the Declaration of Independence, that shows the way to the future. "Be swift my soul to answer him, be jubilant my feet." The soul is plain in the earnest, confident faces, the jubilation is there in the soundless tread of those marching men. It is the moment that followed the Emancipation Proclamation. It is the moment that changed America, released its latent force, delivered to the future the opportunity to escape from the bondage of racial prejudice. The cost is shown there, too; the cost to innumerable, anonymous lives. There will be sacrifice. It will go on for a very long time. "Lay this laurel on the One too intrinsic for Renown." And the end is worth all the means.

For two years the old world and half the new had confidently considered that the Declaration and the Constitution, with its Bill of Rights, were dead and buried under the rubble that had been the United States. England, France and Russia, like

271

Saint-Gaudens' Memorial to the 54th Regiment of Massachusetts
Infantry — Beacon Street, Boston.

hawks over a hen yard, were circling and ready to pounce. A letter from London, January 1863, tells what then happened. "The Emancipation Proclamation has done more for us here than all our former victories and diplomacy. It is creating an almost convulsive reaction in our favor all over the country. Public opinion is very deeply stirred here and finds expression in meetings, addresses to President Lincoln. I never quite appreciated the 'moral influence' of American democracy until I saw how directly it works."

The convulsive reaction was felt over the North like an earthquake. The center of the shock was the state of Massachusetts, of all the states the strongest advocate of freedom. Its stellar governor, John Andrew, long a champion of the rights of black people, at once seized the opportunity to give them equal rights in the fight for freedom. He hurried to Washington, got permission to organize a free black regiment. Garrison of the *Liberator* trumpeted the news. Frederick Douglass, former slave, great orator, began recruiting. Two of his sons enlisted. Luther Stearns, a successful lead pipe manufacturer, quit his office to help. He mortgaged his plant, put up tens of thousands of dollars that neither state nor national legislature would advance, to equip the regiment. Without rest he traveled through the West and into Canada to bring in black recruits. From all over Massachusetts, from all the free states, came black men to Readville to train for the war.

It was necessary to find an exceptional officer to lead it. Governor Andrew was proud of the Second Massachusetts, now at the front in Virginia; of its notable fighting record since its instant response to Lincoln's first call for volunteers. He picked Captain Robert Shaw. A brother officer wrote home, "What do you think of First Massachusetts Black Infantry? One of our officers has had the offer of the Colonelcy, and he has accepted it. As a military measure I entirely believe in it. It is ridiculous for people to laugh this thing down."

Laugh it down, cry it down, condemn it, that was the almost general shout. The *Times* of London outdid itself in vituperation, called Lincoln brute, barbarian, instigator of slave insurrection. The Confederacy proposed draconian punishments for black troops captured. Return to slavery would be but a mild part of the penalty for those blacks who dared with arms to resist it. As for white men caught in such company, the common usages extended to prisoners of war could hardly be expected. Boston was bitterly divided. There were "copperheads," Southern sympathizers whose fortunes depended on cotton, laboring men who feared black competition for their jobs. A majority, not silent, were for freedom. In the army, those who were doing the fighting were glad enough of any help. Before the war would end, nearly ten per cent of the troops of the Union would be black.

Quickly the ranks of the black regiment, Massachusetts 54th, were filled. The rolls of still another, the 55th, had to be opened. The 54th, having completed training at Readville, arrived in Boston on May 28th. There had been some ugly talk of rioting. Special police were out, some conspicuous on the sidewalks, some held in reserve. The regiment paraded through downtown Boston, came up through Pemberton Square and entered Beacon Street from Somerset Street almost opposite the Athenaeum. On some stretches of the parade route there was loud cheering, on others silence.

As the regiment came down Beacon Street there was no sound but the heavy tramp of feet. From a balcony a girl called softly, "Goodbye, Bob." In the silence Shaw heard, looked up, smiled, raised his sword in salute. The regiment turned into the Common, where it passed in review before Governor Andrew, thence down State Street, to the ship that would take it to South Carolina, to the brave desperate attack on Fort Wagner where Shaw, in the lead and falling within the ramparts, would be killed with thirty of his men.

Saint-Gaudens, master sculptor, worked for twelve years, modeled at last the one monument in all the United States that achieves in bronze what only a few poets have suggested in words—what the Civil War was about—why its aspiration is immortal. Time and weather have strangely touched it; enhanced its nobility. The guardian angel, always uncomfortable, floating too close above the gun barrels, has receded into insignificance. Man is his own guardian. Not God nor all his regiments of angels can stand between mankind and what mankind has wrought. The faces of the men stand out now in high relief. And the future lies all ahead. It is what mankind will make it. All humanity marches here with Shaw and the 54th. Whither? The monument requires of each beholder an answer.

A CITY TO WALK IN

*T*he way to civilization is on foot. The legs are the pistons that power the brain. Socrates walked in the Agora, the marketplace of Athens, and the citizens picked up wisdom with their fruit and vegetables. Abelard and the schoolmen walked across the Seine from the old isle of the city to the left bank, and began the University of Paris. Henry Dunster and his students crossed the Charles on a ferry and walked to the cow yard in Cambridge to found Harvard. Emerson, Thoreau and Harry Truman, to name but a few of the famous, were noted walkers.

Boston began as a walking city, because it grew up on a peninsula surrounded by the sea, and around a great hill, almost a mountain, that was unfriendly to wheel traffic. The motorcar has destroyed much of the amenity of city life, even in the old cities of Europe, with the notable exception of Venice. It has all but extinguished life itself in Los Angeles. And as the 20th Century hurries on its way it is a toss-up whether the century or civilization will come first to its end in a gasoline blaze started in the Middle East.

How to curb the motorcar, make it the servant rather than the destroyer of civilization, is perhaps the most urgent problem humanity has to solve. The manufacture of smaller, less gas-guzzling cars could end merely in producing more cars. An attractive solution is to make alternative transportation both cheaper and pleasanter. Of walking there can be no argument. What is worth seeing, the eyes can see leisurely, encompassed in a reasonable space, comfortable for an average pair of feet. And in this quiet motion the mind is free to range the universe. Thus Homer walked along the shore, looking over the wine-dark sea; thus, so Emerson tells us, he found Wordsworth pacing in a garden path composing poetry.

Walking is pleasant in Boston. The motorcar has been forbidden on some of the downtown streets, such as the shopping area of Washington Street and the conspicuously successful Faneuil Hall Marketplace. The old retail area is returning to prosperity. Conspicuous financial success appeals to Americans. The plan will be copied. The next step will surely come, the burial of wheel traffic at important crossings so that pedestrians can move about their city in safety, not breathless with hurry and climbing. The fleeing pedestrian; the pedestrian panting up the stairs of the overpass while the motorist passes smoothly below, gently pressing his accelerator with a touch of his toe, is the travesty of civilization. A little imagination and a small sum of money, compared to the vast sums constantly being spent to make more tunnels and bridges for vehicular traffic, will finally make Boston the model city, the paradise of pedestrians, the most wonderful city in the world; where the eye does not stop in some boxed-in office space, but catching the converging lines of an aspiring tower carries the mind to spaces infinite of imagination.

The opportunity begs to be seized. People, just ordinary people who cannot afford a car, or have sense enough not to drive one into the city, can arrive quickly and cheaply into the heart of Boston, the Park Street Station, from any point in the compass by public transportation. Thence they can take a walk.

What a walk it is! There is more history to be lived again, more architecture modern to old, to be seen, considered, admired in an hour's walking than in a ten days' journey other places. The Common itself is an historical monument. It preserves green space, open sky and the vagaries of human nature such as Hare Krishnas, outdoor evangelists and street musicians. Looking up Tremont Street, just after passing King's Chapel, the spire of the Old North appears under the powerful arm of the New City Hall. And from State Street can be seen, at a single glance, something that cannot be seen elsewhere in all the Americas, three masterpieces of architecture from three centuries, the Old State House of 1711, the Ames Building from the firm of H. H. Richardson, and the New City Hall of Kallmann and McKinnell. Walking west across the glorious Common the Beacon Street houses delight the eye, a facade for all the fine houses that lie behind on Beacon Hill. Then the Public Garden, and Commonwealth Avenue, one of the most beautiful avenues of the world, with its double row of great trees on the mall, its extraordinary blooming of magnolias, its 19th Century architecture, individualistic, sometimes eccentric, but all harmonious, always in scale. Beyond is the wide garden of the Fenway, the Art Museum and the rare jewel called Fenway Court, Mrs. Jack Gardner's single-handed creation.

Preventing the perfection of this whole are traffic crossings. The elimination of wheel traffic to allow the free passage of pedestrians is the certain next step of civilization. Boston should show the way. For Boston has a head start. Cows have been given undue credit for the traffic-slowing quality of Boston's streets. The streets were planned that way by sensible people, all being easy paths to the water's edge, the wide gateway to commerce. Distances to the shore which surrounded the town were made as short as possible and a backpack or a wheelbarrow were often more convenient than a dray or truck. When the problem was the mere transport of people, feet were always more convenient than wheels.

When the motorcar came, Boston people held to their old habit of walking. They were protected from progress by the natural barrier of Beacon Hill, which it was easier for traffic to go around than to go across. And respect for the ancient Common and its extension, the Public Garden, saved the heart of the city. That heart is severed by cross streets, but not irreparably. The task of an enlightened age will be to join it together again. The method is simple and practical.

At major crossings, where a steady stream of pedestrians is blocked by a jet stream of wheel traffic, the roadway will need to be depressed and the pedestrian traffic allowed to pass over it on the level, as has been done between the Harvard Yard and Memorial Hall in neighboring Cambridge. To save expense the roadway need be depressed only eight feet or so and a low bridge raised over it, easy for pedestrian ascent, as the famous Rialto over the Grand Canal in Venice. A beginning could be made at Charles Street to join the Common and the Public Garden. Another pedestrian bridge near Park Street Church, and one beyond George Washington's statue to cross Arlington Street onto Commonwealth Avenue's beautiful pedestrian mall could reveal the possibilities of unifying a city and lead to a great awakening nationwide.

John Winthrop, reading his Bible as the little *Arbella* tossed mid-ocean, put his finger on a verse of Matthew and took its message personally. "Ye are the light of the world. A city that is set on a hill cannot be hid." Yet the only city he ever saw was a little wooden village huddled under a high hill with three tops called Tri-Mountain.

Three centuries later the three tops had been shoveled into the harbor. And the remains of the hill and the Common below it had saved the heart of the city from the most furious onslaught of the latter-day Satan, motor traffic. Winthrop's ghost, if it still walks—it certainly does not ride—doubtless sees a direct intervention of Providence. Perhaps it is.

THE PEOPLE OF THE CITY

*T*he builders and preservers of the city, those who cherish the habitation of man and make the paths to it of civilization and the arts, they are worthy of praise. The stones speak for them. Some only we knew. Of these we tell because in their remembrance is the remembrance of all. The good citizen leaves a crumb of his being for the nourishment of posterity.

There was Walter Whitehill. It was as though, one day, crossing the Common, suddenly one realized that the State House had vanished. Walter Whitehill was an essential part of the landscape. His impressive figure, tailored from London in bright tweed or formal pinstripe, walked in and out of our lives as familiarly as the Athenaeum, King's Chapel and the elegant spire of the Park Street Church.

In fact Walter *was* the landscape. His powerful imagination and his overpowering energy so firmly grasped the shape of the past that he stamped it on the present and projected its lines into the future. The recreated Quincy Market is his personal monument. But the whole city, its architecture and its state of mind, has taken a new lease on life in some considerable measure because of the work of Walter Whitehill.

Many, after the Second World War, labored valiantly for the cause of preservation, spent hours and hours with architects and planners. It was Whitehill who marshaled the hosts.

It seems an age ago, that world of pre-inflation and post Second World War. Cornhill was still intact, a rabbit warren of shoe shops, barrooms and bookstores. Whitehill, typically, was a friend of George Gloss, the impresario of the secondhand book trade; of the Mayor and of the Mayor's spiritual advisors, the editors of the *Pilot*; of the bankers, capitalists and powers celestial and eternal that rule the universe. But all this availed not. The last decision, to demolish or not to demolish, was to be made in a stuffy room, a dirty office in the old City Hall, by three men chewing the stubs of cigars. But when Whitehill spoke, when Whitehill parried their questions, those pols listened; not politicians but pols, that curious subspecies that lies under every city administration. As they listened there came a light in their eyes. They knew and the bystanders knew, as the sympathetic lightnings flashed back and forth, that the Sears Block would be saved to weld the essential link between the past and the future that makes the City Hall Plaza in Boston one of the great places of architecture, worthy of comparison with the Piazza San Marco in Venice or the Parvis of Notre Dame in Paris.

Let us now praise famous men! How we wish we could, with words sufficient to express the fullness of our thought, the largeness of our debt. Who among us but can remember some considerable personal favor, some small kindness, some pleasant word which Walter gave out of the largeness of his good nature, the energy of his endeavor, the keenness of his perception. With a word at the right time he placed many a friend where that friend might achieve the fullest personal satisfaction, more fully serve the end always at the top of Walter's thought, the creation of the Most Beautiful City.

Boston was and would be the Most Beautiful City. It was a large place. It extended from its sparkling harbor and green islands, up from its waterfront, across the Common, down Commonwealth Avenue clear to Franklin Park, the Great Blue Hill and beyond. Beyond lay Charlottesville, Virginia, Monticello and Thomas Jefferson, perhaps the farthest reach of which Walter's normally Federalist imagination was capable. But Walter was most at home, most comfortable, near Bulfinch's State House, among the houses of Beacon Hill, and in the Harvard Yard. London, too, was familiar of course, and Paris and the old universities of the old world. They were all part of that special creation—the Most Beautiful City.

A Topographical History of Boston is one of the very best books about a city that has been written. Boston is a city which can hold comfortably within its limits the house of Paul Revere and Kallmann and McKinnell's City Hall, even the glass tower of Pei and Richardson's Trinity. It is a city where origins are only a path to culture, where the crowds on Boston Common are cheerful, are tolerant, are diverse. Where the way is open to anyone with wit to profit by the universities and libraries, with energy and good will to find his way through crooked streets and into the elevators of high buildings. It is a city where Sam Adams, that old rebel, does not tumble off his pedestal in front of Faneuil Hall because the genial Walter, that essentially establishment man, is smiling up at him in bronze from his secure place at the base of the monument as permanent proprietor of the Walter Whitehill Memorial Park.

It is the Most Beautiful City. Deep in its foundations Walter is still at work. Listen! Can you not hear that faint scratching? That is Walter's pen. And now he clears his throat. Listen! He is about to tell you something worth the hearing.

And there was Charles Hopkinson. Charles Hopkinson was born so long ago that nobody in Boston except Mark Howe, poet, essayist and historian, ever remembered when. Howe thought of Charles as rather a baby. There is a charming portrait of Howe by Hopkinson that now hangs in the Athenaeum. He is looking out at the young painter limning his features. The legend in the corner reads "Pictor 87 Pictus 92."

Hopkinson had all the virtues of a good Bostonian, originality, humor, talent, courage and gaiety, and the supreme virtue of being unlike anybody else, even his fellow Bostonians. To these were added a magnificent head, a mane like a lion's that reluctantly turned white and was more lionlike than before, an athletic figure on which the most elegant clothes that Saville Row could produce as late as 1910 were proud to hang, and a step so light that when in extreme old age he began to carry a cane, his third leg was rattan and bent and curved and cavorted like a young horse in pasture.

Mark Howe, Dean of New England letters, by Charles Hopkinson, master painter of the Boston School.

Other things he added for himself, as a boyhood in Cambridge, four years at Harvard where his uncle Eliot was President, training in Paris as a painter, a wife and five daughters very satisfactory to paint, and a house at Manchester overlooking the changing and restless ocean from a vantage point equaling in beauty even such a famous place as Monreale that looks down over its forests of orange and lemon to Palermo and the Sicilian seas.

His friend Damon Ross, standing there one summer day, said, "Charles, what have you done to deserve to live in paradise?" Words would have been futile to answer. But again and again he answered with the artist's brush. Picture after picture lives to record it. There he stood, in all seasons; in gentle summer; in the hesitant spring frightened by the east wind; in gorgeous autumn; in winter with snow and purple shadow in the foreground and the remorseless leaden sea creeping away towards infinity; seeing the light, recording the color. Color and light were the fabric of his vision. He made them real with the passion, with the devotion of the 12th Century worker in glass, of the artisan of Ming porcelain.

He wrote, "Today I have been painting madly. The blue ocean has been coming in great rollers and smashing in white on these golden rocks. Between them and my window is a wild tangle of orange and purple with here and there a brilliant emerald little pine tree and all in bright sunshine." And again, "The important thing is to have fun with it, even while you are in a worshipful mood at all that beauty you are seeing—and the more you paint the more beauty you will see. I suppose I could go on with my advice till you are tired of it—and who am I to give advice when this afternoon (and every day) I fail to produce the lovely thing I set out to do."

He was never satisfied. He was always experimenting. Sometimes he was successful. Posterity, which is wiser than we, will know just how successful. But we, who are less wise, are at least more fortunate, for we knew him as a friend. He came every day to the city, to paint in his studio, to lunch in an old tavern far down in a dirty alley littered with papers and broken bottles.

The People of the City

Once, on a cold day in winter, coming away up the alley just where it debouched onto Boylston Street, he raised his stick and pointed to the Common, to the blue sky, to the wild white clouds racing across it. "And it's all free!" he cried. A surprised passer-by turned on him a startled glance and saw only a mad old man.

Harold Hodgkinson was designed by a good architect. All his lines were straight and true. He came from Connecticut but he fitted in Boston as comfortably as the latest building just from the drawing board of the International School. Architecture makes the portrait of its time. The restless skyline of New York reflects the hurrying feet of the people far below in the street. The spears of the Conqueror and the bearing of his men are to this day expressed in the towers and front of his Abbey Church at Caen. So it is in Boston at the New City Hall.

There is the excellent monument of our time and specifically of Harold Hodgkinson. It is his monument and the monument of some half dozen others like him, representatives of the best that the city and the region could offer; men of differing backgrounds and diverse race, who knew how to work together and to persuade others to work with them to the common good. The expression is distinctly masculine, as at Caen. It is of the old Boston, the Puritan. The strong horizontal lines are there, firm, decisive, the lines of the mouth of the Boston trustee. There are the square shoulders, as of a man stepping firmly off to his work.

But within there is something different. It is something new in Boston. The imagination has suddenly escaped. It plays with fantasies. It welcomes all races. It could be Irish, Italian, Greek; Middle East or African, from any land or anywhere. It delights in diversity. Here is an immense staircase ascending, a great platform where the ages of man are played every day. Here are vaults rising, mysterious spaces high overhead revealing changing shafts of light, suggesting spaces unseen beyond. Here is room to build. There is no limit here to aspiration.

It was said of Harold Hodgkinson, Hodge as he was familiarly known, that if he met a panhandler on the Common the panhandler might or might not get his quarter, but Hodge would get his quarter's worth of conversation. He had a vast tolerance for other points of view, a curiosity about other backgrounds, an interest in the peculiarities of human nature. He accepted it all and taught it to work for him. Thereby he became one of the world's great rag merchants (his self-title) and made of Filene's Basement a gold mine.

He rose from the job of sorting overshoes in the Basement to be manager of the whole enterprise. The enterprise of the whole city became his province. At his work he met Laura Cabot and accomplished the greatest coup of his life by persuading her to marry him. She was the Conqueror's Matilda. The sensitive impress of a woman's hand is set on that other contemporary monument overlooking the Charles, the Museum of Science, as it is in Caen on the Abbaye aux Dames. In civic virtue, in enterprise for the good of Boston and the state, these two were not a pair but a unity.

In his own words, in the *Proceedings of the Massachusetts Historical Society*, he has told the story of the building of the New City Hall. Of course he has told the story too modestly. But the dredging of Boston out of its long disaster of the 20's and 30's and 40's was in good measure his doing.

"A knight ther was, and that a worthy man, that from the time that he first began to riden out, he loved chivalrye, trouthe and honour, freedom and courtesye. . ." With these words Geoffrey Chaucer begins his description of Leverett Saltonstall. It is no matter that he wrote it some 500 years before Leverett was born. Chaucer is a great poet and great poets can see a long way ahead. He just looked up for a moment from the paper on which he was writing and saw Lev parading through Boston on Evacuation Day, lifting his glossy plug hat—his helmet—in salute to the crowd with that natural and friendly grace which was inherent to his nature. Then Chaucer jotted down his impressions and Leverett took his place in the immortal procession of the Canterbury Pilgrims.

The association of Leverett Saltonstall with Geoffrey Chaucer is an easy one. The 14th Century was a nasty time. Wholesale murder was commonplace; standards of conduct had collapsed. There were still crusades to redeem the Holy Land from the Infidel, but there was nothing holy about the crusades. People knew they had to fight but they had pretty much forgotten why. Except that if they were native Infidels they knew the alternative to fighting was a My Lai massacre, or if they were Christian invaders, that the alternative to being drafted was to be plundered and jailed at home.

When the world—and Saltonstall, then a boy of eight years—entered the 20th Century, civilized warfare was an acceptable term. Civilized nations thought they understood the rules. Armies were expected to mobilize, march, fight battles, capture strategic places, then stop. It had been like that in the American Civil War and in the Prussian war of 1870.

For those who actually experienced the fighting it was a grim business and the people on the path of Sherman's march to the sea, like the people of Paris during the Commune, got a taste of the 14th Century. But most people in 1900 were as innocent as cows in pasture of any understanding of the forces about to be released for the destruction of the human race. The social system had no means to cope with machine guns, tanks, airplanes, poison gas, atom bombs, intercontinental missiles and space satellites. And it was equally unprepared to cope with Karl Marx, or Mussolini, or Hitler.

So when hell broke loose in 1914—the hell that is still loose—civilized man hitched his horse to an airplane and descended into the trenches. Saltonstall was one of those to observe the experiment at first hand. The horse got the worst of it. Ordered to wear a gas mask, he never learned how to breathe in it and nearly suffocated. To pull artillery guns, harnesses were issued in France, but he never saw a horse. And fortunately the armistice intervened in time to prevent any closer view of modern war than a day's walk among the wrecked guns and haunted trenches around Verdun.

The Americans returned, well satisfied with their first crusade; glad to be back; glad to turn their backs on Europe. There was a dandy parade; hours and hours and hours of marching of the men of the Yankee Division down Commonwealth Avenue on a bitter cold day with newspapers blowing about the streets that escaped from the knees of the half-frozen spectators. Leverett always loved parades. He loved people and he liked to be in any cheerful throng on its way to Canterbury or Concord or Lexington or Bunker Hill to pay tribute to past saints whose acts had achieved modern freedom.

He paraded so well, and he managed with such truth and honor both as alderman and as representative in the Great and General Court, that he was elected Speaker of the Massachusetts House. Soon what James Curley unwisely referred to as his South Boston face—and a very handsome face it was—became known not only in South Boston but all over the state. Freedom and courtesy he did indeed love and the electorate loved him for it and made him Governor and then sent him to the United States Senate.

The skillful organization of hatreds has always been one of the customary and successful means of manipulating that body. Into that trap Leverett never fell. His talent, and it was considerable, lay quite in the other direction. What he liked best to do, and what he often succeeded in doing, was persuading his colleagues that insurmountable obstacles left yet some way to go around them. Scholars remember with gratitude his work on the National Historical Publications Commission and his successful effort, backed by President Kennedy, to persuade Congress to appropriate money for it, not as much as they wanted, but a very important part of what they wanted.

His time in the Senate was a time of national groping. The hot war was winding up and the cold war was beginning. America could not make up its mind whether it was a democracy or an empire. With the Marshall Plan it moved with great strength for democracy. Then along came Joe McCarthy riding the inevitable wave of American fascism, with a red under every bed, and loose talk of a new world domination, like the ancient domination of Rome, a Pax Americana; world order on the American plan, room and board included, all arranged for, paid for and bombs away for by the giant of the West.

This required a tough decision. Politics is not an easy game. Probably a majority of Lev's constituents believed in the evil genius from Wisconsin. But there were some good Massachusetts precedents. J.Q. Adams voted for Jefferson's Embargo Act, though it cost him his Senate seat. "Honest John" Davis threw one of only two votes in the Senate against the discreditable war with Mexico. Senator Hoar had the courage to turn against his party, his President and his voters to oppose imperialism and the annexation of the Philippines. His popularity survived the shock, as did Saltonstall's when he voted to censure McCarthy.

The Saltonstall we knew, and Chaucer's vision describes, operated according to a very elevated code. He knew no more than the rest of us whither he was going or why. It was customary to fight the pagans and that was the business of his life. Wherever pagans were to be found he fought them. But he did his fighting in a way peculiar to himself. "And though that he were worthy, he was wys, and of his port as meeke as is a mayde." Never in all his life did he say a disagreeable or unkind word to any person less fortunate than himself. Although his body was covered with the scars of battle his eyes were kind. In an age seldom surpassed for planned cruelty and savage, anonymous hate he set a standard of personal service and consideration in high office later, more enlightened generations may care to imitate. He was "a verray parfit gentil knight."

One more book by Samuel Eliot Morison was on the stands in the fall of 1977. It was not an unusual occurrence. Books by Morison had been appearing fairly often over the previous sixty years; at first only one now and then, but later almost in flocks, like coot over the Cohasset rocks at the call of the autumn northeaster. Now it was indeed the touch of the northeaster. In his own words, the time had come "when death shall break my pen at last."

This was the last book, *Sailor Historian*, a brilliant selection from the immense literary labor of one of the most productive literary lives that Boston, famous for such lives, has known. But though the pen is broken, the life of the life goes on, the life that is not mortal, that does not die with the body of the time. It is two centuries since Gibbon presented the world the question of the fall of Rome and his answer. The world still debates the question and it still reads Gibbon, somewhat for his answer, more for his style. Gibbon knew how to tell a story. So did Parkman. *The Oregon Trail* has the feel, almost the taste and smell, of the Indians and their prairie. So does his story of the French in Canada. Parkman climbed the path Wolfe climbed up to the Plains of Abraham. The stones are felt under the soles of the shoes, the brush of the bushes on the face.

Of these two Morison is the great successor. Always he is the true artist, the individual alone with his art. Because he trained himself rigorously, because he respected facts he is an historian. His interpretation was his own and it will certainly be challenged hereafter. No document, even the United States Constitution, can stand forever without amendment. But he would not write about people till he had been to the places where they had been.

Others will write about Columbus. It is not likely that any other will attempt to write the story of the great admiral after actually tracing his path and making his landfalls from the bobbling deck of a small sailing vessel. No other will write the story of the War in the Pacific with the same authority. He was there.

But being "there" guarantees no history. Millions are "there." Eyewitness accounts are plentiful as maggots in cheese. Very skillful reporters observe and record the present view. Commanders plan, direct events, are absorbed in their own direction, remember what they meant to do, not always what happened. The historian, if he too is an active observer,

The People of the City

must be alert to beware of his own impressions. He must be at once eyewitness, recorder, captain of the whole scene, judge of the immediate event and perceptive viewer of the present age as it derives out of the past and hurries into the future. Morison managed this feat.

His earliest love and his last was the Maine coast. But Boston was home port. For forty years he taught at Harvard, most of that time living in the house on Brimmer Street that a grandfather had built and where he was born. Here he wrote most of the books that made him famous. Here he was living at the 88-year limit of his life. Boston, its physical appearance, its suddenly changing climate, arctic, tropical or delightfully temperate, often in the same season, were of his nature. Its elegance and its roughness were part of him; its practical sense and its great Athenian ambition.

There is an old tavern hidden among the narrow streets of the town. Federalist merchants may have gathered there when the dome of Bulfinch's State House was new. Some of their descendants still do, along with a few writers and painters and the riffraff of State Street and Boston's new glass towers. It was a favorite haunt of Morison and of his friend and contemporary G.P. Gardner. In their faces was peculiarly reflected the qualities that have made New England great, an irrepressible intellectual imagination and shrewd common sense that create commerce and industry out of salt water and stony land and translate them into museums and universities.

When these two were there at ease the tap room became a ship lying at anchor, whence to remember wide seas of life, its storms and its calms and its continents visited. They were both great sailors, great travelers, generous sharers of experience. Gardner was high admiral of conversation. It was his delight to draw out that other admiral, the Admiral of the Ocean Sea, and with a humorous courtesy, subtle as it was generous, enjoy the show. It was quite a show.

— "The Yale map? Of course it was a fake."

— "We owe a lot to the Caribs. Along with syphilis Columbus's sailors brought back the hammock. Before that sailors just

291

curled up anywhere. Hammock is an Indian word. So is canoe. . . ."

— "Sun stones? I used not to believe in sun stones. But I've changed my mind. The evidence of the sagas . . . "

Often we heard that phrase "I've changed my mind." As Sam grew older his passion for firsthand information grew ever more tenacious. He sought facts as an old oak seeks nourishment, pushing its roots deeper into earth.

One winter day we welcomed him home from a trip south— to Cape Horn. In his pocket was a sprig from a rare variety of beech tree that grows at the tip of South America. Sam was not content just to sail through the straits. He had to put his foot on the ground there, where Magellan had put his.

His industry was prodigious. He said, "I read everything I can. I go and see the places. You have to see the places. When you've seen a place you have a feeling for it. I look over my notes, then I write."

ENVOI

*W*rite! How could any one human being write so much, so accurately, with such style? That favorite fountain pen of Morison's was drawn from a magic stone as surely as Arthur's sword.

In too many volumes to count, the *Maritime History of Massachusetts*, the *Harvard History*, the *Naval History of the Second World War*, the *Oxford History of the American People*, Morison has given us his vision of the United States, of the Great Republic. Like Donald McKay's masterpiece, the clipper ship *Great Republic*, the United States has suffered many mishaps from model to voyaging. Its continent discovered by accident, its design brilliantly shaped in the 18th Century with the Declaration and the Constitution, it was burned nearly to the water's edge in the Civil War. Refitted and rerigged, carrying less sail and more cargo than its builders intended, it is yet the noblest vessel ever launched.

Generations now unborn will see it sail, as Sam saw it. Feel the motion of the sea under their feet as Sam felt it. Hear the wind in the rigging.

Now we bid him goodbye. We see him go, as he wished to go, all sails set. He is on the quarter-deck of the *Great Republic*, one hand on the rail, his weather eye aloft. She moves down the ship channel, under topsails only, before a light northwest breeze; past the islands, out past the granite sentinel on Minot's Ledge, unfurling more sail as she goes. T'gallants, royals, skysails are set. Stunsails are spread. She is under a cloud of sail, running steady now and free, out past Cape Cod and Highland Light, out to sea and out of sight.

293

INDEX